Re-HUMAN-izing

THE WORKPLACE

By Giving Everybody Their Brain Back

Re-
HUMAN-
-izing
THE
WORKPLACE

(By Giving Everybody Their Brain Back)

CHUCK BLAKEMAN

"Re-HUMAN-izing the Workplace deserves consideration by thoughtful people everywhere who are concerned about the present, and hoping for a better future."
—DEE W. HOCK, FOUNDER AND CEO EMERITUS VISA AUTHOR, BIRTH OF THE CHAORDIC AGE

"This has not only transformed our companies, it has transformed our lives. I can't thank you enough. We are witnessing how powerful, productive and progressive this approach is, and the amazing results we are starting to experience."
—JIM SPITZIG, PRESIDENT, LEVEL 3 DESIGN GROUP, INC.

"We adopted a Participation Age approach to our business, and as a result, have grown exponentially in the last few years and we are projecting to double in size again next year. We're creating a company that can scale and run without my day to day involvement."
—JESSICA DALEY, FOUNDER & CEO, XCELERATE BUSINESS SOLUTIONS

"We have built our company on the principals of Stakeholders vs. Employees, trusting in adult behavior vs. time clocks and leaders vs. managers. Rehumanizing the Workplace gives its readers the building blocks necessary to be successful and is a must read for owners who struggle with retention, business development and profitability."
—BILL TEUBNER, PRESIDENT, THAT AGENCY

"We have worked on improving processes, focused marketing and the setup of a team leadership structure. There are still many things I need to work on but I am seeing order, and direction. The cloud of chaos is becoming a linear path. Now, if I put the work in, I see progress. I know where I am going."
—FEDERICO TOMASETTI, FOUNDER, CEO, STRUMENTA

"What am I thinking after reading this?! I am thinking of a way to paper my office with it. To distribute it to the people I work with, the management, my friends, elementary school play dates from 25 years ago, and every person I meet on the street. This is an incredibly relevant idea."
—TALIA HAYKIN

Re-
HUMAN
-izing
the Workplace
(By Giving Everybody Their Brain Back)

CHUCK BLAKEMAN

Crankset Group
PUBLISHING

Crankset Publishing, 1324 Shadow Mountain Drive,
Highlands Ranch, CO 80126

10 9 8 7 6 5 4 3 2 1

ISBN- 978-1-7344869-0-2

Crankset publishing books are available at special quantity discounts to use as premiums and sales promotions, or for use in educational or corporate training programs. For more information, please email us at Grow@CranksetGroup.com, or write to the Chief Relationship Officer Crankset Publishing 1324 Shadow Mountain Drive, Highlands Ranch, CO 80126, or contact your local bookstore.

This book is printed on acid-free paper.
Strategic editing by Virginia Lenz
Copyediting by Christine Wilson
Cover design and layout by Olga Vynnychenko
Illustrations by Brie Blakeman

Library of Congress Cataloging-in-Publication Data

Rehumanizing the Workplace (by Giving Everybody Their Brain Back) by Chuck Blakeman

1. Leadership. 2. Management. 3. Entrepreneurship.
I. Title. II. Rehumanizing the Workplace (by Giving Everybody Their Brain Back) III. Blakeman, Chuck

LCCN: 2020934166

www.cranksetgroup.com

DEDICATION

This book, derived from the practical lessons of building twelve businesses in eight industries on four continents, is dedicated to my loving wife Diane, my family, and the amazing Cranksetters who show up every day as self-managed adults living in community, working together with me to change the way work works.

Thank you to our many clients who use these tools and helped us develop them over the years, wanting their stories to be told.

A big thanks to Virginia Lenz, who provided critical strategic editing to help make this book more readable, to Brie Blakeman, my daughter, for the great hand-drawn illustrations that helped humanize this book, and to many others who gave such valuable early feedback, particularly Matt Perez, Tasha Eurich, Megan Kauffman, our faithful Chief Engagement Officer, and Krista Karpowich.

I am indebted to all the giants who came before: Mary Parker Follet, Douglas McGregor, Marvin Weisbord, Bill Gore, Peter Drucker, Dee Hock, Margaret Wheatley, Ricardo Semler, Chris Rufer, and many others who for over a hundred years have been beating the drum, gently and relentlessly, that the Factory System organizational model we inherited wasn't a good idea. In order to rehumanize the workplace, we need only build on the solid foundation they laid down for us.

FOREWORD

Uncertainty is the worst of human conditions. It's why being a hostage for a short period of time can do more damage to the psyche than being a prisoner for many years. As a prisoner, the rules are very clear. You know what is expected of you every day, and exactly when it will all be over, and you might even get out early for good behavior. It's not meant to be meaningful, but just to be endured. For many, work has sadly and ironically evolved to reflect those same attributes of certainty without personal meaning. We can have both.

We still live largely in survival mode and are still hunting mastodons in our heads. The tentative nature of our existence is still dominated by a scarcity mentality that drives the need for certainty. It is the primary force standing in the way of adapting to the emerging work world of the Participation Age; the pain we know is better than the pain we have yet to experience.

We may not like the way we are organized at work, but we have learned to take two mental aspirin every day and deal with it. Many of us have not yet experienced the emerging work world of the Participation Age, and it could be worse, so we hang on to the pain that we know, organizations still strangely dominated by the Factory System hierarchy.

In 1965, Dee Hock, who would go on to found Visa International, was unemployed and depressed, and decided to get a steady, reliable bank job and "retire in place" as he called it. Instead he was drawn into the infant credit card processing world and built a great, and deliberately decentralized organization. He left Visa in 1984 to devote his life to promote the principle of building organizations around both chaos and order, what he terms "chaordic organizations."

The chaordic organization is neither rigidly controlled nor is it anarchic. Participation Age companies are built organically with chaordic-type operating systems that do not require imposed hierarchy to still be highly ordered as well as highly flexible, responsive and innovative.

The Twelve Practices of the Participation Age presented here are not prescriptive. They are our experience as a company, and the experience of others who have adopted these practices as we have shared them with other organizations. These practices have worked for us, but every company is a snowflake and you will find ways to adapt them to your unique culture. The principles behind each tool are what we should cling to. The practices themselves are mere expressions of the principles. Use our practices if it helps you express the principles of the Participation Age, or form and adopt your own.

One of the mistakes we could make moving into the Participation Age is to replace rigid devotion to one form, top-down hierarchy, for another equally rigid form. Management focuses on processes, but leadership focuses on principles. We give you the Twelve Practices of the Participation Age, not as a rigid process you must adopt, but as an example of how we have applied the principles of the Participation Age. Learn and apply the principles of the Participation Age as they are presented throughout this book, and use the Twelve Practices to help you do that as it fits your organization. The emerging work world of the Participation Age is awaiting your contribution to how we can make work a better experience for all.

CONTENTS

Introduction To The Participation Age

The author was recently hired by one of the largest software companies in the world to give them input on how they could recapture their innovative, risk-taking origins. He was on his heels the whole time he was on their campus. There was a deep disconnect between the external perks of blue jeans, ping pong, free lunches, etc., and the true nature of a great, internalized business culture where people are treated like adults.

With all their emphasis on external benefits, this company and many others lack the critical ability to understand what motivates people. Adults thrive through the freedom to both make decisions and control their own personal destinies at work—or as Daniel Pink refers to it—they need autonomy, mastery, and purpose[1]. Adults desire a workplace that fosters community and meaning as part of a fully integrated life. The landscape of business is flooded with people unable to reconcile their personal lives with "What in God's name am I doing here?!" The Industrial Age falsely separated the personal and professional. It's time to bring them back together.

Over two centuries from the development of factories, people still feel dehumanized at work because we haven't dealt with the root cause of why work doesn't work; decisions made by the few for everyone else. The classic top-down hierarchy of the Factory System, upon which we have built the modern business organization, is in trouble. Culturally, it is out of sync with everything we are learning about what makes people free and encourages them to be productive adults. Statistically, it long ago lost the growth, profitability, engagement, productivity, and retention races to companies that focus first on the human side of enterprise. As more companies leave the Factory System behind and embrace Mission-centered Distributed Decision-making, great people flock to them and leave top-down companies struggling to stay relevant.

We need to stop making excuses for a system so clearly broken and unhelpful to business. For over a hundred years, we have done everything we can to work with the Factory System short of replacing it, but over a century of lipstick-on-the-pig solutions has not made it better, and we are finally facing up to it. Fully 90 percent of 11,000 companies recently surveyed understand that in order to stay competitive in the emerging work world, they must "race to replace structural hierarchies with a networks of teams," released to take action[2].

The Factory System, around which most companies still organize, is a tragically broken model, born in slavery, fomented in serfdom, fine-tuned in the militaries of the Middle Ages, and adopted as the most expedient short-term mindset for running today's organizations. Many used it early on not out of spite but because imposed hierarchy was the most prevalent form of human governance, and for two centuries, "Because I told you so," has just seemed easier. Many were aware of the dehumanizing effect exclusive decision-making had, but it was excused with incorrect assumptions about speed and efficiency and rationales like, "You don't have to like your work. You do it to pay the bills." But work should not be an unwelcome interruption in an otherwise great day, and when it isn't, both the company and the worker benefit.

For over a century, starting with the writings of early giants such as Mary Parker Follet, a true prophet of the Participation Age[3], we have been digging ourselves out of an avalanche of data which proves that if you're nice to people and treat them like adults who can make decisions, you make more money. New approaches are adopted slowly, even when, in this case, it is only a return to where we were before the Factory System. Even though a shift to a Participation Age operating system results in immediate improvement and not chaos and anarchy as some fear, the human need for certainty is a powerful and pervasive deterrent to adapting to a changing and increasingly complex world.

Solving for change and complexity rather than certainty may save your company's future. In the late 1990s, Kodak was struggling with spiraling decline and came to the realization that the 35 mm film industry was done; there would be no recovery. As one leader who worked there to the end recounted, the response was to continue to focus on producing 35 mm film, doggedly prolonging their demise. If you were asked to be part of the 35 mm team, it was considered a high honor. It was a classic picture of a band playing while the Titanic sunk. That leader smartly declined to join that team. In January 2012, Kodak filed for bankruptcy, having ridden the decline all the way to the bottom. Their decision-making had solved for the human need for certainty over the need to solve for complexity and change.

How will your company respond to the emerging work world of the Participation Age?

Sixty years ago, even twenty, it was fair to say, as many have said for a century, "I know the Factory System of management has a lot of problems, but I don't know what else to do." Now, we have seven decades of examples of companies such as W. L. Gore, Semco, The Morning Star Co., Nearsoft, Haier Corporation, Buurtzorg, Sudbury Valley Schools, and scores of others like our own Crankset Group, all operating at the top of their professions without imposed hierarchy. We can no longer say they are statistical anomalies or exceptions in some other way. They have given us not just a clear vision of where we should go but all the templates and processes needed to get there. Every industry and profession has shining examples of Participation Age companies leading the way, including government. The data overwhelmingly favors leaving the Factory System behind and reorganizing around Distributed Decision-making (DDM) workgroups.

We can no longer say we don't know what to do or how to do it. The only remaining question is, "Will we do it?" For now, as Kodak reasoned, it might seem easier to continue with what is nominally working, even if something else might work better. Thankfully, companies in every industry and profession are racing to embrace the Participation Age. Those that do will thrive. Those that don't will be left behind. You get what you intend, not what you hope for. Which do you intend to be?

Let's re-humanize the workplace by giving everybody their brain back. Please, come join us in the Participation Age.

Core Elements of the Participation Age

What is the Participation Age? To answer that, we will visit many organizations throughout this book. These organizations all function at the top of their professions or industries, and all of them do so without the Factory System top-down hierarchy we have come to view as the only way to manage an organization. Their varying operating principles and practices reflect their unique positions in a complex and changing world. Some originally employed classic Factory System hierarchies and later transitioned to Participation Age DDM workgroups, while others were born without imposed hierarchy, but they all share a number of things in common that helped them rehumanize the workplace by giving everybody their brain back. The following list is not exhaustive, but captures the major principles Participation Age organizations have adopted:

1. **Participation and sharing** — the hallmarks of the Participation Age are a) participation — people want to participate in building a great organization, not for you but with you, and b) sharing — people want to share in the rewards (not just money) of building that great organization. This is a tectonic shift from time-based bonuses to results-based incentives. Participation and sharing regularly, but not always, lead to ownership of some kind.

2. **Aversion to imposed hierarchy** — the companies in this book have business models with little or no emphasis on hierarchy. No one has a boss, and there is no corporate ladder to climb. They do have at least a background hierarchy, largely organic, where good leadership results in people willingly following a vision together.

3. **Mission-centered** — allegiance is to the mission not to bosses or departments, resulting in a focus on functions, roles, and

responsibilities instead of departments, titles, and ranking.

4. **Distributed decision-making** is the norm — decisions such as goals, metrics, growth, pay, hiring, and firing are all made by collaborating, cooperating, and communicating in community.

5. **Stakeholders, not employees** — Stakeholders are mature adults who think like owners and require leadership but not management. They focus on meaningful work and relationships, not titles, promotions, and competition. The term "employee" has its roots in factories where the average person was under ten years old, where we were all told to shut up, sit down, don't ask questions, live invisibly, and go out quietly with a gold watch. In the emerging work world of the Participation Age, the knowledge economy is founded on inviting everyone to participate in making the decisions that have to carry out, without a specific person or manager having to tell them what to do (teams of Stakeholders guide each other).

6. **Absence of managers** — Distributed Decision-making eliminates the need for managers who used to be the only decision-maker.

7. **Universally Distributed Leadership** — everyone is seen as a leader, using their expertise to create initiatives and form teams to implement them.

8. **Distributed Decision-making (DDM) workgroups** structure — teams and workgroups built on Distributed Decision-making are the foundation of the operating system, replacing top-down imposed hierarchy with decisions made locally where they are carried out.

9. **Principles over policies** — true leaders lead with just a very few principles, providing clarity on how to make localized decisions. They are largely averse to complicated policies and other vestiges of bureaucracy.

Haier — Based in Qingdao, China. Haier has revenues of $35 billion, with 75,000 internal Stakeholders (workgroup members) globally and 90,000 independent truck drivers. It is the largest appliance maker in the world with over a 10 percent share of the global market. The core appliance business has grown by 23 percent over the last ten years. No competitor comes close to matching their success. The present leader, Zhang Ruimin, took over the nearly bankrupt, highly traditional Factory System company and over the course of a decade changed everything to become a Participation Age company. Zhang was inspired to redesign the organization by learning the story of The Morning Star Company.

In 2005, Haier replaced the imposed hierarchy of the Factory System model and reorganized around 4,000 DDM workgroups of ten to fifteen people. All are fully independent microenterprises, each responsible for profit and loss, growth, innovation, and general usefulness to other teams. Every workgroup sources their services from the open market. If they believe they can get better accounting, marketing, or other services outside Haier, they do so with no interference from strategic leaders. As a result, DDM workgroups come into existence or go out of existence based on their usefulness to other DDM workgroups.

Haier is a shining global example of Mission-centered, Distributed Decision-making at its best. They are also one of the best before and after pictures of the inefficiency of top-down bureaucracy and how much better a structure built around DDM workgroups functions in its place. As bosses were replaced with DDM workgroups, Zhang helped them see that they could now listen to their customers, not a potentially tone-deaf hierarchy[4].

W. L. Gore — Based in Newark, DE. W. L. Gore was founded in 1958 by Bill and Vieve Gore in the basement of their house. W. L. Gore is a $3 billion international company with 10,000 people. Bill Gore is one of the pioneers of Participation Age practices, having built the company from the beginning with no managers and an emphasis on a network of DDM workgroups released to make decisions where they have to be carried out. In 1967, Bill Gore published *The Lattice Organization*, a very short document describing the simplicity of a DDM workgroup structure and the speed with which such teams can execute when freed from bureaucracy and specifically from managers[5].

The Morning Star Co. — Based in Woodland, CA. After driving a tomato truck for twelve years, Chris Rufer founded The Morning Star Co. in 1982. When there were still only a few full-time people, he and the others built it around self-management, nearly devoid of all bureaucracy. With over 600 full-time staff, revenues approaching $1 billion, and nearly 4,000 seasonal workers, The Morning Star Company is the largest tomato paste manufacturer in the United States. Every day as the trucks come rolling in, seasonal and full-time staff form DDM workgroups or teams on the spot to handle the flow, and they disband when other priorities take over.

Morning Star is organized around a Mission-centered model with no imposed hierarchy, with leaders who rise up because people are following them. Decisions are all made locally by DDM workgroups, committees are elected to set salaries, no one person can fire anyone, and universal Distributed Decision-making is the norm. In the complete absence of managers, Rufer says, "Everyone's a manager here. We are manager rich. The job of managing includes planning, organizing, directing, staffing, and controlling, and everyone at Morning Star is expected to do all these things. Everyone is a manager of their own mission." Notably different from the Factory System model is that everyone manages things, but no one manages people[6].

Semco Partners — Based in Sao Paolo, Brazil (but with no headquarters). Semco was a pump manufacturer from the 1950s to 1980. When Ricardo Semler took over the company, it had one hundred people, $4 million in revenue, and was teetering for years on the brink of dissolving. He very intentionally rebuilt the company around the two hallmarks of the Participation Age: Stakeholder *participation*, and *sharing* of decisions, information, and profits. In the process he eliminated all managers and developed DDM workgroups who decide their own goals, roles, processes, and metrics. They decide who to hire and fire, and for the last twenty-five years, they even chose their own salaries. Semco has experienced exponential growth for decades, growing into an international and highly diverse company with a few thousand Stakeholders and revenues in the hundreds of millions.

About hierarchy, Semler says, "The organizational pyramid is the cause of much corporate evil because the tip is too far from the base. Pyramids emphasize power, promote insecurity, distort communications, hobble interaction, and make it very difficult for the people who plan and the people who execute to move in the same direction." Semco has three concentric circles of strategic leadership that flow in and out of each other and only exist to serve the DDM workgroups. In this organic way, the direction of the company is determined together. With thousands of workers, they don't track vacation time or office time, and there are no fixed salaries or promotions. The focus is purely on results delivered[7].

Buurtzorg — Based in Amsterdam, Netherlands — a not-for-profit home nursing organization founded in 2006 by Jos de Blok. In the first ten years, Buurtzorg, which means "neighborhood care," expanded with lightning speed to 850 teams of 10,000 nurses and 4,500 home care workers in twenty-five countries, all without hierarchy, bureaucracy, or managers of any sort. Each team of ten to twelve local nurses determine how to run their DDM workgroup and how best to create the next team as business expands.

Client satisfaction rates are the highest of any healthcare organization in the Netherlands, and staff commitment and contentedness is reflected in Buurtzorg's title of best employer. Ernst & Young documented a staggering 40 percent savings to the Dutch healthcare system alone, if all care was provided this way. One of Jos de Blok's oft-stated mottos is "humanity over bureaucracy[8]."

Nearsoft — Based in Hermosillo, Mexico and San Jose, CA. A software company, co-founded in 2007 by Roberto Martinez and Matt Perez. By 2012, Nearsoft was already number six on the Great Places to Work list. Today, with over 300 Nearsoftians, they function without imposed hierarchy (Matt Perez calls it fiat hierarchy) and without managers, titles, or centralized decision-making. They keep completely open books, develop objectives as DDM workgroups, govern via peer evaluations, and encourage anyone to lead by starting something that others will follow.

Nearsoft, like Mars, Starbucks, Quicken, and a growing list of other companies, has banned the word *employee* as "the dirtiest word in the corporate lexicon" because of its history and because of its roots in the Latin word *plicare*, which implies bending to the will of others. Nearsoft was founded not on complex policies but on two simple and profound assumptions: 1) everyone is an adult and should be treated that way, and 2) everyone wants to be responsible[9].

Sudbury Valley Schools (SVS) — No headquarters. SVS is a K-12 school system that was founded in 1968 by a community of people in Framingham, MA. Today, there are over fifty Sudbury Valley Schools around the United States. Like all Participation Age organizations, they shun policies and were founded on three powerful principles: educational freedom, democratic governance, and personal responsibility.

To that end, Sudbury Valley Schools have no class structure (no seniors or first graders), no traditional classes, no classrooms, no curriculum, no grading, and no teachers. Adult staff facilitate whatever learning the students are doing. There is no tenure because SVS is a results-based Participation Age organization. At the end of each year, the students and the staff all get equal and anonymous votes on which staff should return the next year.

Even though the model does not have a bias toward privileged access to the SVS schools, 85 percent of SVS students go on to higher education, including the top schools in the United States. Their biggest complaint about their college roommates is that they won't take responsibility for their lives. A staggering 42 percent of SVS graduates are involved in entrepreneurial pursuits. Even children want to participate and share in building their futures[10].

Spodak Dental Group — Based in Del Ray Beach, FL. Founded in 1976 by Dr. Myles Spodak, Spodak Dental Group is now led by Dr. Craig Spodak, who took over the reins in 2006. In 2013, his son Craig realized his dream of opening a comprehensive, state-of-the-art dental facility, which is now one of the largest single-facility dental practices in the United States, with fifty-five team members in one location. Spodak Dental Group has no managers and no top-down bureaucracy. Everyone is encouraged to lead, not just follow, and "community" is one of their four values.

Each function (front desk, hygiene, accounting, lab) is its own DDM workgroup, responsible for their own profit and loss, metrics, incentives, training, mentoring, hiring, and firing. This high level of interdependent teamwork has given Dr. Spodak the freedom to build a nationally recognized nonprofit and involve himself and his team in other not-for-profit, dental education, and business pursuits[11].

AND MANY MORE

Throughout Rehumanizing the Workplace, we share the stories of many other Participation Age organizations structured around DDM workgroups, including our own, Crankset Group, as well as those of companies with just three or four people in them. Throughout the book, you will hear how Crankset Group applies Participation Age practices, not because we are the best example of how to apply them, but to show that we practice what this book espouses. All these organizations illustrate that Participation Age companies are already present in every industry and profession, in every size, and in every political and economic climate. The organizations in the book range from ten years of Participation Age involvement to over sixty years (W. L. Gore).

Their stories show we're not looking at the lucky or brilliant few but companies that simply purposed to rehumanize their workplaces by giving everybody their brain back. Their strength is not in their brilliance but in their commitment to solve for complexity and change in a world that promotes the stagnation of solving for certainty. Their stories should show you that you don't have to be uniquely visionary, brilliant, or lucky. You simply have to decide that a new organization design, which is really very old, is better than lipstick on the pig we call the Factory System.

Read this book to learn how your organization can be part of the emerging work world of the Participation Age.

RESOURCES

1   Autonomy, Mastery, and Purpose, the Science of What Motivates Us https://www. brainpickings.org/2013/05/09/daniel-pink-drive-rsa-motivation

2   https://www2.deloitte.com/content/dam/Deloitte/global/Documents/About-Deloitte/central-europe/ce-global-human-capital-trends.pdf

3   https://www.amazon.com/Mary-Parker-Follett-Prophet-Management/dp/1587982137/ref=sr_1_4?qid=1581775960&refinements=p_27%3APauline+Graham&s=books&sr=1-4&text=Pauline+Graham

4   https://hbr.org/2018/11/the-end-of-bureaucracy

5   https://hbr.org/1989/09/managing-without-managers

6   https://hbr.org/2011/12/first-lets-fire-all-the-managers

7   https://www.ted.com/talks/ricardo_semler_how_to_run_a_company_with_almost_no_rules#t-391368

8   https://www.buurtzorg.com/about-us/history/

9   https://nearsoft.com/blog/self-management-and-barbecues/

10   https://sudburyvalley.org/theory

11   https://www.spodakdental.com/core-values/

CHAPTER ONE

Lipstick on a Pig

A terrifying 2005 blog post from a programmer in a large technology company:

"Every day I go to work.
When I get to work, I park, leave myself in the car, and head into work.
At lunch, I always try to come back out and reunite with myself for a few
minutes before I have to leave myself in the car, and go back into work.
I do this every day.
And in the evenings, I always hope I get off in time to reunite with
myself…
before I'm gone."

How are we doing at making work, work?

Not well, it turns out. Seventy percent of people at work are disengaged and just phoning it in[1]. Over 50 percent always have their resumes out and are actively looking for something else[1]. Eighty-seven percent say what they're doing isn't meaningful and makes them long to do something else[2].

THE PIG IS THE PROBLEM

For nearly two centuries, we have been putting lipstick on the pig that enables disengagement at work. We call it the Factory System, a top-down organizational hierarchy, born in slavery, developed in serfdom, fine-tuned in Middle-Age militaries, and mimicked in the early factories under the assumption that it was the only way to organize a business. In the twenty-first century, most companies continue to embrace it even though it adds unnecessary management burdens, lowers productivity, disengages people, lowers retention, and lacks innovation.

There is a better way. It existed before we built factories, and we're just now beginning to return to it in earnest: localized, Distributed Decision-making. In the emerging work world of the Participation Age, Distributed Decision-making (DDM) workgroups are proving to be the core practice of a rehumanized workplace.

Forward-moving companies are racing to embrace this DDM model expressed through networks of DDM workgroups, but as with any change, it takes time. There are three major influences on how organizations make decisions. Our reliance on the third one understandably slows the process:

1. **Complexity** — increasing complexity and a realization that every organization is part of multiple complex systems, requires that we constantly adapt and respond and make decisions with input from outside our organization or hierarchy.

2. **Change** — the rate of change continues to increase, forcing us to change when we just got comfortable.

3. **The human need for certainty** — the drive for safety, security, and stability: every day should feel the same.

The Major Influences In Decision-Making

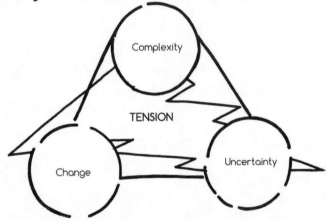

Organizations that solve first for complexity and change thrive, but most organizations still solve first for the human need for certainty. Uncertainty is the worst of human conditions, and when we feel like change causes uncertainty, we slow down. This confounds any attempt to respond appropriately to the influences of complexity and change. Nothing demonstrates more our desire to solve first for the human need for certainty than our continuing adherence to top-down, imposed hierarchy in the face of convincing data that says we should do something else.

There is overwhelming research that confirms uncertainty is a psychologically aversive state for people. Finding the next mastodon to keep us alive still controls most of our behavior, so it is not surprising that in the face of compelling research that we should replace top-down Factory System management with Distributed Decision-making workgroups and still fear the change. This book is designed to help you understand that becoming a Participation Age organization does not create more uncertainty, chaos, or anarchy. We have regularly seen that companies who use the tools in this book to replace imposed hierarchy see immediate improvement in the classic measure of success: revenue, profit, production, and retention. Using the tools in this book, becoming a Participation Age company addresses change and complexity by decreasing uncertainty.

Imposed hierarchy, whether we like our position in it or not, is emotionally satisfying and utterly clear. By a quick glance at an org chart, we know exactly who reports to whom and, as a result, who can control whom. Power and authority are the tools of command and control, and top-down decision-making just seems easier.

As the data now shows, top-down hierarchy impedes growth, profitability, productivity, innovation, agility, and is the main source of high attrition.

In the Participation Age, solving first for the human need for certainty usually leads to obsolescence. Thomas Frey, Google's top-rated futurist, says 2 billion jobs will disappear by 2030, and every existing industry will have disappeared and been replaced multiple times. Most car companies will be bankrupt. Car loans, parking garages, the residential construction industry, and malls will disappear, and cities will lose over 50 percent of their existing tax revenue. Hospitals and pharma companies will be radically smaller, drones will replace umbrellas, and the Internet and teacher bots will replace most schools and colleges,

> **Over two centuries from the creation of the early factories, people still feel dehumanized at work because we haven't dealt with the root cause of why work doesn't work: imposed hierarchy.**

with 20,000 micro industries springing up to replace it all. Change and complexity are inevitable and push against our desire for certainty.

Since the early 1900s, surveys of thousands of companies say the Factory System method of organizing a business is not working, but in deference to the human need for certainty, we have worked hard for over a century to keep the Factory System operating system in place. Over two centuries from the creation of the early factories, people still feel dehumanized at work because we haven't dealt with the root cause of why work doesn't work: imposed hierarchy.

IMPOSED HIERARCHY VS. DISTRIBUTED DECISION-MAKING

Imposed hierarchy, or what is commonly known as the Factory System, is the seminal problem in business today. By 1850, more goods were made in factories than in homes, quickly leading to the demise of the domestic system of production, which began in the late 1700s. The Factory System borrowed it's organizing principles from the military, creating a nearly identical hierarchy of power and control, with different titles.

To be clear up front, hierarchy itself isn't bad. In fact, it's a naturally occurring condition in any healthy business, but imposed hierarchy, as opposed to organic leadership, is dysfunctional in three ways:

a) Where it originates — from the top-down, creating command and control relationships with those at the bottom and an unnecessary management tax (defined later).

b) How it functions — using the people at the bottom for the sake of a few at the top, resulting in a massive disengagement tax and a distortion of capitalism.

c) How it determines status — creating a political and promotion-focused climate that pits people against people that encourages a revolving door of quitting and retraining, resulting in the restaffing tax.

Bill Gore started W. L. Gore (Gore-Tex) in 1958 with an organic approach to hierarchy and the radical notion that people did not need to be managed. Over sixty years later, the company has 10,000 people and no traditional middle managers but is instead organized around teams of people who shun talk about economies of scale and command and control. Early on Bill said, "Authoritarians cannot impose commitments, only commands[3]."

Ricardo Semler, former leader of the very large and diverse company Semco, which developed organically and runs with no middle managers, says, "Put ten people together, don't appoint a leader, and you can be sure that one will emerge. So will a sighter, a runner, and whatever else the group needs. They find their own leaders. That's not a lack of structure; that's just a lack of structure imposed from above[4]."

When hierarchy is working organically and appropriately, it's an innovative, focused profit machine that attracts the best of the best. Presently, only a few hundred very large corporations are operating with organic leadership, developed around what we have observed as DDM workgoups. That is understandable because until the last few decades we didn't fully understand how to make the transition to organic teams, but a few hundred large companies and thousands of smaller ones are not an anomaly; they are the early adapters.

THE PARTICIPATION AGE

The Participation Age is defined by two simple characteristics — participation and sharing. People want both *participation* in building a great company, and they want to become value-adding capitalists (not industrialists) by *sharing* in the rewards of that effort. In a 1994 article for *Harvard Business Review*, Semler wrote, "participation gives people control of their work, profit sharing gives them a reason to do it better, and information tells them what's working and what isn't."

Some large companies, such as W. L. Gore and Semco, have functioned for up to seven decades without traditional hierarchy. Gore was born that way, and Semco made the shift after thirty years in the Factory System. Many others have followed suit in the last few decades. Leaders of Participation Age companies are more satisfied and have an immeasurable competitive advantage by reorganizing around Distributed Decision-making teams. These companies have learned that management creates compliance, while Distributed Decision-making creates engagement.

The author has built twelve businesses in eight industries on four continents. In his experience, organic tactical and strategic leadership has rendered a continuing competitive advantage. It also frees him to focus on the rewarding aspects of developing strategic leadership rather than managing and directing people who have learned to do that as DDM workgoups.

UNHELPFUL DISTRACTIONS

Why hasn't the Factory System been replaced before this? Again, the primary driver is the human need for certainty — the pain I know is better than the pain I have yet to experience. Secondarily, a century of consulting has accepted the presence of this antiquated system without challenging it. For too long, consultants have created nonintegrated, fragmented disciplines that distract us from the core problem. They focus on organizational design (tweaking the Factory System pig), organizational development (training managers), efficiency studies (focusing on machines), perks (masquerading as culture), and technology (to replace the people), as if none related to the other.

All of these are good things, and what is needed is an integrated approach that replaces the core operating system we inherited from the factories. Ironically, advances in technology may accelerate the re-integration and help usher in forms of organic heterarchy that function more like "paper, rock, scissors" than a static top-down system. There is clear authority, but the organic approach releases a network of teams to respond according to the immediate need required by change and complexity.

George Gilder says, "Companies are abandoning hierarchy and pursuing heterarchy because...blockchain technology offers a credible and effective means not only of cutting out intermediaries, but also of radically lowering transaction costs, turning firms into networks, distributing economic power, and enabling both wealth creation and a more prosperous future[5]."

TREAT PEOPLE LIKE ADULTS

Research from the work of Frederick Winslow Taylor in the 1890s all the way through to the present constant drumbeat of data produced and disseminated daily on the Internet by hundreds of organizations all corroborate on thing:

> **When you're nice to people and treat them like adults, you make more money.**

When you listen to, recognize, and respect people and encourage them to make decisions, they bring their full adult selves to work and become fully engaged team members. Great companies already focus on the human side of enterprise, but this simple answer has been ignored by some because it is, in fact, much easier to just reshuffle the hierarchy twice a year, design a faster assembly line, or ask managers to dream up a better process to impose on others. The response to the need for an emphasis on humanity at work was the creation of something called human resources, allowing managers to ignore people so they could focus on "the real business."

The drumbeat of the data on the dehumanization of work is drowned out by the silence of many companies tiptoeing past the graveyard of endless cubicles where people go to put up with another day of making money, with no hope or expectation of making meaning. When will we address the core cause, the Factory System itself? When is enough, enough?

THE FORGOTTEN PRODUCTIVITY FACTOR — PEOPLE

The Industrial Age and its engine, the Factory System, brought us amazing toys and technological advances we could not have dreamed of in 1850, when for the first time in history more goods were produced in factories than in homes and shops, but what impact has that reorganization had on humanity? What if there was an answer that could work better for both the people and the organization?

The technological impact of the Factory System has been amazing by any standard. Food is plentiful. Water is clean. Indoor temperatures are controlled. Distance no longer impedes the transit of communication or goods. Technology makes life more comfortable, and we are endlessly entertained and distracted by tapping buttons with our fingers, but the impact on humanity at work has been equal and opposite, with 70 percent just phoning it in every day.

That leaves about 30 percent who are engaged at work, by Gallup's estimates. Is 30 percent engagement okay? If you had a machine that worked for years at 30 percent productivity, would you put up with that? Our most common response is, "Well, what are you going do? Everybody else has the same problem," but not everyone does. Engaged team members, who are seen as the exception, are now the rule in emerging Participation Age companies.

After WWII, we experienced great gains in productivity, but three things should make us look differently at how it will increase going forward:

1. Virtually all productivity gains from 1800 through 2018 were

driven by advances in technology. Electricity, steam power, internal combustion, central heating and cooling, the airplane, the telephone, batteries, and the Internet all revolutionized our world, but for as long as we've been measuring human engagement in the workplace, about 70 percent of people at work remain disengaged, giving companies with universally engaged people a dramatic advantage.

2. Productivity increases have sharply leveled off since the 1970s, awaiting the next wave of technological innovations that can drive it again, if ever. Many experts say, "Don't hold your breath."

3. The "if ever" people have some short-term proof for their case; despite our recent advances into a digital world, productivity growth over the last ten years has been exponentially lower than in any long recovery since we've kept records.

We can point to significant data that shows work is working better on a production basis than it did a hundred years ago, but our singular obsession with (and historic success with) productivity has obscured three other massive influences on how work does or does not work:

1. The management tax — the unnecessary and wholly unjustified layer upon layer of unproductive management that regularly tops 10 percent of revenues.

2. The disengagement tax — the stunning hidden costs of staff disengagement (US $483 to $605 billion each year)[6].

3. The restaffing tax — management causes disengagement, which results in a never-ending cycle of costly staff turnover and retraining of replacement hires, perhaps the highest hidden cost in any business, running anywhere from four months to two years of annual salary[7].

WHY DO MANAGERS EXIST?

A treasure trove of research has documented how strategic leadership impacts production, as well as the overall health of any organization[8]. Even though the Center for Creative Leadership has found that at least 50 percent of leaders are ineffective[9], studies show that when organizations get strategic, transformational leadership right, they are more likely to function at the top of their industries for a very long time.

The positive impact of good leadership is at the very heart of this book. People need leadership, both on a strategic and tactical level, but they do not need to be managed at any level, and the void of research supporting the need for the organizational role of manager is as telling as the clear research that they need to be led. True leadership, on which we have been vastly misled, is not something provided by people at the top of a pyramid, and management is not something that must be provided by individuals in the middle of an organization.

The research and case studies we review in this book show that everyone should lead, and everyone should manage, not just the few, and it also shows that leadership is for people and management is for things. You will see this principle applied throughout the book:

Manage stuff. Lead people.

People are not stuff and do not need to be managed, only led, and the two are radically different. Peter Drucker said in his book, *Management Challenges of the 21st Century*, that going forward, "one does not manage people. The task is to lead people." Warren Bennis reveals in his groundbreaking book, *On Becoming a Leader*, "management focuses on systems and structure [stuff]; leadership focuses on people[10]." In the emerging work world of the Participation Age, the organizations that understand and apply the difference between leadership of people and management of things will flourish, and those that don't will be left behind.

John Kotter, the Konosuke Matsushita professor of leadership, emeritus, at the Harvard Business School, says, "I can't tell you how many times I've heard people use the words 'leadership' and 'management' synonymously, and it drives me crazy every time." He also believes that viewing leadership in terms of personality characteristics, which leads to the conclusion only a few people can provide leadership, "gets us into increasing trouble[11]."

We invest a full chapter to properly separating leadership from management and another chapter showing how everyone can do both in the many companies where managers no longer exist. Our intent is not to denigrate the people who manage but to show that the position of middle manager should be eliminated by formation of DDM teams. To understand the need to replace the Factory System with a new operating system, DDM teams, we must deal with the management tax head on. The idea that managers make people more productive and without them people would lose focus is perhaps the most untested and expensive assumption we inherited from the Industrial Age Factory System.

DO MIDDLE MANAGERS MAKE PEOPLE MORE PRODUCTIVE?

In the writing of this book, the author asked several highly respected leadership gurus to point to studies that correlated the presence of a manager of a team with higher productivity. To a person, they all pointed me to meta-studies of transformational, high-level strategic leadership, but none could produce a single study that said a manager makes a team more productive.

It is stunning that as one of the most fundamental tenets of management, we have yet to find a single bit of research concluding that a manager, at the team level, makes that team more productive. Endless articles simply assume and then focus on how to fix middle management because it is so broken. On the other side of the coin, there is endless research showing middle managers of teams make people less productive and are the major reason they quit and go somewhere else[12]. When you search the Internet for, "Do managers make people more productive?", it instead returns 139 million hits for:

a) How managers are the problem.

b) What managers can do to fix the problem that they are.

c) Why strategic leadership is so important (and correlated with bottom line profits).

I have yet to find a single study that measures the productivity, engagement, happiness, retention, or any other factor of team performance before removing a manager and after removing a manager. Instead, consultants assume that localized managers of individual teams are necessary. Then, in the face of all the evidence that management of a team by one individual makes people less productive, they have us spending untold billions of dollars attempting to fix a position that no one has proven is necessary in the first place.

The last hundred years of advice to fix a position that has unproven value is simply more lipstick on the pig of imposed hierarchy. Managers are necessary to Factory System hierarchy but not to the success of a company. We highlight many companies who rehumanized their workplace by eliminating middle managers of teams. These companies allowed leadership to be chosen by those who would be led and replaced as many as ten managers with one affirmed strategic leader for these teams. As a result, they increased productivity and reduced staff turnover to levels that managed companies can only dream of. Managers are not the problem, but the position itself is simply untenable in the knowledge economy of the twenty-first century.

The data reliably shows people have no need to be managed, only led, and that these terms — management and leadership — have been so conflated over the last one hundred years that we have no clue anymore what either of them means. The chapter on Universally Distributed Leadership reveals how important it is to understand the very different origins and practices of leadership versus management.

Both the cost savings and the increase in human engagement driven by eliminating managers are game changers. Eliminating the management tax leads to a significant reduction in the disengagement tax and the restaffing tax.

ENGAGEMENT CONSULTING VS. DISTRIBUTED DECISION-MAKING

Employee engagement consulting is a recent distraction to replacing the Factory System. It was coined first in an *Academy of Management Journal* article by William Kahn in 1990[13] and will likely go the way of all other lipstick that promised to beautify the pig by hiding the truth. From our perspective, it is more sensible to approach engagement as an integrated overhaul of how we lead people. People will not become engaged by "employee engagement" but by transforming the structure under which they labor.

This is not a book about engagement. People are not engaged because someone in human resources (HR) came up with "59 Awesome Engagement Ideas" (a real article)[14] but because they have found work that allows them to make decisions as whole, messy, creative individuals.

I'M ALREADY EMPOWERED, THANK YOU

Nor is it a book about empowerment. Trying to empower people is like trying to make an acorn into more of an acorn. I can do nothing to add to its "acornishness." In the same way, people show up fully empowered as who they are, the first day they arrive, and there is nothing I can do to add to that empowerment. To attempt to do so is patronizing and communicates, "I'm still in power, and the only reason you have any power at all is because I granted you a little of mine." True empowerment is not granted. It is the absence of the heavy hand, the absence of black plastic over the seed that inspires someone to use their own empowerment to become a great oak tree where they work.

The primary task of the strategic leaders of a company is to engage their people, not to empower them. People need reasons to use their "acornishness" to become great oak trees. Engagement is the addition of sunlight, soil, fertilizer, water, and pruning. Great strategic leaders provide motivating reasons to get involved — leadership, vision, tools, values, resources, guidance, training, metrics, and relationships. Give people good reasons to give it their all, and they will. Empowerment is fully on them. Engagement is 100 percent on us.

ENGAGEMENT IS A RESULT

Engagement is not a process but a result. It entails one very simple (but not easy) organizational design change—Distributed Leadership. Distributed leadership is lived out through one simple practice, Distributed Decision-making. This organizational design shift will do more to make work actually work than any lipstick applied to the Factory System pig in the last 120 years. Great leaders are important here because they understand that the art of leadership is to make as few decisions as possible and to instead teach others how to make those decisions. The more decisions get pushed across the organization to the people who must carry them out, the more engagement will increase.

These two concepts, Distributed Leadership and Distributed Decision-making, are not new and existed long before the Factory System emerged. We're just proposing that we combine the great technological advances of the Industrial Age with the time-honored ability to make decisions and make localized decisions where they must be carried out. These are the same two concepts that made work meaningful for the shoemaker before we put him in the factory and told him to bang a nail into the left boot. All we're proposing is that we go back to where we came from before the Factory System, rehumanizing the workplace by giving everyone their brain back.

REHUMANIZING WORK

Whether you're pushing a broom or writing code, work shouldn't be demeaning, nor should it be an unwelcome interruption in an otherwise great day, and it shouldn't be a place filled with office daycare centers where we are supervised like seven-year-olds. It should be a place we run to because it is one of the many places in our integrated lives where we have the precious opportunity to make meaning, not just make money.

We've done a great job of addressing productivity through technology and by making machines more productive. Now it's time to fully address why only around 30 percent of people at work are giving it their best shot. It's time to pay attention to improving the lives of people, not just the performance of the machines they run. Let's replace the Factory System management model that has been our tired default operating system for nearly two centuries.

REPLACING IMPOSED HIERARCHY WITH DISTRIBUTED DECISION-MAKING

We all intuitively know this is the right thing to do. The Deloitte Human Capital Trends survey says fully 90 percent of companies surveyed understand that in order to stay competitive in the emerging work world, they must "race to replace structural hierarchies with a networks of teams," released to take action[15]. We are not proposing better engagement processes, a more human resources focus, better management, or any other quick fix. We're proposing reorganizing business around Distributed Decision-making, the one simple practice that rehumanizes work for everyone.

Organizations that have eliminated managers aren't outliers or exceptions. There are hundreds of large ones and thousands of smaller ones in every industry, some with over six decades of Participation Age success. How have they all learned to make meaning, not just money?

They have rejected the drumbeat that says, "Well, everyone has the same problem," or the self-fulling prophecy, "This is just the best we can do." Too many businesses have proven otherwise. We can no longer ignore the decades of accumulated voices calling us into the emerging work world of the Participation Age.

MORE LIPSTICK ISN'T THE ANSWER

Ironically, the software industry is one of the most archaic, organized slavishly around imposed hierarchy while attempting to distract people with perks masquerading as great culture and autonomy. The

Introduction opened by highlighting one such company that lacks the critical ability to understand what motivates people. They are in the majority. In most companies today, people are still unable to reconcile their personal lives with their work lives. The Industrial Age falsely separated them, and it's time to bring them back together.

> **It is the absence of the heavy hand, the absence of black plastic over the seed that inspires someone to use their own empowerment to become a great oak tree where they work**

Again, the question is no longer, "What can we do?" but "Will we do this?" Let's join the thousands of companies racing to embrace the emerging work world of the Participation Age. Let's replace the worn-out Factory System with a new operating system founded on the practice of Distributed Decision-making. DDM workgroups are the new operating system.

Please, come join us.

THE NEXT ONE THING

At the end of each chapter, we provide a place to summarize something you might want to apply from the chapter.

1. What is the Next One Thing we can do to continue responding to change and complexity without creating unnecessary uncertainty?

---

2. How do we measure the success of doing that?

---

3. What might keep us from doing it, and how do we get past that?

---

4. When will we do it? ____/____/____ by ____:____ am/pm.

5. Who will take responsibility to make sure it gets done (an individual, a team)?

_____

_____

_____

RESOURCES

1 State of the American Workplace https://www.gallup.com/workplace/?g_source=link_NEWSV9&g_medium=related_tile1&g_campaign=item_180404&g_content=State%2520of%2520the%2520American%2520Workplace

2 If You Love Them Set Them Free https://www2.deloitte.com/insights/us/en/topics/talent/future-workforce-engagement-in-the-workplace.html?id=us:2el:3pr:dup2725:awa:dup:MMDDYY:

3 https://guides.shiftbase.net/wl-gore/

4 https://hbr.org/1989/09/managing-without-managers

5 https://www.amazon.com/Life-After-Google-Blockchain-Economy-ebook/product-reviews/B072NYKG2G

6 The Global State of Business https://www.gallup.com/workplace/238079/state-global-workplace-2017.aspx?utm_source=2013StateofGlobalWorkplaceReport&utm_medium=2013SOGWReportLandingPage&utm_campaign=2013StateofGlobalReport_Redirectto2017page&utm_content=download2017now_textlink

7 Employee Retention Now a Big Issue - https://www.linkedin.com/pulse/20130816200159-131079-employee-retention-now-a-big-issue-why-the-tide-has-turned?trk=aff_src.aff-lilpar_c.partners_pkw.10078_net.mediapartner_plc.Skimbit%20Ltd._pcrid.449670_learning&veh=aff_src.aff-lilpar_c.partners_pkw.10078_net.mediapartner_plc.Skimbit%20Ltd._pcrid.449670_learning&irgwc=1

8 https://sites.fas.harvard.edu/~soc186/AssignedReadings/Thomas-Matters.pdf

9 https://www.ccl.org/articles/leading-effectively-articles/how-first-time-managers-can-avoid-flaming-out/

10 https://guides.wsj.com/management/developing-a-leadership-style/what-is-the-difference-between-management-and-leadership/

11 https://hbr.org/2013/01/management-is-still-not-leadership

12 Managers Make People Disengaged https://www.google.com/search?client=firefox-b-1&ei=2TxLXMapMqrP0PEPtK-zwAQ&q=why+people+quit+their+jobs&oq=why+people+quit+their+jobs&gs_l=psy-ab.3..0.27767.32476..32647...0.0..0.683.2701.5-4......0....1..gws-wiz.......0i71.VLBl8NL1asM

13 https://www.researchgate.net/publication/275697337_Psychological_Conditions_of_Personal_Engagement_and_Disengagement_at_Work

14 https://www.snacknation.com/blog/employee-engagement-ideas/

15 https://www2.deloitte.com/content/dam/Deloitte/global/Documents/About-Deloitte/central-europe/ce-global-human-capital-trends.pdf

CHAPTER TWO

The Mission-Centered Organization

"The organizational pyramid emphasizes power, promotes insecurity, distorts communications, hobbles interaction, and makes it very difficult for the people who plan and the people who execute to move in the same direction."

— RICARDO SEMLER, SEMCO

Peter Drucker said, "What motivates workers is what motivates volunteers. They need to know the organization's mission and to believe in it." This radical focus on being mission centered is a foundational principle and practice of Participation Age companies, providing a model of organic leadership. In Mission-centered organizations, both strategic and tactical leaders find their true north for how to make decisions.

THE MISSION-CENTERED ORGANIZATION

A few years ago, my friend Doug Kirkpatrick, a seasoned practitioner and adviser for self-management who was part of building The Morning Star Co., shared with me, "What we teach people is that the mission is the boss"— a simple, powerful, and life-changing approach for any organization.

Everything lines up when you fully embrace the empowering practice of being mission centered as the basis for building a great product or service and creating happy, loyal customers. The mission statement is bigger than the delivery of a product or service; it embodies the entire customer experience. Thanks to Doug's simple summary, we've put it all under the principle of the Mission-centered organization. When you fully embrace the idea of being mission centered, it impacts your organization at every level:

1. Being mission centered moves the focus from bosses, departments, and departmental rivalries.

Factory system organizations are either boss centered, department centered, or a combination of both. Because the manager has the gun (I can fire you), for survival alone you are boss centered or focused heavily on making that boss's department highly successful.

Organizations that suffer under the Factory System hierarchy deal with ongoing wars between departments. Sales and ops are always at odds, accounting is on our backs, administration is underrated, upper management is considered clueless, and nobody understands what marketing does. The localized fixation with a boss or department results in an ongoing effort to protect and broaden the influence of the department, often with no connection to the company's objectives.

Managers come by this honestly because we tend to pay them for how many people they have under them, how big their budget is, and how many assets they manage. In order to get a raise, they feel compelled to chase and control more of those three things, and in the process, they can completely lose sight of what serves the entire company.

In a memo to all Tesla staff, Elon Musk decried the cumbersome, political nature of management layers and issued an edict that "two people should just talk until the right thing happens." He went on to say that any manager who required that they be in the loop on all decisions would find themselves working in another company. At the end of the email, Musk expressed a clear desire to have a Mission-centered organization:

We are all in the same boat. Always view yourself as working for the good of the company, and never your dept. Thanks, Elon.

This is the essence of a Mission-centered organization, which is refocused on the success of the mission, not on the success of a boss, partment, or team.

2. The second implication is that to declare the mission as the boss is to place ourselves under it. All of us.

If the mission is now the boss, I'm not. I work for and serve at the pleasure of the mission statement. No one person is a boss anymore. Everyone is now a servant of the one boss, the mission statement.

One manager at Concentrus who rejoined the team after learning this principle immediately changed the way he responded to people when they asked him what they should do. In the past, he believed he added value by telling them what to do and how to do it, and they all appreciated that, but with this new approach, he began reminding them, "I'm not your boss, who is?" Then, he would get them to recite the mission statement and ask them, "So, what do you think the mission statement, the boss, would have you do?"

He didn't just throw this at them and walk away. That isn't leadership. It's abdication. Instead, he hung in there with them to work through how to relate each of their issues to how it helps support the mission statement. He trained them on how to do this because as we'll learn in the next chapter—managers tell, leaders ask, and in the process of asking, they train.

THE POWER OF A FULL RESET CEREMONY

Imagine the power of this moment: A strategic leader stands in front of the entire organization and says, "I'm stepping down as your boss, and all the other bosses are stepping down as well. We'll still be here as strategic leaders but not bosses. We now all serve only one boss, the mission statement. If you ever see me doing anything that does not serve that boss, you have the freedom, but more importantly, the responsibility to help me get focused again on serving only the mission, and if I ever see you not serving that boss, I'm asking for the same permission to help you refocus. Let's all make every decision going forward by asking, 'How does this support fulfilling our mission?'"

That is a powerful moment, and I've witnessed it. It immediately begins to flatten the hierarchy in a healthy way and gives us all a true north to guide every decision.

The Mission-Centered Organization

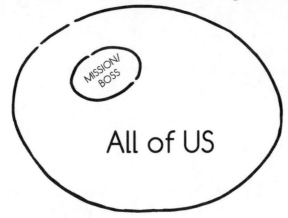

OTHER IMPLICATIONS

As with every tool and practice we present, the Mission-centered approach turns hierarchy on its side to encourage us to relate horizontally, not vertically. When fully implemented, it eliminates power positions and power titles that power-rank people, such as president, vice president, director, manager, and supervisor. None of these gives insight to someone's contribution or value but are focused solely on who is above or below me in the power struggle.

At Crankset Group, everyone is titled functionally by the greatest contribution they bring to the business. We are all chiefs, and some of us have the same functional title: chief hospitality officer, chief results officer, chief transformation officer, chief relationship officer, chief connecting officer, chief operations officer, and so on. Everyone proudly wears a title that proclaims their greatest contribution in a results-based world, not a ranking system that focuses on competition and politics.

One powerful implication of becoming mission centered is a shift away from titles and departments to an emphasis on roles and functions. A strategic tech leader no longer owns the technology department but uses the technology function to serve the mission. We stop thinking about boundaries created by departments and focus instead on cooperation between functions for the sake of the mission. Territorial squabbles cease, and we are compensated for how well our function serves the mission, not for the size of our budget, staff, and square footage.

Needless political rivalries become taboo in a Mission-centered organization. People who want to hoard money, staff, and assets must reset their values. It's no longer a sign of a powerful leader to accumulate more control but a sign of self-focus that does not serve the mission or the company. Remember, as Musk said, "We are all in the same boat. Always view yourself as working for the good of the company, and never for your department."

HOW BEING MISSION-CENTERED WORKS

The Participation Age organizational model aims to increase revenues, grow faster, increase productivity, and attain exponentially higher staff retention. As we make the pivot to being mission centered, our mindset about leadership and who is responsible for what begins to shift.

Imposed Hierarchy -The Managed Model-	Organic DDM Hierarchy -The DDM Workgroup Model-
Person/leader — who is the person who can lead this? A single-person leadership mindset — always solving by finding a person who can lead everyone else (manager-report model).	**People/leadership** — who are the people (not person) who can solve and lead this? A team leadership model.
Titles/reports — VP, director, manager, supervisor — emotionally satisfying, utterly clear hierarchy that slows everything down and stifles innovation. Are these people following me or just pretending to because I can fire them if they don't?	**Functions, ideas, and followers** — three people generate an idea and people follow them. Ideas and innovation come from every corner of the organization, without regard to title. Titles, if any, describe what people contribute, not how much power they have.
Result — how do I impress my boss and make his/her department stronger? (border wars, politics, budget envy, competing for resources, guarding of knowledge).	**Result** — how do we accomplish the mission and make the company stronger? (collaboration, cooperation, communication, community, laser focus on the mission).
Scarcity mindset — we have to get ours before other departments get theirs — more budget, people, resources, square footage, knowledge.	**Abundance mindset** — the more we help other functions succeed, the quicker we all achieve the mission. We are rewarded for giving, not for getting.

KNOW YOUR BOSS INTIMATELY

We must all know the mission statement like we would know a boss. In a Factory System company, we quickly learn if the boss is married, the spouse's name, how many kids, if any, what they like to eat, what kind of car they like, hobbies, humor, politics — it's amazing how much we get to know about that person. Why? Because they hold our work life in their hands and can color us gone with a pen stroke. In turn, we exist to serve that boss.

In a Participation Age company, we purpose to serve the mission, not a boss. That is now the one boss that guides DDM workgroups and the decisions they make in community. If we are truly committed to being mission centered, we will all become as intimately acquainted with the mission statement as we did before with our human bosses. We need to know what every word means, how we interact with its values and vision, how it is being measured, what our customers are saying about it, and how everything we do relates to it.

This does not replace knowing each other. As you will see in the chapter on community, building deep relationships with everyone on our team and living in community across the organization is central to full engagement, increased productivity, and retention of team members. We got to know our human bosses because they had our careers in their hands. We get to know each other and the mission for much better reasons.

MISSION-CENTERED COMPANIES

The following six companies are just a few we would say are mission centered. Most of them are very good at emphasizing functions, DDM workgroups, organic leadership, and cooperation to accomplish the mission.

Haier Corporation — They eliminated managers and reorganized in 2012 around thousands of DDM workgroups. The organization has only three kinds of roles; the "*platform owner*," the "*microenterprise owner*," and the "*entrepreneur*." These develop and dissolve organically; a powerful testimonial to Distributed Decision-making, Universally Distributed Leadership, and being mission centered.

The Morning Star Co. — Chris Rufer and his team brought early and simple clarity to the idea of being mission centered as a way of replacing allegiance to hierarchy, departments, and managers. They train everyone to make localized decisions by asking if it supports their mission. We owe Morning Star a debt for their contribution to being mission centered.

Buurtzorg — The Dutch-based visiting nurse company that went from a startup to thousands of nurses worldwide in less than a decade, all without managers. They put an emphasis on accomplishing the mission through localized DDM teams of twelve nurses per team who self-organize, find their own offices and distribute responsibilities amongst themselves[1].

W. L. Gore — Bill Gore created a flat, lattice-like organizational structure where everyone shares the same title of "associate." There are neither chains of command nor predetermined channels of communication. Leaders replace the idea of "bosses." Associates choose to follow leaders rather than have bosses assigned to them. Allegiance is not to departments but to the mission[2].

Buffer — This company is the creator of a social media management platform. They are "fully distributed" across the United States with an emphasis not on headquarters and departments but on functions, teams, sharing of resources, and getting things done together. They also share all revenue, salaries, profits, etc., openly with each other and the public[3].

GE Aviation — Distributed decision-making teams carry out traditional supervisory tasks such as planning and scheduling production, setting overtime and vacation policies, and improving manufacturing processes. Team members sit on "councils" alongside company leaders and have input into promotions, firings, and overtime decisions. GE leans on team members to understand and take ownership of their work — a key way to engage employees almost immediately[4].

STAY IN RELATIONSHIP WITH YOUR MISSION

When we all serve at the pleasure of the mission, it levels the playing field and invites everyone to stay focused on accomplishing the only thing that really matters. Being mission centered appropriately flattens the entire organization, nudging us into community rather than pitting us against one another.

Let's stop guarding fiefdoms and work together for the good of the company by serving the mission.

THE NEXT ONE THING

Review the examples of ways to focus on being mission centered and decide what could be a next course of action for your organization. What is the Next One Thing you could apply?

1. If you have an "annual report" mission statement that really hasn't meant anything, don't come up with a new one yourself. Get everyone involved via things like Slack.com and have them elect representatives to help design it. Input equals ownership, and people commit to what they create. The more input I have, the more I'll own it.

2. Have a reset meeting to declare our commitment to the mission statement as our one and only boss.

3. Give out copies of our mission statement, with accompanying values and vision statements, with a review of the major things to highlight about the mission statement.

4. Post the mission statement prominently and refer to it regularly.

5. Have strategic leaders (or anyone who can contribute) regularly take a word or short phrase from the mission statement and write something about it, talk about it, describe what it means, how it impacts us when we buy a copier or decide to create another product. Doing this regularly creates a powerful ongoing drumbeat for others to follow.

6. Give out awards once a month or more often for people who were nominated by their peers for going out of their way to serve the mission statement this month.

7. To open any meeting, have someone recite the values, vision, and mission, then ask them for examples of where these have been lived out since we last met. This is one of the simplest and most important ways to keep the values, vision, and mission alive as a guide to daily decision-making.

8. What is the Next One Thing we can do to become more mission centered?

_____

_____

_____

9. How do we measure the success of doing that?

10. What might keep us from doing it, and how do we get past that?

11. When will we do it? _____/_____/_____ by _____:_____ am/pm

12. Who will take responsibility to make sure it gets done (an individual, a team)?

RESOURCES

1   https://www.buurtzorg.com/about-us/buurtzorgmodel/
2   https://www.gore.com/about/our-beliefs-and-principles
3   https://buffer.com/values
4   https://www.hrdive.com/news/ges-self-managed-teams-are-raising-productivity-employee-satisfaction/444498/

CHAPTER THREE

Leaders Are Not Managers 3

"Most of what we call management consists of making it difficult for people to get their jobs done."

—PETER DRUCKER

I n 2012, Haier eliminated the entire middle management of their organization, releasing 75,000 full-time and 90,000 outsourced team members to build DDM workgroups. Traditional thinking might predict this would create a dip in production, but it only served to build on the Distributed Decision-making work Haier had already done[1].

As with Haier's experience, as Participation Age concepts are introduced, we do not see dips, pauses, or instability but immediate improvement in both production and engagement. Only when organizations make the mistake of first taking away a traditional support function does this occur. A move away from imposed hierarchy to organic leadership is an additive process: we add practices and tools that create horizontal relationships that, by extension, reduce or eliminate dependency on a vertical relationship.

Don't eliminate management or imposed hierarchy as a first step, but simply add practices and tools for people to rely on, gradually replacing the Factory System structure. In the next chapter, we propose implementing the practice of having everyone be a leader as one step to eliminating management. In this chapter, we clarify the difference between leadership and management and why leadership should be pervasive throughout the organization where management of people no longer exists.

While some companies understand the importance of leadership,

their misconceptions about managing people stand in the way of
developing effective leaders

Are managers necessary in business, or could we replace them with
fewer strategic leaders who perform none of the traditional management
functions? A few thousand companies of every size have operated
without managers, some of them since the 1950s. Many of the ones we
profile in this book have discovered that the role of management is both
unnecessary and unhelpful. These innovators outperform their peers in
productivity and staff retention by understanding that management is
the problem, not the solution.

To introduce the practice of Distributed Leadership, we need to deal
with the confusion surrounding the difference between management
and leadership. Even though managing people versus leading them leads
to radically different outcomes, most universities and management
consulting firms have conflated these two ideas so much over the last
one hundred years that we no longer know the difference.

Another way to see the vast difference between leadership and
management is to trace the historical roots of both. Leadership is much
harder to trace than management, largely because true leadership is an
organic thing that arises when people decide they want someone else to
impact their life, situation, or performance. Management, however, is
easily traceable throughout history to people with power and authority,
subjugating others with little or no input.

Leadership rises organically throughout history, starting with
human awareness and the search for meaning and later with the rise
of democracy and other social, political, and technological shifts.
True leaders have always emerged without regard to hierarchy or birth
situation. Gandhi, Martin Luther King, and countless other citizens
with no rigid social ranking became heads of state or influenced their
culture for good in democratic countries because people willingly
followed their compelling mission.

The first written mentions of people being managed is in writings
by Hammurabi a few thousand years ago related to slavery. This makes
sense. Any time you require people to work with little or no visible
possibility of gain, the only way to get them to produce is power and
control. We see this management model carried through Middle Age
serfdom into the professional military, which was mimicked by the first
international merchants. When factories arose, they just kept going

with the same military management model, and the Factory System was born and canonized as the only way to run a business.

The Engines of Manager & Leader

In the Participation Age, businesses no long feel the need for this hierarchy and see the long-term damage it has done to business and the reputation of businesses in general. Theodore Roosevelt said, "People ask the difference between a leader and a boss…The leader works in the open, and the boss in covert. The leader leads, and the boss drives[2]."

As individuals, we intuitively see that management and leadership are in direct opposition to one another. When I meet a manager, I get the sense they are important. When I meet a leader, I get the sense I am important. What's the difference? Let's look at the manager first.

> **Management**
> The use of power and authority to command and control, for the benefit of the management.

I have a great cartoon that reflects the above definition. It shows a manager poking his head into a staff person's cubicle, with the caption, "Don't forget. I need to take credit for your report by 3:00 pm."

The two hallmarks of the Participation Age are participation and sharing. If we assume people want to participate in building a great organization and also want to share in the results, they don't need someone to control and command them. It dehumanizes them to know that they are being used for the sake of the organization. Nothing increases the disengagement tax faster than when people who have no input are being used for someone else's benefit.

NAKED CO-DEPENDENCE

Traditional Factory System management is nothing more or less than unadulterated co-dependence. If we called management what it truly is, co-dependence, we would be less likely to inflict it on people in our organization.

Co-dependence has an enabler and someone who is enabled (the dependent). Managers are enablers. Verywell Mind defines enabling as "doing for someone things that they could and should be doing themselves[3]." Note this is very different from helping, which is doing for others what they are incapable of doing. It is also different from training, which is teaching others how to do something for themselves.

Psychology Today gives three attributes of an enabling parent[4], which apply equally to the position of a manager. Manager-employee relationships create the same unhealthy co-dependence:

1. **Being inflexible** — "Because I told you so" or "Because I'm the boss." Most of the time these aren't even spoken. They are already in place due to the utterly clear hierarchy that gives one person the ability to hire, fire, and generally make all the important decisions that affect the lives of the team they manage. As reflected in Scott Adams' *Dilbert* cartoons, management is an insecure position that does not respond well to being challenged, even though the open secret is that the team as a whole generally already has arrived at a better solution on their own.

2. **Having your child [employee] meet your needs** — Management is about using power and authority to command and control childlike employees who wait to be told what to do. It is an inherently self-promoting occupation with misdirected allegiance. Management serve the boss and many times unconsciously uses others to meet their needs for advancement.

3. **Wanting to solve problems for them** — Managers are taught they should be better at solving problems than the people they manage. It's one of the rationales for why they make more money, but it is pure co-dependence (again, "doing for others

things they could and should be doing themselves"). People begin to adapt the false narrative that they are not competent or responsible enough to figure things out for themselves, and then they learn to like it. After all, their home life already includes enough stress and decision-making, so why add more? They'd just be on the hook for more measurable performance at work too. So, the manager likes telling, and the team member likes being told. Co-dependence.

Management struggles with all three of these, but the last one, solving problems for others, creates the most negative impact. An organization design strategist at a giant software company asked me how they could enhance their flagging innovative spirit. I responded that the first thing they needed to do is look around for the people who are serving others. These natural leaders should then train others how to arrive at great solutions together and then get out of the way by diminishing their own role. She responded, "Well, that's going to be a problem here because we promote people specifically for their personal ability to come up with great ideas and solve problems, not for helping others do that." We call this the *heroic genius* model.

In this software company and thousands of similar companies, this is how it works. The heroic genius develops an idea and then recruits others to work with them to make their idea legendary. As a result, the heroic genius gets promoted, and everyone else learns the same "everybody for themselves" mentality. It is a classic example of a manager exerting control, power, and authority for the sake of the manager, yet this software company views it as their most valuable kind of person. It is no wonder they are losing their innovative spirit. People commit to what they create, not what you create for them to run.

Input equals ownership, but since the governed have little input in the decisions that they must carry out, they have no ownership of those initiatives. One manager at this company was baffled because he switched people's career paths without discussion (because it served the manager and the company to do so) and was surprised that they were getting pushback. As in most companies, telling people what to do is the prevailing co-dependent behavior. Let's start calling the role of manager what it really is, co-dependent enabler. Realizing this helps us eradicate it from business.

SOLVE AND DECIDE, OR BECOME LESS IMPORTANT?

As this software company illustrates, the manager's most co-dependent habits are to:

a) solve and decide things, then

b) tell others what to do based on that solution.

If you audit a manager-led meeting, you notice that telling is the default way to communicate with others. Asking, on the other hand, defines the leadership style. Having a manager tell you what to do it is the opposite of empowering. When a manager gives the order to "put this nut on that bolt, at this rate," those receiving that command can feel used and dehumanized, but the only obvious choices for them are to either comply or quit. Managers who solve, decide, and tell dehumanize the workplace by treating people like machines. Leaders do it quite differently. They train others in ways that engage them in meaningful work by first asking as many questions as possible.

Since it is the job of the manager to solve, decide, and tell, managers regularly delegate *tasks* ("put this nut on that bolt"), which makes people feel used. Leaders want to train, so they delegate *responsibility* ("make a great washing machine"), which creates ownership. A waiter has all the responsibility and none of the authority, which lies with the host, cook, and restaurant manager. The waiter just executes orders. Imposing a task like this without authority causes burnout. Delegating responsibility with authority fosters participation and eliminates co-dependence.

Co-dependence is the hallmark of the management system, creating an unhealthy organizational design. The solution is to turn all managers and team members into healthy, interdependent leaders.

Managers tell. Leaders ask.

Leaders use questions to train others to solve problems and make decisions and then get out of the way. You might have been inadvertently labeled a manager, but if you're focused on asking questions, training, and becoming less and less important in your position, you're leading. Your title should be changed to reflect your contribution as a leader.

Leaders delegating the responsibility for a result, as well as the task. Unlike managers, the leader trains the team members to gather the data, develop the report, and analyze it along with the strategic leader. Perhaps surprisingly, great strategic leaders react to data coming at them, whereas managers hold on to the clipboard and do the data gathering and report writing themselves.

Dave Thomas, founder of Wendy's, had one number come and find him every day, the number of buns sold. From that one number, he could extrapolate a wide range of financial and sales information. He worked proactively up front to help set it up but then led reactively to the number coming at him. **Ownership** Others weren't responsible for simple tasks but for **is the most** the entire process of getting that data to Dave. **powerful** This is important because, as we shared previously, when we delegate tasks, people feel used, but **motivator in** when we delegate the broader responsibility for **business.** the result, the metrics, the process, and how to improve all those, that responsibility creates ownership, and ownership is the most powerful motivator in business.

EVERYONE SHOULD BE A LEADER

Yes, everyone. No exceptions. In a Participation Age company, every single person working in your organization can and should be leading others daily.

How can everyone lead? As a general rule of inclusive and Distributed Leadership, we use the following definition to capture all the ways people can lead:

> ### Leadership
> Any act that improves the life,
> situation, or performance
> of another individual.

By this definition, anyone can lead, and everyone should. You can see the striking contrast with our definition of management earlier: "the use of power and authority to command and control, for the sake of the manager."

THE CONTINUUM OF LEADERSHIP

In the Factory System model, leadership is for the few, the strategists, but in a healthy Mission-centered organization, leadership is for everyone and exists on a continuum from strategic leadership to tactical leadership. Most of us are doing both.

Universally Distributed Leadership, as with all the tools and practices in the book, is designed to turn hierarchy on its side and encourage us to relate horizontally, not vertically. All four expressions of leadership are both equal and necessary and should be celebrated and developed by the organization.

The Leadership Continuum

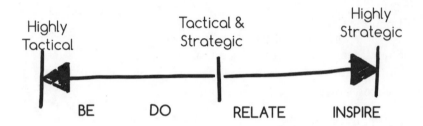

People with broad or expansive views of issues and opportunities are more strategic leaders. A tactical leader has a deeper, more detailed local impact. This isn't a qualitative division, simply a practical one where people find their best contribute to the mission.

Many people function both strategically and tactically to varying degrees. Even in the pyramid scheme hierarchy of the Factory System, many managers (thankfully) don't function like the managers they were hired to be but more intuitively like leaders. While their title may be "manager," they focus instead on improving the life, situation, or performance of others.

When people tell me about a great manager they've had, it is likely that the manager was functioning as a servant leader, not as a manager. They were asking great questions, pushing others forward, mentoring, resourcing, connecting, and training. Most importantly, they were getting out of the way so decisions can be made locally where they are lived out.

The following graphic highlights the leadership continuum. It emphasizes heterarchy, which is organic leadership springing up as needed and then stepping aside as its purpose is fulfilled. The four categories more appropriately would be swirled around together, not layered on top of each other. This reorients us to see organization design and contribution of people from "the edges to the middle and out again," not "top-down and bottom up."

The Mission Centered Organization

Formal Informal Org Function SeamLessly Together

3 Circles of LEADERSHIP

Can exist without management

MISSION/BOSS

Strategic Leadership

Strategic/Tactical Leadership

Tactical/Local Leadership

This transition to Distributed Leadership can happen quite smoothly, but it does not happen overnight. After 200 years of the Factory System, it's hard to say, "You're now all leaders. I'll be in my office." It will take a concerted effort to reawaken the innate leadership potential of everyone in the organization.

THE BEST LEADERS MAKE THE FEWEST DECISIONS

The art of traditional management involves planning, organizing, staffing, controlling, and the shameful act of "manipulating human capital[5]." (I found all these practices embedded in the operations of the giant software company mentioned previously.) The term "human capital" relegates me to being a "resource," but I am not a human resource. I am a human being. In Factory System management models, people are "capital" to be manipulated and controlled. In the DDM workgroups model, they are human beings trained to make decisions locally. Leaders train others because they embrace this principle:

The art of leadership is to know how few decisions the leader needs to make.

Good leaders are passionate about training team members to make decisions that managers used to make. Distributed leadership creates a healthy wave of decision-making throughout the organization. Jack Dorsey, CEO of Twitter and Square says, "If I have to make a decision, we have an organizational failure[6]."

In the Participation Age, a manager making individual decisions for others is failing at strategic leadership, but when you're focused on asking questions, you're training others to make decisions, and you're leading.

MANAGE STUFF. LEAD PEOPLE.

In our company, we only manage stuff: computers, numbers, software, processes, systems, delivery of goods and services, accounting, marketing, sales, etc. Everyone managers stuff, and we all lead each other by asking questions, creating vision, guidance, training, and support.

The leader's quest is to ask questions first, then follow through by training others to solve and decide, rendering the leader less necessary every day. It's important enough to say again: *the art of leadership is to know how few decisions the leader needs to make.* Become a leader — stop solving and deciding and focus instead on asking questions. Everyone and your business will be better off if you do.

THE THREE RESPONSIBILITIES OF A STRATEGIC LEADER

If managers delegate most of the tactical responsibility to their teams, what does leadership look like? Some managers fear they would have nothing left to do, but they will have a more critical focus. Strategic leaders have three main responsibilities:

1. **Guard the values** — the belief system, the values, principles, vision, and mission. These comprise our true north, the compass that tells whether we are wandering or are properly focused. The primary responsibility of any leader is to guard and tenaciously promote the values of the organization. The more we guard the values, the more likely others are to focus properly on production, marketing, sales, revenue, and profits.

2. **Champion the people** — the needs of those who are directly responsible for production, marketing, sales, revenue, and profits. A hundred plus years of research confirm that when we take care of the people, they take care of the business. Too

often, leaders act like managers, making an end run around others and running the business themselves. Then, they wonder why no one is engaged. Great leaders work through others, not around them.

3.   **Pilot the results** — the alignment between the desired corporate result and the process used to get that result. Managers hope that by micromanaging (focusing on the process) they will get a better result. Leaders, on the other hand, focus on the result by consulting with the team A leader asks questions until there is alignment between the process and the result. They delegate figuring out the process to the workgroup.

The Three Leadership Pesponsibilities

Guard The Values
of Principles, Vision, Values, Mission

Champion the People
Train, Mentor, Guide, Support, Resource, Step a side

Pilot the Results
On top of Metrics/Results, Monitoring agreements

Beat the Drum, Gently and Relentlessly

The three action verbs of guard, champion, and pilot should consume most of a strategic leader's attention while also being a secondary responsibility of tactical leaders. Great companies have people who focus on these three simple but never easy actions. What are you focused on? It will tell you whether you are managing or leading.

A DAILY TEST FOR STRATEGIC LEADERS
How can you know if you are leading or falling back into the habit of management? Here are two simple daily measures you can monitor:

1. Ask yourself, are you chasing data, waiting for reports or information? If so, you are managing and not leading. Delegate that to others who are responsible to provide you with the information you need. Lead reactively, not proactively.

2. Ask yourself, are you assigning specific tasks to others or delegating responsibility? If you are merely assigning tasks, you are managing and not leading. Responsibility requires decision-making and creates ownership; completing a task merely requires one small action without reference to the whole.

THE LEADER'S GREATEST ASSET — TRUST

In the Participation Age, trust is the primary asset in every relationship. Without it, there is suspicion, wariness, or simple lack of engagement. Nothing matters more to the strategic or tactical leader than building mutual trust.

THE LEADER'S GREATEST PRACTICE — CONSISTENCY

Consistent behavior is the only way to build trust. Say what you will do and do what you said regarding values, metrics, support, and processes. Nothing hurts a leader's credibility more than acting in opposition to what was agreed upon.

Our greatest asset is trust. We build it with consistent behavior; say what you will do, then do what you said.

When my team senses that I'm overreaching as we interact, they know that they have the freedom and responsibility to speak up. A billionaire connected with me to ghostwrite a book for him and help launch a new initiative. As I began to work on the project, two of my teammates sat me down and expressed concern that working with him was not consistent with four of our five values. With their help, it was an easy call to guard our values instead of taking on this project. We moved on quickly.

GOOD MANAGEMENT OF PEOPLE IS NOT POSSIBLE

When we help leaders see the difference between managing and leading people, some respond that we're just talking about bad management versus good management, but confusing managing with leading is paralyzing.

There are indeed good and bad leaders and good and bad managers. Here is a review of the major differences:

1. **Organic vs. imposed** — Leaders rise up organically because people voluntarily follow them. Managers are imposed and exert power and authority to control the people they manage.

2. **Others vs. self** — Leaders exist to serve others, while managers exist to promote themselves. Some people are promoted not because they're good at helping others but because they are singularly good at what they do, as in the heroic genius we mentioned earlier. Good leaders, on the other hand, gradually make themselves less important and eliminate co-dependency by training others to do things for themselves.

3. **Provide vs. accumulate** — Leaders provide vision, guidance, tools, access, support, training, opportunities, and connections to champion their people, but managers are about accumulating bigger departments, more people, and larger budgets, which serves the manager and their department, not the mission.

4. **Ask vs. Tell** — Leaders train by asking good, open-ended questions. Managers command by telling. Managers partially justify their positions by saving others from making mistakes or having to figure things out. Their position requires them to be the most competent, highly skilled expert in the room. Conversely, great leaders understand that their job isn't to be the only ones who generate new ideas or develop processes, but it is to teach, equip, and free the team to do this.

The following T-Chart shows a few summary comparisons of the position of manager versus leader. You can see that they are very different roles with very different outcomes. Leadership is essential to building a great Participation Age company, while management is the central problem in the Factory System model.

Manager	Leader
Imposed — People are reports	Organic — People are followers
Self — I am prominent	Others — They are prominent
Accumulate — People, budget, resources	Provide — People, budget, resources
Tell — I make decisions	Ask — I train them to make decisions
Delegate task (people feel used)	Delegate responsibility (creates ownership)
Focus on process	Focus on results
Manage by policies, HR	Lead by vision, principles, mentors
Proscriptive — I forbid and limit	Prescriptive — I recommend and release
Roots in slavery, serfdom, & military	Roots in movements, ideas, values, beliefs
Unnecessary Factory System artifact	Timeless and necessary in every organization

Many misnamed managers focus on serving and should be correctly renamed leaders. Remember, manage stuff. Lead people. In the next chapter, we see how teams can take over the management of stuff. How can everyone be a leader? Let's dive in.

THE NEXT ONE THING

1. Learn to ask, not tell.
    a. When I think of something I would like to tell someone, I turn it into a question that invites them to problem-solve and respond.
    b. If they are confused, I demonstrate with a question I would ask myself to arrive at a solution. I walk them through the process.
2. List the few decisions.
    a. For a month or a quarter, keep a running list of all the decisions you make.
    b. Take an hour to separate the ones you need to keep making from the ones you can begin to delegate. (Strategic leaders need to make very few decisions.)
    c. Prioritize just the top three and come up with a plan to delegate them to someone else.
    d. Repeat until you are making as few decisions as possible. (The art of leadership is to know how few decisions the leader needs to make). You should find that most of the decisions you keep for yourselves as strategic leaders fall into the category of guard the values, and even then, you will know you are being successful in building a great company because you rarely have to make any of those decisions because everyone else has embraced and owned the company values, vision, and mission.
3. Focus on the three responsibilities.
    a. Never do strategic work in the same location as your tactical, everyday work. It won't get done. Have a strategic place away from any tactical distractions (an idea pond, a path, a home office, a library, a coffee shop).
    b. Make a standing appointment to meet yourself there and treat it as your most important meeting with your most important client. Never violate it. Review your values, people,

and results, and develop one or two actions each week related to them.

   c. Share it with others, with dates for completion — get a support buddy (accountability has negative connotations).

4. Implement a one- or two-question survey that goes out every week or month to everyone.

   a. Example: On a scale of one to ten, how well did we trust each other this week?

   b. Example: On a scale of one to ten, how consistent were we at keeping our commitments to each other?

   c. Ask others what one question we should all be asking that week.

   d. Use this to set the bar high and then keep raising it.

PRACTICES TO DEVELOP

All of these, when practiced consistently, help us develop trust, our greatest asset.

Practice #1 — Ask, don't tell. Remember, managers tell, and leaders ask. Great leaders ask questions on an ongoing basis that get us moving in the right direction, not to guide us to their answer but to help us all find the best solution together. There is no more positive impact than adopting this one behavior. It rehumanizes your workplace and gives everyone their brain back.

Practice #2 — Train, then get out of the way. The mental muscles for making decisions in the workplace must be developed. Training is the process of walking someone through a thought process so that they can make their own decisions. "Telling" should only happen in the context of training — "I will tell you how to approach this unfamiliar process so that you can learn how to do it, and I can get out of the way after you do."

Practice #3 — Invest your time on the three responsibilities of a leader. If you are a strategic leader, relentlessly guard the values, champion the people, and pilot the results. When you focus on these three things, others can pilot the processes, production, marketing, and other core business operations.

Practice #4 — Be consistent. Say what you're going to do, then do what you said. It is the only way to build trust.

Practice #5 — Trust in adult behavior. Believe others are smart, motivated, and want to participate in building a great company. Distribute the decision-making, being aware that making mistakes is part of the learning process. The rewards of working together can yield a corporate core of rich wisdom, experience, and satisfaction. Early in the transition, you may feel like you are pushing water uphill with a rake. Remember that people have decades of experience living as co-dependents in the Factory System model and, in some cases may need to re-learn how to make decisions.

THE NEXT ONE THING

1. What is the Next One Thing we can do to create more strategic and tactical leadership (add leadership, don't yet remove management. That will happen naturally).

_____

_____

2. How do we measure the success of doing that?

_____

_____

3. What, if anything, might keep us from doing it, and how do we get past that?

_____

_____

4. When will we do it? ____/____/____ by ____:____ am/pm

5. Who will take responsibility to make sure it gets done (an individual, a team)?

_____

_____

There are several other practices associated with Participation Age leadership that we share in workshops, retreats, presentations, and papers, but this is not a book focused solely on leadership. If you'd like more information on how to lead in the Participation Age, contact us at Grow@CranksetGroup.com

RESOURCES

1   https://corporate-rebels.com/haier/

2   https://www.goodreads.com/quotes/401364-people-ask-the-difference-between-a-leader-and-a-boss.

3   https://www.verywellmind.com/enabling-alcoholic-is-not-helping-63297.

4   https://www.psychologytoday.com/us/blog/business-success-therapists/201108/are-you-raising-codependent-child

5   universalteacher.com/topic/management/

6   https://www.businessinsider.com/square-ceo-jack-dorsey-management-decision-making-2015-5

CHAPTER FOUR

Everybody Is a Leader

"Knowledge workers have to manage themselves. They have to have autonomy."

—PETER DRUCKER

To deconstruct the traditional Factory System organization, you can't start by subtracting managers or their responsibilities. To do so invites the risk of chaos. The right approach is to share the vision and gradually add actions that help create movement toward DDM workgroups and away from the Factory System hierarchy.

In the early 2000s, Google declared very publicly "the end of managers," and then just a few short months later, reeled it all back in. It didn't work because Google removed them without presenting a clear vision for what could more effectively replace them or any options for how to organize differently. It was a free-for-all. Distributed leadership properly provides the first step and the structure needed to allow the managed model to melt into obsolescence in a very organized manner.

DO MANAGERS MAKE PEOPLE MORE PRODUCTIVE?

As we have said previously, we assume managers make people more productive, justifying their presence by supposedly adding profit to the bottom line. Surprisingly, the only study I am aware of in the last 120 years that attempts to prove this assumption is Google's Project Oxygen. Published in 2008 and updated in 2018, it outlines ten behaviors people at Google need from someone else:

1. Good coach
2. Empowers the team and does not micromanage

3. Creates an inclusive team environment
4. Is productive and results-oriented
5. Listens and shares as a good communicator
6. Supports career development and discusses performance
7. Has a clear vision for the team
8. Has key technical skills to advise the team
9. Collaborates across the company
10. Is a strong decision-maker

As a result of defining these ten very helpful behaviors, in 2008 Google announced, "managers matter," and the 2018 update reaffirmed, "We now know that managers *still* matter[1]," but the conclusion was fatally flawed by confirmation bias, sampling bias, and false correlation.

Confirmation bias interprets new evidence as validation of one's existing beliefs or theories. One of the co-leaders of Project Oxygen, Neal Patel said, "We ended up trying to prove that managers don't matter. *Luckily* we failed[2]." Similar sighs of relief came from others at Google who depended on the study to affirm the existence of managers.

The bigger evidence of confirmation bias is found in the sampling bias. Sampling bias excludes data that would not support a desired outcome. A study designed to broadly answer the question, "Do managers matter?" would have sampled a wide range of organizational models and companies, not just one model in one company. A neutral study would not have ignored the few hundred highly visible large corporations and the thousands of mid-sized to smaller companies that have run for over sixty years without managers of any sort. A quick glance at these hundreds of companies, most of which function at the top of their professions or industries, would have provided the clear message that indeed managers don't matter. If they mattered, there could not be so many companies across all industries operating at the highest levels without them. Something else matters.

MANAGERS DON'T MATTER, THE TEN BEHAVIORS DO

Another issue is the flawed correlation between the ten behaviors and the need for managers. As we know, correlation does not imply causation. Students of causation are taught that crime rates rise along with ice cream consumption, and divorce rates rise as people use more margarine, yet there is no causation between them.

As a reminder from Chapter Three, we and many others make a

clear distinction between management and leadership. Leadership, both tactical and strategic, is critical to the success of any organization. Management (of people) does more to stand in the way of success than anything else we do.

Google rightly identified ten behaviors that people want from others at work and then assumed that managers are the only way to deliver those behaviors. The study didn't prove that managers matter at all; it proved that the ten behaviors matter. This is a form versus function problem. Google identified ten functions (behaviors) that Googlers identified as necessary for them to do their jobs and then summarily decided there was only one form that could deliver them — a manager. What if all ten of those behaviors could delivered better by teams of people to themselves as a workgroup?

PEOPLE, NOT PERSON—TEAM, NOT MANAGER

We give kudos to Google for identifying the ten necessary behaviors, but the way we deliver those ten behaviors is a problem of mindset. The Factory System taught us to look for a single person (manager) to deliver them when the better answer may be to look for a group of people to deliver them to each other. The better answer seems to reside in the plural, as in people, not one individual, because multiple people are always more successful at delivering those ten things than any one heroic genius. It is too much to ask of any one person.

I don't know any manager who exhibits all ten of these behaviors consistently and very few who could even deliver most of them. In Participation Age companies like ours, teams of people divide up the list according to individual strengths, so the teams can deliver more consistently on all ten with each other than any one manager would. Haier's 4,000 teams of ten to fifteen people each demonstrate this very well. Each team functions as an independent business, with responsibility for its own vision, strategy, tactics, processes, production, wages, personnel issues, hiring, and firing.

A reset in our thinking may be in order, leading to reorganizing around DDM workgroups, not top-down management. The success of the many companies thriving without managers signals to us that we may not have to find an individual person to be *the* leader or manager. Form should always follow function. The essential

Form should always follow function.

functions here are the ten behaviors, but there are multiple forms that could deliver these functions, and the top-down management structure we borrowed from the military is only one of those. History teaches us that the manager form is one option, but we believe it is not the best one.

To summarize, Participation Age companies demonstrate we can look to a team of people to successfully co-lead through the practice of Universally Distributed Leadership. According to the data, there are better ways to bring those ten qualities to bear than attempting to find them all in one superhuman with the title of manager.

Nothing replaces hierarchy with horizontal relationships better than Distributed Leadership. Most teams, regardless of their education, collectively own more of the behaviors, skills, and talents necessary to manage themselves than any one manager can normally provide. Decision-making by a few in a hierarchy cheats the company out of the full-orbed perspective it could gain from acting on more than one or two viewpoints. Everyone across the organization is needed for optimal decision- making.

Education level is not a factor in Distributed Leadership. The Morning Star Company, with approximately 4,000 people and a large percentage that has no education beyond high school, has no managers and practices Universally Distributed Leadership. The reality is that people with more practical experience, common sense, and good intuition generally make better decisions, regardless of their educational level.

THE FOUR MODES OF LEADERSHIP

Everyone can lead. No exceptions. The problem is with our definition of leadership. When someone says the word "leader," what image comes to mind? For many of us, it's the guy on the white horse out front giving motivational speeches and leading the charge: General George Patton, Tony Robbins, Mahatma Gandhi, President Kennedy, Margaret Thatcher, Martin Luther King, or one of my favorites, Mary Parker Follett, who was a true prophet of the Participation Age from the 1920s.

Steve Jobs, Elon Musk, Jeff Bezos, and Warren Buffet all have at least one common trait — they are inspirational. They inspire us to attempt greater things than we might without their vision.

Inspirational strategic leadership is by far the rarest form, but it is the most celebrated. *The Gladiator, Rob Roy, Braveheart, Gandhi, Black Panther, Lincoln* — movies about "leadership" are almost always about the guy on the white horse out front. If this is leadership, then most of us truly have no shot at leading, but there are at least three other, much more common forms of leadership that invite every one of us to be great leaders on an everyday basis to those around us, and they are practiced through Distributed Leadership.

THE FOUR MODES OF LEADERSHIP

In the Distributed Leadership system, the following four verbs—be, do, inspire, and relate— describe what everyone on the team does.

BE

Honesty, integrity, sincerity, tenacity, joy, patience, kindness, gentleness, being level-headed, detail-oriented, strategic-minded, loving, etc. All these character traits are clear and powerful forms of leadership when they are used to improve the life, situation, or performance of another individual. Any one of us can lead by simply being. Without saying a word, we can inspire people to improve their lives.

DO

Whether it's baseball, oral hygiene, typing, music, reports, training, coding, writing, or running a process consistently, we can all find a way to contribute to the well-being of others. Anyone can lead by doing something with excellence that impacts the life, situation, or performance of another individual.

INSPIRE

This default image of leadership is limited to highly visible, very dynamic personalities, yet I can inspire someone by being or doing something or talking very quietly in a private conversation. We can all be inspiring. It's not about whether we can fill a lecture hall or get on the evening news but whether we can inspire one other person in a way that improves their life, situation, or performance. Anyone can be inspiring simply by practicing one of the other three leadership modes.

RELATE

Can you be a friend, counselor, mediator, adviser, reconciler, peacemaker, party host, small circle leader, or best yet, a good listener? Every one of us can lead others in some relational way that makes them better.

The Four Modes of Leadership

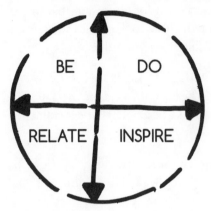

Anyone can assert one of these four forms of leadership to improve the life, situation, or performance of another person, and most of us lead with multiple expressions of leadership. The questions I want to ask are:

a) to what degree am I improving the lives of others, and

b) what form is that influence and improvement taking?

OPEN SPACE LEADERSHIP

Open space leadership is practiced by strategic leaders in Participation Age companies and by good leaders everywhere. It encourages Distributed Leadership by requiring everyone to lead in some way. Open space leadership is the act of throwing out an idea or a need and inviting everyone to jump in and address it. Conceptually it's a little like starting with a blank canvas and probing about to see how it is filled, which is quite different from asking if people like or dislike an already finished painting. We throw out an idea and invite people to help create the painting. If someone likes the idea enough, they will pick up their brush and begin to paint with us.

Distributed leadership, or leadership by everyone, is a deep shift away from the military-style reporting structure that is at the core of the dehumanizing Factory System. The military is aggressively studying how to decentralize more as they enter an asynchronous world of resistance. Traditional centralized militaries are like spiders; cut off the head, and the organization dies. The asynchronous world of resistance is more like a few species of starfishes. If you cut off some arms, the arms grow back, and the severed arms grow new heads and bodies. All you did was multiply how many starfishes there are.

Distributed leadership allows businesses such as Haier, the Morning Star Company, Nearsoft, and our own to respond like starfishes to an asynchronous, complex economic world.

DISTRIBUTED LEADERSHIP IN ACTION

Captain David Marquet inherited the Santa Fe, the worst-rated submarine in the entire US Navy, yet in one year he turned it into the best rated sub in the whole fleet, and here's the kicker: he did it with the same 134 people who had made it the worst for a few years in a row. In just one year, with the same people, the same sub, and the same entrenched military organization outside the sub, they went from worst to first. Stephen Covey visited his sub and called it "the most empowering organization I've ever seen[3]."

What changed? One thing, the leader, and in reality, you don't have to switch leaders because the real difference here was not brought on by a different leader but by a different belief system that the leader adopted. This had nothing to do with charisma, motivational speech, steely-eyed bravery, or brilliant solutions. It was simply about one thing: Distributed Leadership. Captain Marquet invited the other 134 people to participate by both allowing and requiring them to lead.

To make that happen, he and his officers formally redesigned as much of the hierarchical pyramid as they could, so that that decisions would now be made locally whenever possible. Captain Marquet lived out one of our core Crankset Group principles:

The art of leadership is knowing how few decisions a leader needs to make.

Managers make a living by making decisions. Great leaders make an impact by asking questions. Marquet called it all "intentional leadership" and insisted that even in crisis situations he would not revert to command and control. He always insisted on localized decision-making.

He wasn't out of the loop, but he taught people to come to him with answers and plans for execution, and instead of telling them what to do, he would ask probing questions, resolve the questions, and the submariners would institute their plans.

LEADERSHIP — A CULT OF SYSTEMS

This is the first major lesson of Distributed Leadership. Great leadership is a cult of systems, not a cult of personality. For many years after Marquet left the boat, and through subsequent submarine captains, the Santa Fe continued to produce more Navy leaders than other ships or boats. It wasn't the ghost of Marquet's aura that brought it about but the presence of a system of Distributed Leadership that lived on long after he was gone.

As Marquet's example shows, Distributed Leadership is a system that creates its own legacy and impacts the organization long after the trailblazing leaders who put it in place step back. A "heroic genius" is only effective while he or she stays with the company, but when leadership and decision-making wash through the entire organization as a system, it carries on without you.

Distributed leadership is a radical departure from the idea that leadership is about a single, powerful leader with vision and an unflinching personal tenacity to move everyone forward in the face of adversity. The cult of personality only lasts as long as the hero is up front on the white horse.

Distributed leadership is a cult of *systems*. The leader makes Distributed Leadership systemic by getting everyone to embrace and practice it. Distributed leadership doesn't rely on one person, so it is self-sustaining; everyone owns the decisions and results. As part of our business, we help CEOs and other leaders build a system that everyone can embrace and operate.

We see that in great business organizations such as W. L. Gore, Semco, and many others, the originator of Distributed Leadership is no longer there, yet the businesses thrive because leadership is systemic, not individual. This should encourage any leaders who feel inadequate to be a George Patton or a Tony Robbins. They just have to believe that everyone wants to participate in building a great company and have the resolve to champion that into existence.

THE ORGANIZATION MUST CHANGE

This is the second major lesson of Distributed Leadership. To be effective, we must structurally change the way we organize. Taking someone for a walk to encourage more involvement won't suffice. The traditional Factory System structure must be replaced and redesigned. Any attempted syncretism of the old and new systems will fail. Organic leadership, as demonstrated by all our examples, is a thing of beauty, but it must be allowed to thrive without the overload of imposed hierarchy.

Some organizational leaders make impassioned pleas to help them lead, followed by the old "open door policy" comment. Most of them truly want that input, but the top-down hierarchy remains in place. The missing ingredient is formal redistribution of leadership responsibilities from managers to everyone.

We can't just say we want people to "lead from your seat." That is empty hyperbole. Frankly, if they took our advice, it would require them to buck the very hierarchy of imposed management they suffer under. The invitation sets everyone up for a showdown. Most people are smart enough not to take a manager seriously when they're invited to join in leading, knowing that it may get them into trouble.

We won't get people to participate and share, the two hallmarks of the Participation Age, unless we are willing to radically change the imposed management reporting structure. This means formally pushing leadership responsibilities across the entire organization instead of being held closely by a few at the top. Only then can we expect localized decision-making of the kind that will be a cult of systems and not a cult of personality. We must swap out the Factory System hierarchy for DDM workgroups and teams.

LEADER-LEADER

The third major lesson of Distributed Leadership is a leader-leader model of organization design, where there are no managers, and everyone is a leader. That may seem like inviting chaos, but it is remarkably simple and effective.

To get there, we need to deal with two imposed hierarchy issues that stand in the way of leader-leader:

1. Manager-report relationships — Managers have "reports," people who report to them. This manager-report relationship

must fade away. Leaders have followers who choose to follow because that leader is adding value to their work lives. It's important to say here again that many managers act like leaders instead of managers, and as a result, people who have been assigned to report to them end up following them as well, but that shouldn't be something we just hope happens. The opportunity to follow or not follow should be built into the system because that tells us who really wants to be there and who is only reluctantly going through the motions.

2. Imposed hierarchy — Imposed hierarchy is designed and implemented from the top down. No matter how poorly it functions, the people in an organization do not have the power to resist or change it. All they can do is be disengaged and dehumanized or leave. In the Distributed Leadership model, we replace the imposed hierarchy with organic leadership. At Crankset Group, organic leadership comes from the edges in and center out, bringing 100 percent engagement for everyone who works in our company. We arrive at an utter clarity division of roles and responsibilities and create pervasive engagement because we all work together to align the responsibilities with the right people to carry them out. At Crankset Group, people have full say in who leads them, and in many cases, it ends up being two or more people on the team who lead together. Power and authority are no longer associated with an imposed hierarchy but with expertise, ideas, vision, service, mentoring, action, skill, character, and other attributes of leadership that people choose to follow. When hierarchy, which is normal and natural, is arrived at by consensus, it becomes leadership in the best sense and really only of the word.

AUTHORITY BY EXPERTISE

After two centuries of embracing the Factory System as the only option for organizing a business, the idea of organic leadership and hierarchy can be confusing or even baffling. Our lens is deeply colored by the models we are already immersed in, but if we look at history, we see that most strategic leadership over the centuries has been organic, brought about by someone's expertise or vision.

Participation Age companies allow and require leadership to be chosen by those who would be led. At Haier, leadership comes to those who develop viable new product concepts or can put together a team to solve complex problems. This has encouraged creativity and innovation throughout the company. At Menlo Innovations, a software development company in Ann Arbor, Michigan, there is no formal hierarchy and no imposed reporting relationships. Instead, they encourage people to naturally become leaders by being "gentle, empathetic, and trusting teachers." This organic approach is based on peer reviews and leaves it up to team members to award raises and leadership positions to each other, which turns out is much less political than having a manger decide.

The great initiatives, ideas, disruptions, and revolutions (like our own American Revolution), and the great strategic leaders themselves primarily rose outside of any imposed structure and no ability to coerce people to follow. Heroic geniuses have their place as initiators (Google was started by two of them), but they are at their best when they immediately start practicing Distributed Leadership, as Gandhi did in the early days of India's freedom.

These are not new ideas. In the 1920s, Mary Parker Follett wrote on "authority by expertise" and the "giving of orders":

> *"One person should not give orders to another person, but both should agree to take their orders from the situation. If orders are simply part of the situation, the question of someone giving and someone receiving does not come up. Both accept the orders given by the situation. Moreover, we have now to lay somewhat less stress than formerly on this matter of the leader influencing his group because we now think of the leader as also being influenced by his group[4]."*

She had an early following, including Teddy Roosevelt, but her writings were lost and largely unheralded until the last decade. She wrote against the "giving of orders" as missing a great opportunity to invite the worker to *participate* in decisions that affected them. Instead, she developed the ideas of the "authority of expertise" and "power with" instead of "power over." She was ahead of her time.

ELIMINATING THE MANAGEMENT TAX

Distributed decision-making results in the elimination of what my friend Doug Kirkpatrick so rightly labeled the management tax[5].

Billions of dollars are spent every year on the untested assumption that managers make people more productive, pay for themselves, and add profit. In a small company with profits of $150,000 a year and five managers making $80,000 each, they could easily acquire another $240,000 to $320,000 directly to the bottom line by distributing the leadership among team members. By operating with one fully strategic leader instead of five managers, that leader can be paid more.

Spodak Dental Group in Delray Beach, Florida, has fifty-five team members (including dentists and the founder, Dr. Craig Spodak), and one strategic leader, Erika Pusillo, who still dives in tactically here and there when needed. They save hundreds of thousands of dollars every year by eliminating managers through the practice of Distributed Leadership. It's a great example of how companies can eliminate the management tax. In a large organization like W. L. Gore with 10,000 people, the savings gained by adopting Distributed Leadership also creates a measurable increase in team member engagement and retention.

Through Distributed Leadership, you can replace every seven to ten managers with one leader. Since this is an additive process (don't start by eliminating managers), it is orderly and usually takes care of itself through natural attrition as managers become leaders or change their function on a team.

Rarely, people with a deep need for command and control self-identify and leave quickly. One company we worked with had a manager turn in his resignation the day they proposed Distributed Decision-making. Not surprisingly, it turned out to be a great thing. For weeks afterward, the CEO told me about the regular stream of people who shared with him how relieved they were that this person was gone and how much better things were. Nobody missed what the CEO had seen as an indispensable contribution. The organization improved instantly as he self-selected to go someplace where he could continue telling people what to do.

Distributed leadership is a fundamental shift from relying on an imposed management hierarchy to developing everyone's four leadership traits (be, do, inspire, relate). They use these traits to make localized decisions. Distributed leadership lays the foundation for a great organization where everyone participates and everyone shares in the rewards. It starts the process of rehumanizing your workplace by giving everyone their decision-making brain back.

KIDS CAN LEAD

As we highlighted in the prologue (A Few Organizations to Get to Know), Sudbury Valley Schools has no headquarters, no K-12 class structure (no seniors or first graders), no traditional classes, no classrooms, no curriculum, no grading, and no teachers. Adult staff facilitate alongside whatever learning the students are doing. On the first day of school, the students and the facilitators decide together how the year should be organized and what they will commit together to accomplishing. Everyone has one vote, including the facilitators.

Most of us would assume children would not be able to create and run their own Distributed Decision-making organization, yet that happens every year in every Sudbury school throughout the nation. Eighty-five percent of students go on to higher education, and 42 percent are involved in entrepreneurial pursuits. Even children want to participate and share in building their own futures. People commit to what they create, and Sudbury students are very committed[6].

THE NEXT ONE THING

1. Distributed leadership discovery exercise — a powerful, simple exercise to help everyone see how they are already leaders:
    a. Have everyone write the name of each team member at the top of separate sticky notes (one for each team member).
    b. With one teammate in mind, review the four modes of leadership (be, do, inspire, relate). On the appropriate sticky note, write one to three ways that person leads you right now. The four modes are just reminders — it might be something much more specific.
    c. Have everyone collect the sticky notes from their teammates. How do others see you as a leader? Share that. You should feel free to ask a teammate to amplify on a response if needed.
    d. Post the sticky notes where you can see them and are reminded of how you already lead in the world around you. Work at developing those leadership strengths.
2. Have a reset meeting to teach people to stop coming to strategic leaders for answers but to come instead with solutions in hand, ready to answer questions. Talk openly and regularly about how decisions can be made locally where they must be carried out.
3. Have managers make a list of their decision-making responsibilities

and discuss together which one they think they can distribute to the team first, how (usually through some form of training), and by when.

a. Meet regularly (weekly? bi-weekly?) to support each other in developing others as leaders.

THE NEXT ONE THING

1. What is the Next One Thing we can do to create Distributed Leadership?

_____

_____

_____

2. How do we measure the success of doing that?

_____

_____

_____

3. What, if anything, might keep us from doing it, and how do we get past that?

_____

_____

_____

4. When will we do it?_____/_____/_____ by _____:_____ am/pm

5. Who will take responsibility to make sure it gets done (an individual, a team)?

_____

_____

_____

RESOURCES

1   https://rework.withgoogle.com/blog/the-evolution-of-project-oxygen/
2   https://hbr.org/2013/12/how-google-sold-its-engineers-on-management
3   https://hbr.org/2015/05/6-myths-about-empowering-employees
4   Mary P. Follett. "Dynamic Administration: The Collected Papers of Mary Parker Follett", ed. by E. M. Fox and L. Urwick (London: Pitman Publishing, 1940)
5   https://www.amazon.com/Beyond-Empowerment-Age-Self-Managed-Organization/dp/1944878386
6   https://sudburyvalley.org/theory

CHAPTER FIVE

Your Beliefs Determine Your Destiny

5

I n a Participation Age organization, a solid working set of values drives every decision. You want everyone in your organization to be able to recite your values reflexively and describe how they live them out.

Neither managers nor employees produced the Factory System. That system stems from a particular view of the world and how we think about people, business, success, organizations, leadership, money, and our work. If we were just thinking straight about these things, the Factory System would never have happened. It is simply incongruent with creating the most productive business environment.

At Crankset Group, the values, vision, and mission we work out together become our belief system. Most companies write important-sounding statements in their annual reviews, but few rarely live them out as the heartbeat of their day-to-day decision-making, yet our values, whether written or not, form our culture.

You don't create a culture; you simply live out what you believe.

What do you believe? I'm not talking about what you wrote in your annual report. What values inform each decision? As Maya Angelou said, "When people show you who they are, believe them." Most organizations tell people who they are and then show something very different, but what you believe is what you will act on. Your values dictate your decisions and your business culture. Peter Drucker famously stated, "Culture eats strategy for lunch."

My friend Alan Wyngarden understands the priority of beliefs above production. Alan had a successful mortgage company for a few decades. He had crafted a great life and was deeply respected by other business owners who all attested to his success. Then, Alan clarified his Big Why, or lifetime goals[1], and everything changed. Alan wasn't driven by mortgage processing but by the unrelenting desire to "help people get from where they are to where they need to be."

After clarifying his personal Big Why, his values, vision, mission, and business came into even better focus. Within five years, he was out of the mortgage business and had built five very successful assisted living centers for Alzheimer's sufferers, all in alignment with what he really believed about why he was in business. The company was named by some (one?) of its Alzheimer's residents, Applewood Our House. To live out his Big Why, all the centers were built around Distributed Decision-making. Each facility is its own profit-center, and all team members are participating leaders and capitalists who split (50percent) of the profits, with the rest going to the company.

For Applewood Our House, the absence of managers is an asset. People work instead through a network of teams, so turnover is significantly lower than the industry standards, and engagement is exponentially higher than the 30 percent national average.

Alan will tell you what we say all the time: doing this is simple but not easy. Ultimately, the result is far better because Alan and the organization own mutually shared values, driven by the Big Why.

EVERY COMPANY IS DRIVEN BY ITS VALUES

Enron was driven by a set of values. So are companies we admire. We all bring business beliefs to work with us, but we aren't likely to write them down to use as our true north for every decision. Instead, by default, we tend to employ situational ethics, with no attachment to a bigger plan. When we don't know what guides our decisions, the result can lead to chaos, confusion, and bad decisions.

Great strategic leaders know their beliefs and values, write them down, and drive them to every corner of the organization. They learn to beat the values drum, gently but relentlessly, which helps create true adoption of the mission across the entire organization. You can never over-communicate your values.

CULTURE IS NOT A PROGRAM

Culture is not something you take on as a project or a program. Any company attempting to overtly build a better culture is misdirecting its efforts. If they focus instead on what they believe, the culture develops naturally around that. In fact, if you don't like what you see, chances are that some unspoken and less than desirable cultural attributes have adversely affected your organization. Lack of clarity about a true north creates a culture where anything that gets a great short-term result is acceptable, while ignoring any long-term negative effect.

Culture can be constructive or destructive, healthy or unhealthy. If you don't like your culture, change your belief system. In Netflix's famous slide deck on Freedom and Responsibility[2], slide number twenty-four says, "A great workplace is *not* day-care, espresso, health benefits, sushi lunches, nice offices, or big compensation."

Netflix only espouses activities that support:

Freedom and responsibility.

The belief that every single person should be a stunning colleague, and because of this, you will want to work at Netflix.

HOW DO BELIEFS DETERMINE OUR DESTINY?

The following Why Beliefs Matter diagram divides our work world into three sections on the continuum:

1. The world in our heads — Contrary to the pragmatic approach that says only production matters, this is as much a part of the "real world" as anything we can see. What is in our heads *defines* everything we can see.

2. The visible world — Because this is the one-third of the world we connect with through our five physical senses, our actions and habits seem largely driven by what we see, despite the fact that all our actions actually stem from what we believe and value.

3. Our future world — legacy is an artifact of beliefs and values lived out consistently in the visible world. This is true for failed companies as well as successful ones — our beliefs determine our destiny.

Enron was named "America's Most Innovative Company" six years in a row right up to the year it declared bankruptcy in 2001 from some very deceptive accounting practices. CEO Jeffery Skilling was sentenced to twenty-four years in prison, and accounting giant Arthur Anderson, the main auditing firm for Enron, was convicted of obstruction of justice and driven out of business with the loss of thousands of jobs.

I cite Enron here because they didn't just have a values statement on the inside flap of their annual report. They developed and widely distributed a booklet called *The Enron Code of Ethics Manual,* a sixty-four-page swearing of allegiance to all things ethical. The gap between the visible world of their ethics manual and the world in their heads that drove their true behavior was a Grand Canyon.

The story of Enron is instructive. People should not listen to what we say we believe but should instead look at what behaviors are being carried out in the visible world, which reflect our true beliefs. When companies tell you who they are, thank them. When they show you who they are, believe them. Do you want to know what a company (or an individual) believes? Look at what they do, not at what they say they believe.

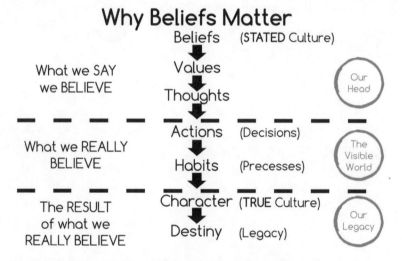

Why Beliefs Matter

YOUR BELIEFS DETERMINE YOUR VALUES

We must get our actions in the visible world to line up with what we say we believe. Here's how it works:

1. **Our beliefs determine our values.** If you believe people are smart and motivated, and I believe they are stupid and lazy, we may treat them very differently. At the very outset, before we have left our heads and entered the visible world, we have diverged toward two very different outcomes.

2. **Our values determine our thoughts.** If you value people

highly, and I see them as disposable, we also think about them in vastly different ways. I think of them as disposable, and you think of them as precious.

3. **Our thoughts determine our actions.** Now we enter the visible world, where it becomes clear how much impact our differing beliefs have on day-to-day decisions. Depending on our perspective, we may make vastly different decisions about how we treat others, how or whether we attempt to retain them, and how or if we develop their potential.

4. **Our actions determine our habits.** Driven by what we believe, we act predictably with a defined set of decision-making biases, forming a habit, which in business terms can be called a process. In the workplace, these are "default" processes, meaning they are not something anyone has written down. Rather, they are deduced by interactions with the boss, who creates a pattern of predictable behavior based on similar past situations.

5. **Our habits determine our character.** In business terms, our character is our culture. It doesn't appear by focusing on external culture, blue jeans, free lunches, ping pong tables, or clever sayings on the walls. Through what we believe and a long-term habit of action based on those beliefs, our business character, or culture, is established.

6. **Our character determines our destiny.** Every company culture is built one decision at a time. It is one of the three responsibilities of leadership, to guard the values, which ensures everything that happens in the visible world reflects what we *say* we believe. Nobody at Enron was guarding the written values. That organization didn't get to the depths of accounting depravity by having a meeting and deciding to go there. They ended up there because someone made one bad decision and got away with it, and the next person saw it and mimicked it. There was no true north compelling anyone to challenge the acts that became habits, which became their character and ultimately determined their destiny.

WRITING WHAT WE BELIEVE

At Crankset Group, we have found that confirming and listing our values is the most important strategic work we can do as a company. We have a widely divergent group of people from a myriad of backgrounds, but we all believe the same things about our mission.

Whether you are a company of three or 3,000, you can profit from investing in the time to clarify and write down your organizational values. Take a representative sample of people from around the company, or all of them if it is a small company, for a three- to four-hour session to discover your core values using the process that follows, or make a full day of it and do things to build relationships that enhance the meaning of your values. Our small company did this together in about two hours.

The following is a sample list of topics and examples of business beliefs to discuss. It might be good to do the following exercise without showing people the T-Charts below and see what they come up with, then show the T-Charts for further discussion.

Beliefs About Business

Business Should Win	Business Should Add Value
Business is War	Business is Service
Dominate the World	Add Value to the World
Destroy Competition	Be The Best
Depts & Teams Compete	Depts & Teams Serve Other

Beliefs About the Company

We're a Machine	We're a Community
Rigid Structure	Organic Structure
Regid Rules	A Few Principles
Focus on Process	Focus on Results
Status Quo	Innovation/Creativity
Authority & Control	Freedom & Responsibility

Beliefs About Work

Make Money?	Make Meaning?
Necessary evil	Big part of my life
Resent going to work	Love going to work
Run the process	Innovate, Create, Improve
No meaning in work	Work is satisfying

Beliefs About People at Work

Stupid & Lazy	Smart & Motivated
Childish	Adult
Want to be Users	Want to be Owners
Want to make money	Want to Make Meaning
Reactive	Proactive
Threaten & Cajole	Self-motivated
Work when watched	Self-managed

Beliefs About Leadership

Manage People?	Lead People?
Solve & Decide	Train Staff to Solve/Decide
Regular threats	Cast Vision/invite them
Daily quota mgt.	Weekly/Mthly Results
Focus on Process	Focus on Results
Delegate Task(used)	Del. Responsibility(ownership)
Supervise	Get out of the way

Beliefs About Success

Big Bucks	Big Impact
It's about the toys	Use the toys - bigger things
I succeed	We all succeed
I got more/better	My world got more/better
Use others to serve me	Serve others so I succeed
Money	Legacy

Summary
What Do You Believe?

About Business?	About YOUR Organization?
About Work?	About People?
About Success?	About Leadership?

Write a statement or manifesto about what you believe. Make elegant physical copies of it and share it with everyone to post. Make *that* your motivational poster, not the canned sayings you can buy on the Internet. Refer to it during discussions within the organization or in other important communications. We have listed our five values on ours, and it hangs in a prominent place in our training room. We refer to it before every meeting, then ask for an example of how someone has lived it out since we last met, and we like to catch people doing something right. Highlight when people are practicing your business beliefs regularly.

YOUR VALUES DETERMINE EVERYTHING ELSE

Here's a simple and powerful exercise to check your core values. It will help you determine what you truly believe, not what you say you believe. This is for every company of every size. The smaller you are, the more you need this because outside influences have more impact in smaller organizations. If you don't have a handle on your values, you may end up living out someone else's.

1. Brainstorm around the question, "What are we really good at that we're also very proud of?"
   a. Make a list, then combine and delete until you have it down to the top three to five things. It can be anything: production, customer service, teamwork, culture, benefits, vision, pricing, quality, innovation. You get the idea, but pare it down to a few.
2. Put that list aside and ask a second, similar question, "What are we really good at that we're not so proud of?"
   a. Make a similar list with no constraints. Then, get it down to no more than two things: the thing(s) that you would not like your name to be associated with. Nothing is off limits: the way we treat each other, communications, gossip, customer service, profit, growth, vision, etc. Be honest and respectful, and then focus on the very few.
3. Ask, "Why?" Why is the least asked yet most important question in business (see my first book, *Making Money Is Killing Your Business*, #1 business book of the year.)
   a. Why are we so good at those things we're so proud of?
      i. Brainstorm the beliefs and values that are driving you, then get it down to three to five that best express what makes you good at these.
   b. Why are we so good at those things we're not so proud of?
      i. Brainstorm the beliefs and values that are behind this bottleneck, then get it down to three to five that best express why you struggle with these.

      It's important to do both questions 1) and 2) before answering the two questions in number 3). When answering, "Why?", use value or belief words to answer the question.

      Example: A dental clinic we worked with had a tough time getting their patients to agree to expensive treatments they really needed. They realized the value that was driving this was an over-emphasis on the desire to be liked. They got help tackling this unhelpful value. By approaching it this way, you are uncovering what drives everything you do.

      Tip: When Crankset Group does this exercise with companies on day-long summits or annual meetings, we don't want people to know about the "Why" questions until after they've done the "proud" questions.

4. From the short list of positive beliefs and values, decide together what you will write down as the values that will guide every decision of the company going forward. It can be a simple, powerful values-laden sentence or a list of three to five words that are themselves values that express your deepest beliefs as a company.

CONSISTENCY

When Crankset Group did this exercise for the first time years ago, we identified the five core values that we still use as our true north:

1. Abundance
2. Community
3. Clarity
4. Conation
5. Trust

Five is a long list. Fortunately, someone realized it spelled ACCCT. We ACCCT on our values, which makes them easy to remember. It's better to keep your values to just three or less unless you can find a way to remember them (don't create an acronym and then values based on the acronym).

Everything we do at Crankset Group must be fully consistent with these values. They infiltrate everywhere. Crankset Group hires and moves people along based on these five core values. Upholding 4.5 of the five values is a four-alarm fire. (More on this later.) Every decision, from buying a copier to opening a new office or starting a whole new product line, is evaluated according to our five company values.

BROADLY HELD AND WIDELY SHARED

In Participation Age fashion, we got everyone as involved as we could. Initially, my list looked very different from what the team came up with. Their list proved better than I could have imagined.

Because we all participated, we jointly own these values deeply, and that commitment gets communicated in spades to any new people who come on as we grow. This is important to understand. The classic definition of culture is,

"a set of norms and values that are strongly held and widely shared throughout the organization[3]."

If your beliefs are strongly held and widely shared, you have consistency between what you say you believe and what you really do.

KEEPING THE VALUES IN THE CENTER

We do what is important. My mother once said, annoyingly, "Chuck, there are no excuses. There aren't even reasons. There are only priorities." Most companies run inconsistently on a few core values without writing them down, which would help to keep them focused, and rare is the company that knows how to sustain their values day by day. It needs to be a priority.

Following are some simple strategies:

1. Every meeting in our company, without exception, starts by asking someone to recite the values. We all know them by heart. Everyone in your company should, too — this is part of being mission centered. Someone then provides an observation about how our values were lived out since we last met. The example can be gleaned from anywhere in their life, a book they're reading, someone they saw helping an aging man cross the street, a client, or someone else in our business. That simple ritual of starting every strategic or tactical meeting this way demonstrates the importance of these values as the true north for every decision.

2. Put your values in your recruiting ads. Have people interview you and let them know how important these values are. We don't put the job description in the ad until after we have listed our values. Our applicants need to know these first, or we don't want them to apply. Netflix requests that new recruits go through their full Freedom and Responsibility document before applying. It's the right statement to make about who you are and what drives you.

3. Develop a kudos program to celebrate people carrying out your values at an exceptional level.

4. Catch people doing something right and affirm them to others. We send out communications to everyone when we see someone striving to uphold our beliefs under difficult circumstances.

5. Set up a volunteer leadership team of those who are most passionate about guarding your values. They should meet regularly to promote your values through activities, quiet

initiatives, events, simple videos, etc.

6. Have a weekly short focus on the values as a whole company, like.

These are just a few ways to help keep the company focus. If our values are a priority, we will find great, innovative ways to breathe life into everything we do.

THE MINDSET OF HIGHEST COMMON DENOMINATOR (HCD)

Leading by principles is a highest common denominator practice. When Zang Ruimin first took over Haier, he recounted, "We had just over 400 refrigerators in the warehouse. We inspected them one by one and found seventy-six problem fridges. I had to change the perception of our quality: If products left the factory, they should be first rate." Zhang had his incredulous employees take the seventy-six defective refrigerators into the street and publicly destroy them with sledgehammers. He could have sold them or given them as political favors, but the message was clear. Never again would Haier sell products it could not be proud of.

When Alan Mulally took over as CEO of Ford, one of the first questions he fielded in an auditorium packed with Ford employees was, "What kind of car do you drive?" He responded, "I drive a Lexus. It's the finest car in the world." Everyone knew instantly that the bar had been raised.

In our company, the highest common denominator principle helps us select nothing less than "stunning colleagues," as in the earlier example of Netflix. If we encounter a situation where a person's work behavior doesn't consistently meet this standard, someone talks to the person confidentially, pointing out examples of others who are managing the issue well. We provide support for the person as they work out the issue, watching them return then to the ranks of stunning colleagues. We refer to our stunning colleagues as Stakeholders.

A first step in attracting stunning Stakeholders is to lead by HCD principles rather than by lowest common denominator policies that don't lend themselves to making adult decisions., For example, Netflix, rather than requiring expense reports, encourages everyone to act on a simple principle: "Act in Netflix's best interest." With one statement, they eliminated a costly process of monitoring expenses.

STAKEHOLDERS ARE EVERYWHERE

The long and the short of it is that HCD leadership companies don't wonder where they will find five, fifty or 5,000 stunning Stakeholders. Remember the 50 percent-plus from Chapter One that regularly have their resumes out? They're climbing the walls to get into these great companies.

You can find great people right under your nose. Remember Captain Marquet's experience? He took his sub from worst to first in one year with the same 134 people. Invite ownership and involvement, and the people you work with will raise their game. You will have 80 percent functioning as stunning Stakeholders, and when you get to 80 percent or more, that tipping point will cause the other 20 percent to step up or step out. In a Participation Age organization, 100 percent stunning Stakeholders is the norm.

NOT SQUISHY

In closing, I'm compelled to say it again — if you want longevity, stability, consistency, continued growth, and an organization of committed, fully participating people, defining your values together is the most important work you will ever do. Start by clearing the schedule and getting this work done. Then, make sure the values you settle on permeate everything you do. The rest of the Distributed Decision-making tools described in this book are ineffective until you've done this work and are practicing it.

THE NEXT ONE THING

1. Beat the drum gently and relentlessly concerning your values and beliefs. The following are some suggested steps:
2. Do a participative review (or creation) of your values statement. DDM workgroups can send representatives, and a lot of the interaction can be done via tools such as Slack.com or Workplace.com.
3. As part of every meeting, have someone repeat your values, vision, and mission, and as each one is shared, ask someone to volunteer a way they saw it lived out since we last met, either at work or elsewhere. This takes three to five minutes, sets the right tone, puts tactical issues in the right perspective, and reminds us why we're are all here. Most of all, it communicates that these things are of primary importance.

4. Catch people doing something right. Stop the train, recognize them for things that demonstrate your values, vision, and mission. Verbal affirmation is important. You can also give ad hoc rewards for people you see who went above and beyond and demonstrated a deep commitment to the company's values.

5. Put your values in your hiring ads and hire right up front. We don't look at resumes unless someone has demonstrated a commitment to our values. (See the chapter on hiring.)

6. Focus on values in your peer recognition surveys (see a later chapter for how these can eliminate annual reviews and other unhelpful practices).

THE NEXT ONE THING

1. What is the Next One Thing we can do to ensure our values are strongly held and widely shared?

_____

_____

_____

2. How do we measure the success of doing that?

_____

_____

3. What, if anything, might keep us from doing it, and how do we get past that?

_____

_____

_____

4. When will we do it? ____/____/____ by ____:____ am/pm

5. Who will take responsibility to make sure it gets done (an individual, a team)?

_____

_____

_____

RESOURCES

1   https://www.amazon.com/Making-Money-Killing-Business-Build/dp/0984334327/ref=pd_rhf_se_p_img_2?_encoding=UTF8&psc=1&refRID=HSR82SF65C6M9YA6195K

2   https://www.slideshare.net/BarbaraGill3/netflix-culture-deck

3   O'Reilly and Chatman, 1996, https://www.homeworkmarket.com/files/module6files-20181011-zip

CHAPTER SIX

A Network of DDM Workgroups

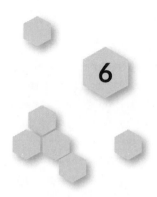

6

"A lattice organization involves direct transactions and natural leadership, and lacks assigned or assumed authority. Every successful organization has a lattice organization that underlies the façade of authoritarian hierarchy. It is through these lattice organizations that things get done, and most of us delight in doing things the straightforward and easy way."

—BILL GORE, FOUNDER OF W. L. GORE

It's the start of the day, and there are hundreds of associates at the unloading docks of The Morning Star Co., waiting for the first wave of trucks carrying tomatoes. There are no managers or supervisors, and many of the colleagues have yet to form a team or workgroup today. As the trucks roll in, people begin to organize into workgroups to handle the nuances of today's unloading.

Every morning is another opportunity to reorganize based on what needs to get done. There are other workgroups that have formed on a more stable and long-term but not permanent basis who carry the work forward to clean, stew, and can the tomatoes.

SIMPLE PRINCIPLES, POWERFUL RESULTS

In the 1990s, Chris Rufer organized Morning Star around elegantly simple principles that provide powerful, practical, day-to-day guidance for how to get things done. They have two simple guiding principles:

1. Use no force.
2. Keep your commitments.

The first, use no force, such as imposing your will at the point of a gun, is the motivation behind having no managers or individual bosses. Managers are bosses who have a gun: "I can fire you." In the DDM model, no one person hires or fires; the team/community makes those decisions together. The mission statement serves as their boss, and Morning Star Company's colleague letters of understanding, or CLOU, tell them how to serve the boss.

The second principle, keep your commitments, is the driving force behind a civil society. If we all agree together that red means stop and green means go, traffic runs smoothly. Each individual's CLOU, which colleagues write annually with input from others, describes in detail the roles, responsibilities, deliverables, metrics, and outcomes that are required of each person to make the wheels go around at The Morning Star Company.

Does it work perfectly? No one claims it does. In the Participation Age, we are not shooting for perfect, just better, and The Morning Star's model of Distributed Decision-making (DDM) workgroups is exponentially better than imposed hierarchy, both for the company and the people who work there. For over twenty years, organic leadership has proven to be a better solution for them.

We opened this book by looking at the Global Capital Trends survey revealing that over 90 percent of companies are racing to replace hierarchy with a network of teams released to make localized decisions. Distributed decision-making teams are central to rehumanizing the workplace. They allow for an elegant, orderly, and simple replacement of the traditional managed team model that is pervasive in the top-down hierarchy of the Factory System.

Input Equals Ownership

Unlike most teams in the Factory System model, DDM workgroups can form for a day, a week, a project, an event, or for years depending on the need of the company. They can also disband as quickly because they are not tied to politics or necessary for someone's future promotion. It's all about the mission, not the department.

In a Mission-centered business, departments become functions, titles become fluid but clearly defined roles, and teams exist only to serve the mission.

At Haier, each of the nearly 4,000 DDM workgroups of ten to fifteen people functions as a microenterprise, with full responsibility for its decision-making, personnel selection, and profit distribution. These teams are not linked by administrative mandate to work together but by a market-driven contracting mechanism. If a team thinks the HR, accounting, or marketing functions can be better resourced outside the company, no one questions that decision.

This is another way in which capitalism reigns at Haier; every DDM workgroup flourishes or goes out of business based on its real contribution to the world around it. No one is insulated or protected by a mandate from on high that you must use internal services.

At Crankset Group, we never protect team stability. We use "team" to accomplish the mission, and when a clearly defined team has served its useful purpose, it should dissolve. As we've recounted, in a Mission-centered business, departments become functions, titles become fluid but clearly defined roles, and teams exist only to serve the mission.

DDM WORKGROUPS REPLACE THE MANAGED MODEL

After Haier CEO Zhang Ruimin eliminated all managers at the giant appliance manufacturer, he told a reporter, "The most difficult thing is that in the past the employees would listen to their bosses, but now that they don't have any bosses; they listen to the users." The users, who have no political motivation to advance up the hierarchy, gave them much better direction, leading to exponential growth at Haier.

As we have said previously, bringing leadership to every corner of your organization begins by understanding that the position of manager is unnecessary and counterproductive. The question becomes, "Do we need a single person at the head of a team, or can a team accomplish the tasks of a manager more effectively?" The second option, teams that distribute the manager's responsibilities amongst themselves, is a core motivator for the establishment of DDM workgroups.

In this chapter on (DDM workgroups, we lay out specifically how the myriad of responsibilities we place on the shoulders of one human being, the manager, can and should be distributed among multiple team members.

SELF-MANAGED DDM WORKGROUPS

Following is the model for distributing the former responsibilities of a manager to a DDM workgroup. You can see how DDM workgroups turn the hierarchy on its side and encourage building horizontal relationships of trust.

Factory System vs Participation Age

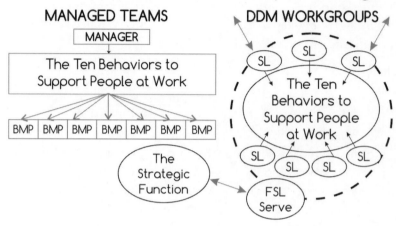

On the left, the managed team relies on one heroic genius to be everything for everybody. On the right, the DDM workgroup divides up the very few things the manager used to do that were important to them, among the SLs (Stakeholder-leaders) who are a) individually good at few of those things and are b) energized by doing them with, and for, the team. We redesign the structure so the workgroup can redistribute the management. A team of three people almost always has more of the ten behaviors among the three of them than any one manager.

REPORTS BECOME FOLLOWERS

As an example, one of our clients was about to fire a manager. She performed well in many respects, but there were some problem areas as well. As they restructured with DDM workgroups, they asked her if she would like to switch from her managerial position to a DDM workgroup where she could keep doing the things she excelled in. This would allow others on the team to pick up the rest of the necessary responsibilities.

The former manager was delighted with her new position on the team because she knew she could succeed without having to be a heroic genius, and the rest of the team found great satisfaction in taking over the things that were not the highest and best use of her time. In reality, the team still looked to her for much of their strategic direction, but a tectonic shift had occurred in their relationship with her. She was no longer a command-and-control manager but a leader serving them from her greatest strengths. The creation of a DDM workgroup realigned the relationship between her and the other Stakeholders.

ALLOW AND REQUIRE DECISION-MAKING

When I first consciously worked to release Stakeholders into my businesses a few decades ago, I thought I could just invite everyone to start making decisions, and they would all jump at the chance. My language was around "allowing" people to make decisions, which it turned out was a little bit like saying, "You're now all adult Stakeholders; I'll be on the golf course." You can't just free team members with no sense of what freedom means. Either they crawl back into their cubicles, or chaos and anarchy ensues, and usually it's the former. Few people are initially comfortable making decisions because it's been so long since that has been part of their responsibilities at work.

I very quickly had to change the statement to, "We must allow *and require* everyone to make decisions." Making decisions is central to rehumanizing the workplace, being a Stakeholder and an adult, and is not optional. We would much prefer that people make decisions at work because they are allowed to function as adults, and that should be the emphasis, but everything in the structure of the Factory System mitigates against Distributed Decision-making. That is the job of managers. It might take some time for us all to relearn how to make decisions, but we all need to get there. It is central to rehumanizing the workplace, and if at some point, you decide making decisions isn't for you, we'll work to find you a position in another business.

After nearly two centuries of being rewarded for leaving their brain at home and just doing what they're told, a small majority of people may need to be retrained to do that at work, but it must be very clear that we aren't going back. We've freed the pig, burned the bridges, or whatever metaphor works for you to replace the Factory System, but we are now going to live as Stakeholders who leave none of their brain at home or in the car.

FUNCTIONS VERSUS DEPARTMENTS

You'll also notice in the above graphic that some people in the DDM workgroup, like the floating Stakeholder-leader (FSL) are half in the circle and half out. That works well in a system where our allegiance is to the values, vision, and mission — a Mission-centered organization, but it doesn't work in a department-centered hierarchy where we inherently want to protect our fiefdoms. In the DDM workgroup model, departmental boundaries are de-emphasized or eliminated in favor of getting things done by anyone who can contribute. Someone might be 80 percent in the sales function but have some skills the marketing function finds helpful and vice versa. The emphasis is moved from guarding the sales or operations departmental turf to refocusing on accomplishing the function of sales or operations. This is an extension of the Mission-centered approach to organizational structure.

In a Participation Age company, the focus is on upholding the values and the vision and working together to fulfill the mission. Every function in the company exists only for that purpose. Nothing is sacred but the values, vision, and mission. Nobody owns a department called IT, operations, sales, accounting, etc. Teams of people have utter clarity on what teams or workgroups are responsible for what functions, and we all simply use the functions to fulfill the mission. No more fiefdoms. No more fights over resources.

DDM WORKGROUPS REDUCE POLITICS

Early in my career when I was leading in manager-centric companies, no manager ever came to me and said, "I just thought of a great way to dissolve my department into Joe's — we'll save a ton of money." I regularly had managers suggesting the opposite. Managers feel they add value by adding resources to own and manage. The bigger my fiefdom, the more I should get paid. In a Participation Age model, people are paid for results, and teams are incentivized in a result-based system, not a time-based or power-based system. Aside from common human frailties, politics can become a thing of the past, and we can now get on with the business of building a business. Instead of lipstick, we see real, lasting change.

STAYING NIMBLE AS YOU GROW — THE LATTICE ORGANIZATION

One of the most elegant and easily understood illustrations of a DDM workgroup comes from Bill Gore's 1976 landmark paper, "The Lattice Organization[1]." He and his wife built W. L. Gore around this idea from its inception in 1958.

The Gore organization flattened their hierarchy altogether with a lattice organizational structure where everyone is an "associate." In the lattice, there is no chain of command or power-based communications channels. To become a leader, you must attract followers; you don't get there by being the boss. Since there are a lot fewer leaders at Gore than bosses in a traditional company, they effectively eliminate the management tax. Associate contribution reviews are based on a biannual peer rating system, not the dreaded management review. These peer reviews also determine pay for everyone at Gore.

Bill Gore defined the lattice organization this way[2]:

1. No fixed or assigned authority
2. Sponsors (mentors) not bosses
3. Natural leadership defined by "followership"
4. Person-to-person communication
5. Objectives set by those who must make things happen
6. Tasks and functions organized through commitments

The following simple diagram is reprinted directly from Gore's 1976 paper:

Attributes of the Lattice Organization
Everyone interacts directly with everyone
No intermediary (manager)

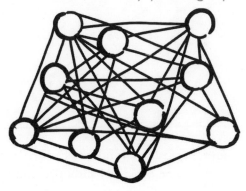

Your first reaction might be, "That looks really complicated," but this is an incredibly simple, elegant approach to business that, when applied, gives rise to whatever complex and intelligent behavior is necessary to accomplish complex tasks better than in a managed environment. It is simpler than imposed hierarchy, but it is not simplistic in any way. What you see are dozens of opportunities for people to connect and communicate. Let's look at how DDM workgroups work in this example.

ANTON TALKS TO LAURA

In the following illustration, you see Anton needing to communicate with Laura to get something done, or Team A needing the same from Team L:

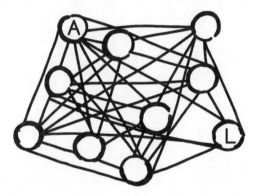

All by itself, it looks like this:

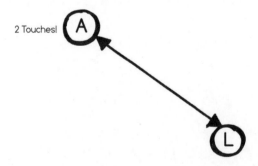

Utter simplicity. If Anton needs to talk to Laura, they talk and get things done. It sounds so reasonable, but the Factory System hierarchy complicates this in the name of power, authority, command, control, ego, possessiveness, and politics. To avoid chaos and anarchy, these two simple touches are supported and performed in community through two-step decision-making, which is introduced later.

Earlier in the book, we alluded to an Elon Musk email to "All Tesla Staff." Please look at the prior illustrations as you read this remarkably revealing email:

From: Elon Musk

To: All Tesla Staff

Subject: Communication Within Tesla

There are two schools of thought about how information should flow. By far the most common way is chain of command, which means that you always flow communication through your manager. The problem with this approach is that, while it enhances the power of the manager, it fails to serve the company.

To solve a problem quickly, two people in different depts should simply talk and make the right thing happen. Instead, people are forced to talk to their manager, who talks to their manager, who talks to the manager in the other dept, who talks to someone on his team. Then the info has to flow back the other way again. This is incredibly dumb. Any manager who allows this to happen, let alone encourages it, will soon find themselves working at another company. No kidding. Anyone at Tesla can and should email/talk to anyone else according to what they think is the fastest way to solve a problem for the benefit of the whole company. You can talk to your manager's manager without his permission, you can talk directly to a VP in another dept, you can talk to me, you can talk to anyone without anyone else's permission. Moreover, you should consider yourself obligated to do so until the right thing happens...

We are all in the same boat. Always view yourself as working for the good of the company and never your dept.

Thanks, Elon

Fantastic email, and amazingly insightful about how work should get done. I don't know if Musk has ever seen Gore's illustration, but he intuitively understands the power of the lattice organization, but one thing went missing after this memo came out—he didn't fundamentally change the existing imposed hierarchy that was deeply entrenched and ran counter to everything he put in his email.

If I worked there and got this email, I would be very inspired, then go on about my job because as much as I would love to skip layers of bosses to get things done directly with other people, the reality is that the one person above me in the imposed hierarchy still holds my work life in their hands. The Factory System hierarchy was not any different after the email than it was before. In spite of his impassioned plea to work efficiently to just get things done with whomever you needed, I would still feel I need to go through the boss that can fire me, and that boss could do whatever he wants with my suggestion, if I would even share one.

The above communication between Anton and Laura or Team A and Team L seems so simple, but is it better than going through managers? Here's what it looks like in most organizations:

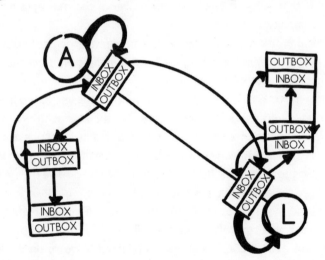

The above illustration is the nightmare Elon Musk described in 2016 that Bill Gore had already solved in 1958. As we look at this, is it any wonder that the bigger an organization gets, the less likely they are to invent anything, achieve ongoing innovation, or even keep the quality up? Is it any wonder that important things move glacially or that the majority of people are deeply disengaged?

DDM workgroups reengage people. They are built as a network of teams that have all the power they need to talk to each other and get things done. This is more organized, communicative, and orderly than imposed hierarchy. In the chapter on two-step decision-making, we show how simple it is to ensure everyone in the organization has all the input they need to make every decision. Keeping it simple improves communication.

DDM WORKGROUPS — A TEAM SPORT

Netflix says they are like a pro team, not a kid's recreational team[3]. For many years, we have compared DDM workgroups to specific team sports like soccer, hockey, field hockey, hurling, and others where the ball or puck is regularly touched by everyone. There are several great parallels:

1. **Two to ten team members, sometimes more:** Except for some creative work, two people can get a lot more done together than each of them by themselves. Bigger teams begin to get unwieldy and preclude people with more deferring personalities. If the team is focused more on running a process and producing, it can be bigger, but they might want to send representatives to get together for strategic discussions related to the team and keep strategic discussions smaller. For collaborative discussions, three to six people seems to be the sweet spot, and odd numbers are better than even ones for tie-breaking[4].

2. **Well-defined roles and positions:**

   a. To the uninitiated, games such as hockey and soccer can look chaotic or disorderly, and it's hard to follow who plays what position or who is in charge of what, but if you ask the coach and the players, they all know exactly who plays what position and their responsibility is when they are in the game.

   b. Why does it look like there is no order?

      i. Results-based work — The result is more important than the process.

         1. In the Factory System, we call things teams when they are more like a linear assembly line of people doing tasks. I do my task, then pass the product or service off to you to do yours. If you're swamped or having trouble with something, that's your problem. The Factory System likes that kind of highly segmented and specialized work. It lets me leave my brain in the car, which is fine because I have enough decisions to make at home

ii. Fluid teamwork — Working together like a soccer team,
covering for each other, and sometimes taking over someone
else's position, is the best way to get the result.

1. In a DDM workgroup, we still have even clearer personal
responsibilities than through Factory System job
descriptions, but we prioritize getting the final result over
doing our individual jobs. The focus isn't on my list of
tasks but achieving the result as a team. Teamwork isn't
just segmentation of work but is more like a hockey or
soccer game — I know what I need to do, but if I can
help the team get a better result by pitching in somewhere
else when my work is slow, I'll do that.

3. Well-defined results and processes:

a. Intended result — put the puck or ball in the goal. By facilitating
strategic leaders (coaches), we agree together on the intended
result. Remember, managers tell, leaders ask. A manager
tells the team what the objective is and what metrics define
success. A leader facilitates a discussion, casts their vision, and
collaborates to design the intended result because the more
input I have in a decision, the more ownership I can take. If I
can help design it, I'm much more likely to work to achieve it.
A director of one of the largest software companies in the
world shared that his VP had decided on a new, outrageously

expanded annual revenue objective. He conveyed it to the managers, and it sifted down to the few thousand staff who were supposed to get that result, but the informal feedback he was getting was that the staff found the new goal ridiculous, had no commitment to get it done, and were laughing about it. Since the VP, director, and his managers had told people the intended result and had even given them a process for getting it done, they thought it should suffice. The director's frustrated response to me was, "People keep wanting to talk about this." Input equals ownership, and they had none of either.

b. Strategy/processes to achieve the result — A manager uses his/her brilliance to design a perfectly plausible strategy and process for achieving the result and then tells everyone how to achieve it. A leader, having achieved agreement on the intended result, then does something the Factory System manager would rarely do — turn the process over to the team and say, "Figure out a way to get the result that you came up with." Like a soccer coach, a leader wouldn't leave them on their own but would act as an adviser to the process (see two-step decision-making).

4. **We cover for each other** — fullbacks go forward, forwards go back, etc.

a. This flows naturally from designing a process with very clear personal responsibilities but where the result is more important than the process, and teamwork is doing anything and everything together to achieve the result, not just a specific assigned task. I may be a midfielder on my team, but I play anywhere I'm needed in the moment.

5. **The coach is on the sidelines** — This is such an important part of the analogy.

a. In a hockey or soccer game, where is the coach? On the sidelines. Does that make the coach unimportant? No, the coach remains very present and involved. He is not on the field directing every move.

b. Helpful input, not micro-direction — Imagine a soccer coach who gave everyone ear pieces to guide the process, "Number Four, kick the ball to Number Eight; Number Eight, push the ball up the sidelines; Number Three, cross it to the other side," etc. This would communicate a lack of trust in the ability of the players to bring their full humanity on to the field and figure out how to achieve the goal, yet this is exactly what we do to people on a subtle but regular basis on a managed team. In contrast, the leader's biggest responsibility is to help everyone agree on a result, and that process is everyone's responsibility.

6. **In soccer, if you're called a manager, more often it's someone who takes care of stuff** — balls, grass, benches, uniforms, equipment, etc. Managers manage stuff. Leaders lead people.

7. **Whoever gets to the ball/puck first is the leader** — What do you do when you see a loose ball on the field? Do you ring up the forward and say, "Hey, there's a ball loose on your side of the field. I just happen to be over here, but it's your ball. Come get it."? That would get a soccer player pulled from the game, and a repeat of it would likely have them off the team.

    a. Leader-leader — This is central to the idea of leader-leader. Everyone leads in some way, described earlier, that replaces the manager-follower model. People become leaders by: Seeing an issue or opportunity and grabbing it, and/or

        i. Getting others to follow, form a team or workgroup, and address the issue or the opportunity.

        ii. In the Factory System, there are balls left lying all over the field. "That's not my job" or, "Somebody should do something about that" are common responses. At Crankset Group, "That's not my job" would be a firing offense. Whoever gets to the ball first and can bring together other people to address it — that's your leader. That is organic leadership. In the former system, nobody ever truly knows if a manager is leading because people don't choose to follow organically but are assigned as "reports" for the manager to command and control.

8. **There is room to be a creative individual** — Creativity happens more on our own, and collaboration follows to develop the idea. Teams do not replace the creative juices that one person has by working alone for a day to come up with possible solutions to a problem or insights on an opportunity. At Crankset Group, we

have time alone as well as together. Both the teamwork and the creative alone time help us build a great organization.

Soccer, hockey, or a similar sport is a good analogy for how a DDM workgroup should operate when it's healthy. Coaches cast vision and get people to agree on the intended result. They train, provide resources, connect, mentor, and then release them out onto the field to design the process and get the desired result.

STABLE AND DYNAMIC DDM WORKGROUPS

DDM workgroups form where there is a need and then disband when they are no longer serving the mission. Some teams may exist for many years. The Morning Star Company has some teams that form and disband daily. In a DDM workgroup structure, anyone can suggest the creation of a new team. Allowing teams to form as needed alerts the strategic function that something important is happening on the edges of an organization. The strategic function doesn't make the decisions for the edges; the edges inform the strategic function as to which direction it might want to go next.

HOW DO WE FORM DDM WORKGROUPS?

STEP ONE — AGREE TOGETHER

To form DDM workgroups, agree together that this is the direction we want to go. If people are scared of becoming adults at work, you need some patience to get them there. That patience is justified because for too long we enabled them to be children at work by telling them what to do.

Cast the vision — Share some TED talks, (here's mine https://www.youtube.com/watch?v=ewA2BqbWhUQ), give one or two other companies as an example, and show how they did it. Do whatever you need to do to give a clear picture of what Distributed Decision-making can look like when you're done. We have simple slide presentations that can also help.

Talk together about the vision and how it works through DDM workgroups, then give plenty of time for asking questions. When making any transition that threatens the status quo, people can be very reluctant at first. In one company, it took a few months for people to begin to engage regularly, largely because they had been such a task-driven, "do this" culture for so long. They had a lot of great things in their culture and took great care of their people, but their roles were so defined and inflexible that it bordered on adult daycare, so it wasn't surprising that the employees took a while to respond to the challenge of asking questions and making decisions.

The more co-dependent (heavily managed) and top-down your organization has been, no matter how open and supportive, the more patience you will need to build agreement around becoming a Participation Age company. We've seen companies grasp Distributed Leadership and DDM workgroups overnight and make the full transition in a few months, but others have taken longer. In no case have we seen a fall-off in production. Just the opposite — the metrics always improve as people are allowed and required to take ownership.

We're Done Talking

At some point, the discussion about building DDM workgroups must end and move to the action phase. Moving forward is an art not a science, requiring intuition, emotional intelligence, and possibly an outsider view of things. If you move overnight and people aren't ready, you may look behind and realize no one is following—you're not the leader. You're just out for a walk. If you move too slowly, people may sense a lack of conviction and resolve, and those who never want to take ownership will find all kinds of reasons why this won't work.

The Benevolent Dictator

Remember, the art of leadership is to know how few decisions the leader needs to make. One decision we do not put up for a vote is Distributed Decision-making. Everyone is a Stakeholder, we will have DDM workgroups instead of managers, and we will never look back.

You may have caught the irony here. We're requiring participation and sharing. In every instance where we have seen an organization move away from imposed hierarchy to organic leadership with DDM workgroups, there has always been a very committed, highly resolved, benevolent dictator (or a team) who is committed to the emerging work world of the Participation Age and lets nothing stand in their way getting there.

Some of my friends recoil at this wording—find another if you choose—but the reality of it is that very deeply committed strategic leadership is required to replace decades of co-dependent, inappropriate structure. Leaders make as few decisions as possible, but this is one of those that you need to make and never release for a vote: we will all be adults at work, with no opportunity to go back to being co-dependent children and managers. Read the book, *Maverick*[5], by Ricardo Semler, and you will see a great example of a benevolent dictator at work who made the transition. Since then, for more than thirty years, the nearly billion dollar company he owns, Semco, has grown and flourished without managers of any kind. He has backed off completely and makes no decisions at all (they have six co-CEOs, and he's not one of them). A strong conviction up front resulted in great freedom for all on the back end.

Can We Please Go Back?

At Crankset Group, we are developing an ongoing list of the *very few* things that may never be up for discussion, to help us keep going in the right direction. This is because the human condition, from hunting mastodons on through hunting a job, seeks safety, security, and stability—every day should look the same. This stunts growth, both as human beings and as companies.

One of the most attractive features of the Factory System hierarchy is that it provides such clarity around who has the bigger and smaller guns. For that reason, even if we're not satisfied with our position in the ranks, it is still clear and emotionally satisfying. Couple that with the comfort provided by being in an environment where I don't have to make decisions or take responsibility for them, and you can see that the inertia is always in the direction of the human need for certainty and not in the direction of DDM workgroups. For another reminder on this, review the three major influences of decision-making with which we opened Chapter One. I need to review it regularly.

W. L. Gore is one of the great examples of a Participation Age company, but they also struggle with this. Bill and Vieve Gore started it in their basement in 1958 without managers, and today it is a $3 billion company with 10,000 Stakeholders. Acquaintances of mine who have worked there say there is an ongoing resistance movement to create managers and titles and at least some form of imposed hierarchy. It is perfectly understandable and alluring but not helpful.

STEP TWO — MAKE A LIST OF HELPFUL TEAM RESPONSIBILITIES

1. Make a complete list of the few things the manager used to do that added value to the team. Since it is an unsupported myth that they make people more productive by their existence, managers must invent ways to justify their jobs. Don't look at the company's description of managerial duties. Create your own list. It might (or might not) include things like:

   a. **Strategic communications** — Link us to the rest of the company by going to meetings outside our team, communicate back, put our work in that context, etc.

   b. **Community at work** — Build relationships, be human together, kudos and recognition, mentoring, training, building teamwork. Building relationships is key to great teamwork.

   c. **Planning** — Procure supplies, inventory, production forecasting, think about the future of the team and the members of the team.

   d. **Organizing** — Scheduling, staffing, running internal team meetings, following up on those meetings to ensure action and results.

   e. **Data, metrics, reports** — Focus on results (process exists only to get a result); measure what we do so we have utter clarity on whether we're producing what we should as a team.

   f. **Support (most companies call this accountability)** — Assess effective incentives, disincentives, performance reviews, corrective actions (what we call Carefrontations), hire, and fire.

Note: The list is not always this comprehensive. These are just categories to sniff around in. You might also have some things that aren't on the list.

STEP THREE — DISTRIBUTED LEADERSHIP

Decide together who is best at fulfilling these roles and responsibilities. Discuss each responsibility on the list one at a time. I love the sticky note approach my friend Doug Kirkpatrick taught me. Put the responsibilities on 4 x 6-inch sticky notes and stick them on a wall. Address each one separately and ask if anyone wants to volunteer, or if someone would like to volunteer another person. One person stands up and physically takes the sticky note off the wall, but as they do, the rest of the team must confirm that this is the best fit for the person and the team. If not, find someone else to cover that. Go through each of the responsibilities one by one as an open question.

Everyone's Highest and Best

This isn't about equal distribution of responsibilities. This is about finding out what is in the best interest of the organization, the team, and the individual. Simply put, people who are good at things should do those things. If the team decided there were seven contributions the former manager made, one person (the former manager?) might end up with four of them, and three more people might end up with one each. The team chooses based on matching the need with the person who can meet that need because, as Mary Parker Follett put it, leadership is by expertise and voluntary choice. One person might end up with a lot more responsibilities than others, but a team of just two people can distribute the responsibilities a lot better than dumping it all on one manager.

STEP FOUR — FREEDOM MAPS — PROCESSES, ROLES, RESPONSIBILITIES

DDM workgroups must also have utter clarity around the day-to-day delivery of goods and/or services. At Crankset Group, teams create what we call freedom maps — simple one-page process maps that show every major step in the process, the result intended for the process, who owns the map, who owns each step, and most importantly the very few metrics that show we are doing the process correctly (timeliness, accuracy, transition, etc.)

Freedom maps are one of the Twelve Practices of Distributed Decision-making we use to make things run smoother, with better processes, clearer metrics, and support than I ever experienced in a managed environment, and because the teams built the processes and the maps, they own them, run them, and update them regularly. The chapter on freedom maps also gives more input on how to keep these alive, so they don't just become "shelf-help" documents, sitting on your shelf with other books just to look nice.

STEP FIVE — ONGOING SUPPORT

Support begins with community. At Crankset Group, we want workgroups to function at the level of community, above the level of even a high-performing team. Research shows that when people like each other and get along well, they are much more likely to solve problems, accomplish tasks, and produce more than teams that are focused on production. Great support starts with great community, but it extends into going to lunch together, occasional happy hours, and even doing things outside work together. Good sports teams coalesce around the task. Great ones build deep, committed relationships off the field that brings them to another level when they're on the field. We're all better off when we take care of each other as human beings first, then tackle the task at hand.

A word on accountability as it relates to Factory System legacy. Although we sometimes use both, we prefer the word *support* because accountability has gained some baggage through association with the Factory System. Too often a manager comes up with a goal for all of us to hit, we pretend to agree, and then the manager spends the rest of the year chasing us, to hold us accountable to a goal we never honestly embraced in the first place.

In a word, accountability is too often someone chasing something that others are running from.

If I participate in setting the goal, I will achieve it with some guidance and encouragement along the way. The difference between the words *support* and *accountability* may seem small, but it is meaningful for us. Use the word *accountability* if it works better for you.

Either way, we need it. We are mammals made to live in community, and when we share our goals by supporting one another, we are more likely to reach them. Pearson's Law (also associated with the Hawthorne Effect) says, "That which is measured, improves. That which is measured and reported, improves exponentially." When we see as a team how each of us is doing, we all want to do better.

A good system requires that we measure the result, report it, and decide what it means to us as a team and as individuals. For ongoing support, we tie production metrics to our processes and use peer surveys (see the chapter on that tool) to measure and measure our commitment to community. We combine these to give us our incentives (and corrective actions).

We need support to run a team and a business, and that comes by clarifying the processes, roles, responsibilities, metrics, incentives, and corrective actions. This isn't unique to Participation Age companies, but I find they generally do a much better job of providing support or a healthy version of accountability.

STEP SIX — FINE TUNING

Fine tuning a DDM workgroup is an ongoing, dynamic process. One of the responsibilities of strategic leaders is to help us raise the bar and shoot for something better on an ongoing basis. All five of the previous steps need to be revisited regularly. A good way to do this is to put something on the schedule quarterly, (i.e., the first Thursday of every quarter) where we review the big picture related to these five steps, assign champions and due dates, and get moving again. The best way to do anything like this is somewhere other than where the tactical work gets done. Get out of the office, go to a hotel or board room or a pond; anywhere that allows you to be free of the day-to-day pressure and promotes thinking more strategically and creatively.

There are other things that will need to be addressed regularly by any DDM workgroup:

1. Kudos/recognition
2. Team and individual evaluations
3. Carefrontations and conflict resolution
4. How to run, improve, and kill meetings
5. Community-building amongst the team
6. Training and mentoring
7. Hiring and dismissal
8. Things specific to your own business

In the following chapters, we cover the above ways to foster DDM workgroups in detail.

THE NEXT ONE THING

1. Review the "How Do We Form DDM Workgroups?" section and commit to going through the steps.
   When will we start? ____/____/____
   What challenges need to be addressed before we start? Note: Planning doesn't create movement. Movement creates the plan. Get moving and be aware of issues. Deal with them as

you go. Only a few things are true challenges that need to be addressed before you get moving.

2. Visit the FAQs chapter and see if there are questions there to help you get off the dime and get started or that might make you aware of a true challenge to address before starting. List the very few, if any, that need to be addressed here:

a. _____

_____

_____

b. _____

_____

_____

c. _____

_____

_____

RESOURCES

1   https://folk.uio.no/terjegro/materials/Gore_lattice.pdf

2   https://folk.uio.no/terjegro/materials/Gore_lattice.pdf

3   https://www.slideshare.net/reed2001/culture-1798664/24-Were_a_team_not_a

4   https://sheilamargolis.com/2011/01/24/what-is-the-optimal-group-size-for-decision-making/

5   https://www.amazon.com/Maverick-Success-Behind-Unusual-Workplace/dp/0446670553

CHAPTER SEVEN

Two-Step Decision-making   7

—DEE HOCK, FOUNDER, VISA INTERNATIONAL

A t Nearsoft, everyone participates in the decisions that need to be made, starting with the recruitment process. Then, they develop mutual expectations and a peer recognition feedback process concerning how they live in community. A five-year vision statement is developed together, and as in other Participation Age companies, the financial indicators are visible to all, requiring the teams to take them into account. This DDM workgroup approach guarantees that no decision is made without broad input.

Strategic leaders at Nearsoft don't make decisions for others but function as facilitators who bring information, tools, practices, methodologies, and examples to the table to aid others in that pursuit. As Anabel Montiel says, strategic leaders do this to "facilitate what otherwise might have been very difficult (or inefficient) to solve on their own." Those who work at Nearsoft are involved in every decision that impacts them, but if everyone and anyone can make decisions, it can be a recipe for chaos and anarchy.

The simple two-step decision-making process described later not only alleviates the fear of chaos and anarchy, but it is orderly and more likely to create good mutual communication, as well as being safer than management-focused decision-making. Two-step decision-making ensures the right people are involved in the most important decisions. While it is a simple approach, companies can struggle to grasp it at first, not because it is hard, but because it disrupts everything we were taught about how to make a decision in the antiquated Factory System of the Industrial Age.

THE CORE PRACTICE OF THE PARTICIPATION AGE

Decision-making and problem solving are central to what makes us human and especially to what defines us as adults. If you reintroduce decision-making to everyone throughout the organization, the purposeful humanity flows back into people who once saw themselves only as extensions of machines without a voice. It is a deeply satisfying and freeing maturation of any business. I believe two-step decision-making is the central, most important practice of the Participation Age. If every company adopted two-step decision-making, the work world would be a different place.

As a reminder, localized Distributed Decision-making is both allowed and required. The historical pattern is that natural Stakeholders are eager to do this, the majority may have to relearn it, and some small percentage just won't adapt.

From the Roman Empire through the early 1800s, the overwhelming majority of free people owned their own business, farms, shops, and stores[1]. Outside of slavery, serfdom, and other oppression, very few people worked for someone else their entire life. People apprenticed with others to run their own shop someday. In your own ship, decision-making was a way of life at work, not just at home. Ownership of our work and the corresponding desire and need to make decisions is in our DNA. The 4,000-plus DDM workgroups that comprise the white-goods manufacturing giant Haier are a perfect example of this.

THE DEHUMANIZATION OF WORK — THE TECTONIC SHIFT

By the middle 1800s, most business owners were taken out of their shoe shops and inserted on an assembly line where we followed commands, put a nail in the left boot, and passed it to the next guy. For the first time in history, free people worked like slaves, with no responsibility or authority to make decisions. In that one way, the Industrial Revolution and the corresponding Industrial Age of management and hierarchy were tectonic shifts in the very fabric of what it meant for the average person to work. We no longer worked to make meaning, but we worked simply to make money so we could go make meaning somewhere else in our lives. Work became an interruption rather than being integrated

---

1   History of Small Business, https://bebusinessed.com/history/history-of-small-business

into our lives.

The result was that those at work waited for someone else to tell them what to do. For those who grew up when the average company was still using the Factory System as their operating system, decision-making will seem new and foreign. Those who no longer rely on that old system must be patient because that history has affected our ability to make decisions at work, but patience does not mean capitulation. We need to see consistent and measurable movement toward full decision-making at work. A growing desire and ability to make decisions indicates progress. While some natural Stakeholders may immediately jump on the bandwagon, others may take up to six months to feel comfortable. We have found that with patience almost everyone will eventually participate.

THE NON-ADOPTERS

Throughout history there has been a small minority who never wanted to own their own business, make decisions, or essentially grow into adulthood at home or at work. A few may eventually quit, or we will need to move them along, but we have never seen it be disruptive. To the contrary, when they are replaced, the right hiring process vets for Stakeholders and things can improve dramatically very quickly (see the chapter on Reverse Hiring, Becoming the Employer of Choice)

TWO SIMPLE STEPS

If everyone is allowed and required to make decisions, how do we implement this safely in the absence of managers? Two-step decision-making is the tool that facilitates quick, inclusive decisions by everyone in every localized corner of the organization.

As a reminder of why we want localized decision-making:

The more input I have in a decision, the more I take ownership in that decision.

Therefore, decisions should be made locally (where they must be carried out), whenever possible, and it's almost always possible

With those principles in mind, here are the two very simple steps that we should practice for every decision:

> **Step One** — Ask, "Who has to carry out this decision once it's made?"
> Those people should make the decision together.
> **Step Two** — Ask, "Who else is impacted by this decision?"
> Whoever is affected/impacted should have input.

Yes, it is utterly simple but not easy. Communication of any sort is the most prominent issue in any company. Two-step decision-making, once grasped, greatly enhances communication.

Step one rehumanizes through localized decision-making and ownership. Step two ensures that chaos and anarchy are avoided and that everyone who wants input into a decision has the opportunity to speak up.

It is important to understand that step two keeps the process safe from chaos, but it is also step two that people may inadvertently skip, thinking it is somehow covered in step one, by initially gathering others to make a decision. A simple solution is to implement step two immediately after asking step one, not days or weeks afterward. Make sure those impacted are brought into the decision-making process as early as possible.

ABOVE THE WATER LINE

Bill Gore, co-inventor of Gore-Tex and founder of the manufacturing giant W. L. Gore, had an elegant picture of step two that he used to help guide decision-making at Gore. If a few people made a decision that might result in shooting a hole above the water line in the Gore business boat, they would not be stopped or chastised afterward. They would have to patch the hole, and in the process, they were likely never to make the same mistake again. The end result was that more people knew what to do next time and were less co-dependent.

But if they appeared to be lining up a shot that could be below the water line and risked sinking the boat, a lot more people got involved to prevent it. The decision to open a new plant at Gore is not done by a few geniuses at headquarters, but it involves a lot of people who must live with the decision after the building is occupied. Step two of two-step decision-making ensures every decision has the appropriate number of people making it, commensurate with its impact on the organization. If you just ask both questions in two-step decision-making, you can ensure you don't shoot a hole below the water line or get too many people involved in a small decision.

THE TWO-STEP PROCESS IN PRACTICE

Remember the soccer/hockey analogy from the DDM workgroups chapter? Whoever gets to the ball first (sees the issue first), is the leader until they step aside, or other leaders are agreed upon. The willingness to take initiative and grab things that were traditionally left for "the boss" is central to two-step decision-making.

Just as in soccer, there are no conditions under which we can look at a loose ball on the field and say, "It's not my job to kick that ball; it should be kicked by somebody else." Kick the ball and figure out later who should have kicked it, if not you. This is leader-leader in action; no followers, just people everywhere in the business making sure there are no loose balls on the field. If you don't feel competent, kick it as quickly as you can to someone you want to be the leader.

GRAB THE BALL

To play out that analogy for two-step decision-making, let's suppose Jenna makes copies and perceives that the copier is on its last leg and might need to be replaced very soon. Jenna has done something people have done at work ever since the Factory System took over in the 1800s: she has recognized a situation. The people on the ground and in the trenches are almost always the first ones to notice, but in true *Dilbert* cartoon fashion, they have been taught to wait around until the manager sees the problem, then praise the manager for being in front of the issue.

Two-step decision-making diverges from that at the outset. Instead of Jenna thinking, "It's not my job," or "Somebody (the manager) should do something about that," since she is the first one to recognize the issue, she is now the leader, at least early on. She *must* grab the ball by asking a step one question:

Who uses the copier regularly and has to deal with the copier decision over the long term?

Jenna makes a short list in her head of the three other people besides her who make 90 percent of the copies. Jenna is now forming a team of leaders who will address the situation. No manager has been inserted into the process, and none is needed. A temporary DDM workgroup is forming, and no one at headquarters need be alerted. (Permanent teams can form the same way).

FORM THE TEAM

Jenna asks the other three people if they think the copier is on its last leg. Everyone agrees, so they set up a short fifteen-minute meeting to discuss next steps. Jenna may ask someone else to lead the process going forward (pass the ball), or the four of them split up leadership responsibilities ("I'll run the meeting, you research new copiers, you be our step-two presenter," etc.). Jenna could keep some of the leadership around organizing and pushing the issue forward and distribute the other leadership needs such as research, doing the numbers justification, or presenting the issue to other teams or leaders, etc.

In that meeting the first question they should ask is:

Step Two: Who doesn't make many copies but would still be impacted by this decision?

SLACK.COM OR OTHER COMMUNICATIONS OR PROJECT MANAGEMENT SOFTWARE

In this example, there are at least three possible constituencies they would need to bring into the process: 1) whoever holds the purse strings (accounting, the founder, etc.), 2) customers (internal or external) of the copies being made, and 3) the IT function, to ensure systems integration. The team could miss some of this or not be exactly sure who is or isn't affected. An easy fix is to use Slack or another simple communications tool to touch everyone in the office once and let them know they have "X" hours/days to respond, or the team will assume they aren't affected or do not wish to provide input.

People who are affected might ask to be part of the full decision-making process or might just have something they want you to consider, and then they're out, but don't let the decision-making team get bigger than the decision. It's an intuitive process; small decisions should have small teams, and big decisions should have larger teams (above and below the water line). You might have a professional meeting-goer who wants to join everything. If they aren't measurably impacted, ask that they give their input to someone on the team to communicate for them.

OTHER THINGS TO SETTLE IN THAT FIRST MEETING

At the beginning of the meeting, these are some good things to get out of the way:

1. The one who called the meeting is the facilitator or decide otherwise.
2. Set a meeting length and a time period to reach a final decision.
3. Determine how you will decide (e.g., majority vote of 51 percent, 70 percent, etc., but rarely 100 percent).
4. Touchy subject? Invite someone with good mediating

skills to facilitate.

THERE ARE NO MISTAKES, ONLY SEMINARS

People who are relearning to make decisions must be encouraged to take small risks. We must celebrate decision-making, even if the outcome isn't always what we desire. If people feel no freedom to experiment and learn, and the specter of failure looms over them, they will have no interest in relearning how to make decisions. We should reframe "mistakes" as "seminars" where the focus isn't on "we did something wrong" but on learning something from the experience. As an example, in a writing seminar, you wouldn't focus on "I wrote that wrong" but on the continual process of writing better and better.

We need to substitute the notion of mistakes with the concept of how we learn. Mistakes are only bad if you don't learn from them, or if they are irreversible (below the water line). Mistakes are part of the natural process of getting things right. If people never get to make mistakes, they will continue their co-dependency with the manager, which is helps the manager add perceived value.

We encourage them to not think in terms of mistakes but in terms of attending a seminar. Learning in a seminar helps you to avoid mistakes by making more informed decisions. We have two rules around seminars (formerly mistakes):

1. Keep the seminar as short and inexpensive as possible. Time and money are at a premium.
2. Don't repeat seminars you already took. If you take the same seminar repeatedly, it's no longer a one-time seminar but a pattern of not learning.

FIVE STEPS IN THE DECISION-MAKING PROCESS

1. People should come to you with "I intend to do 'x'." With rare exceptions, no one can come to a leader with just a question. They must start with a solution — "I intend to."
2. Who else could answer this question for you? They should come having answered as many questions as possible by talking to their peers and tactical leaders first. It's important that we retrain people to engage the concentric circles of Distributed Leadership for their answers. Send them back to other people who could have helped them answer the question.
3. Have you done as much homework on this as you can? Come

with possible solutions, not questions; no co-dependence.

4. Ask, Ask, Ask — Help them think of the implications they have not explored: the challenges, the opportunities, the people who may need help adapting, etc.

5. Strategic leader: "Make it so." (Captain Picard — *Star Trek*) — Once everyone feels the plan is sound, have them carry it out.

Everyone will struggle at first with step two, "Who else is affected by this decision?" but it is important because people should never make decisions in a vacuum, which is independence. We should shoot for interdependence, working together, and using the wisdom of crowds.

FINE TUNING

One of the objectives of two-step decision-making is to streamline decisions to the point that some no longer require the two steps. At Crankset Group, when people have formed a habit of making good decisions in a particular area, they can then bring the decision to just one set of outside eyes for a quick review, while we celebrate the trust that comes from knowing they've "got it." Two-step decision-making should not create an ongoing burden by throwing every decision out for everyone to flog, but it should facilitate learning how to involve fewer people as the decisions become more sound. This is a somewhat intuitive process and is an effective use of a strategic leader's time and talents. Streamlining the two-step process across the board encourages more adult Stakeholders to grow into their roles.

MY INDIVIDUAL RESPONSIBILITY

Two-step decision-making is designed to create as much communication as possible with everyone who might be affected by a decision, within obvious time constraints. It is still the individual's responsibility to chase down things they have been made aware of and to give input. Nobody gets to say, "But I wasn't asked that specific question." Adult Stakeholders don't blame the process, which is never perfect. They proactively get involved when they hear of something that might affect them and aren't offended by perceived slights, saying, "I wasn't asked clearly enough to do this!" Instead, they ask themselves how they can be a leader, get involved, and give input.

A FINAL IRONY — WE ALL WANT TO MANAGE

We were working with a very frustrated Stakeholder on a team who recounted that she and a few others on the team had fully vetted a situation, explored all the possible solutions, and had chosen what they felt was the best one. They shared this with their former manager, who was now functioning as a strategic leader and who annoyingly started asking questions. The team member said this really took the air out of the balloon, and when I asked why, she said, "Because we had already figured out what was best and just wanted to tell him what we had come up with."

It was a blinding flash of the obvious, or a BFO for me. Here was a DDM workgroup member who was attempting to do to her former manager exactly what he had done to her for years: come up with a solution without input and just dictate it. When we explained it to her, she got it. The simple solution was to get the strategic leader involved (step two) much earlier in the process so he could ask his questions along with everyone else. Step one and step two should happen almost simultaneously, not in a gapped sequence.

SUMMARY

Two-step decision-making is inherently simple but not easy. Don't take it lightly and make sure it is being used universally. Everyone will find that they continually need to help each other recognize and honor step two.

Ownership is the most powerful motivator in business, and the best way to create localized ownership is with localized decision-making. Nothing defines me as an engaged adult more than knowing I'm both allowed and required to make good decisions, not in a vacuum but through collaboration, cooperation, communication, and in community.

THE NEXT ONE THING

1. Role Play

It's good to take a look back at a recently made decision and role play how two-step decision-making lines up with how that process went down, or take a live opportunity to role play two-step decision-making.

It could be that your company is nailing this already, but there is likely either some fine-tuning or fairly significant changes to make. Remember the objective, rehumanizing the workplace by giving everybody their brain back, which happens through Universally

Distributed Decision-making. Two-step decision-making is the core practice of great Participation Age companies — take it very seriously and practice it well, and always look for a good decision, not a perfect one.

Choose a real/hypothetical issue to solve (preferably a look back on a recent decision):

1. Who noticed the issue first? Did they take the ball and run with it? Why? Why Not?
2. How would we use two-step DM to verify that it is a decision that needs to be solved? (think step one).
3. Who set that meeting (if there was one)? A manager? Who could set it using the two-step process?
4. Did we ensure that everyone affected had input? How would we do it differently with the two-step DM process?

a. Openly, Regularly Celebrate Seminars (mistakes)

Devise a prize, or regular prizes, to celebrate people who complete a seminar (mistake) and announce the award regularly at team or company meetings. Have the winners share with others what they learned at the seminar and why they won't likely need to take it again. If we don't encourage experimenting and learning through "trial and seminars," people will not take us seriously about Distributed Decision-making.

THE NEXT ONE THING

1. What Next One Thing do we need to do to implement two-step decision-making?

_____

_____

_____

2. When will we start? _____/_____/_____

3. What are the one or two challenges that need to be addressed before we start?

_____

_____

_____

TWO-STEP DECISION-MAKING PROTOCOL

"Good decisions create healthy interdependence"

—CHUCK BLAKEMAN, CRANKSET GROUP

What is the issue to be solved?

Note: Many times, it's not a problem but an innovative or creative idea.

1. If one or two others have confirmed this is an issue (either through conversation or even a Slack channel on the topic), then call a meeting of people based on answers to both questions that follow.

- The bigger the decision, the more people who might be in the room. Fewer is always better, as long as those who have to live out the decision are there.

Meeting Attendees:	

Question 1: Who must live out the decision?
 	
    Whoever must live out the decision should make that decision.
 	
    Usually means more than one person should make the decision.
	Question 2: Who is affected by the decision?
	• Whoever is affected by the decision needs to give input.
	• Consider who is involved from the back end (internal) to front end (customer) Note: The "customer" is many times internal.

	It's easy to skip Question 2. Make sure you always a) figure out who is affected and b) get their input.

Starting the meeting:	During the meeting:
Person calling the meeting is the facilitator, unless they or the team suggests otherwise. If there is someone at the meeting not affected by the problem, thank them for their interest and reduce the team size. At the start, set how much time for the discussion. Determine how decision will be made (simple majority, super majority) and if even number, who is the tie breaker (don't go for 100 percent). Agree as a group that when done, all are on board regardless of how they each voted.	Ask "why" at least three times. This encourages strategic thinking of how this problem/solution affects the whole organization. Refer to freedom maps (see that chapter) for clarification of processes discussed. Facilitator honors the established discussion time and calls for a vote or consensus on extension. Look for a good decision, not a perfect one. Honor the "no" votes to see if the group feels there is passion/validity that needs addressing as part of the solution.

CHAPTER EIGHT

Community at Work

8

We believe reestablishing the idea of community at work may be the next big focus on how to improve the workplace. For Participation Age companies, it always has been.

We are mammals. We are made to live in community, not just at home but at work, too. By 1850, more goods were made in factories than in shops and homes, and for the first time in history, people were doing something very unnatural, leaving home and going to work, eventually at great distances. Separation of work and personal life is unhealthy, unnatural, and largely unprecedented for most people before the Factory System made it pervasive. It became a mantra, "Leave your personal life at home!" because being human at work got in the way of becoming like the machine you operated.

We believe organizations that place an emphasis back on community at work are emerging as the big winners in the Participation Age. To that end, our company bias is that work should be organized not around teams but around building community at work. Super-performing teams are a result of great community. Davita, a 65,000-person dialysis machine provider, sees itself as "a community first, a company second[1]." Since adopting this mindset in 1999, they experienced exponential growth. Strategic leaders in Participation Age companies focus on developing community first and then encourage the community to figure out how to accomplish the task at hand.

Teamwork organized around a task gets the job done, but vast research over the last 125 years shows that relationships organized around community both rehumanize the workplace and get the job done even better. Friend groups widely outperform acquaintance groups in both decision-making and motor tasks[2]. Research across forty-seven countries found that nearly half of the top fifteen drivers of company greatness are about building peer team community[3].

Before the Factory System, we worked with and sold our products to friends, had them over for dinner, invited them to our weddings, and built life-long relationships with them, yet because of the persistence of the Factory System into the twenty-first century, only half as many people claim to have a close friend at work as those who did in the 1980s. The research shows community works better, but we're going in the wrong direction.

HIRE FOR COMMUNITY

Community is best promoted through both formal and informal means, and community at work is no exception. It starts with the hiring process. Pivotal Software, with 2,500 people, hires first for empathy and emotional intelligence, not programming skills. Collaborating closely with other programmers on an everyday basis in DDM workgroups is essential to their way of doing business[4].

At Crankset Group, we hire for community. We don't even look at resumes until at least halfway through our eleven-step hiring process. We look at business beliefs and values, the desire to integrate personal and work life, emotional intelligence, empathy, and a deep commitment to living in community. Community is one of the five core values we prominently post at the beginning of every hiring ad. We want to hear how people respond to our core values before we take another step to hire them. For your organization to function at the level of community, not just team, you must hire with community in mind.

INFORMAL COMMUNITY

We're not a family but a community. We don't all go out for happy hour all the time, but everyone at work has a few deep friendships that in some cases rise to the level of family, and all of us get along on a relational level, not just at the task level.

In my book, *Why Employees Are Always a Bad Idea*, we described the seven common culture types. By far, the most common is the *allies culture*, where the mantra is, "you don't have to like each other, just get the job done." As a result, companies hire for learned skills and experience while largely ignoring innate talent. Companies put up with highly productive heroic jerks who drag down the productivity of everyone around them and send the message that getting along with others doesn't matter. Then, they wonder where their customers get that message, too.

Participation Age companies hire people who put other people first. Strategic leaders not only encourage others to build relationships informally but actively engage in doing so themselves. Happy hours, lunches, whole company events, sports, inviting people over to play cards—basically, anything we would do with our neighbor, we should see going on between people at work.

All great relationships, whether at work or at home, are built on two principles: recency and frequency. How recently did we talk, and how frequently do we talk? It's not only about "quality time" but also about just being together. Great sports teams at any level don't focus first on the task but on building camaraderie through off-the-court relationships. Those deep relationships, built in community, are the secret sauce of super-performing teams. Great strategic leaders invest time in building relationships informally whenever the moment arises.

FORMAL COMMUNITY — SEVEN PRACTICES

The very intentional and consistent practice of informal, relational community is foundational, but giving it formal priority in our weekly work schedules demonstrates to everyone how it truly matters. When my wife, Diane and I had young kids, we made sure we had "date night" every Thursday. Being purposeful about building relationships is not inauthentic. Just the opposite, it demonstrates that it is a priority.

There are at least seven formal practices to build community at work, all of which work together to deemphasize imposed hierarchy and encourage horizontal relationships:

1. **Communication** — the number one skill and consistently the number one complaint of everyone at work: nobody communicates enough with me.
2. **Coaching** — teaching human skills that help us relate to one another.
3. **Mentoring** — an advocate for each person and his/her development.
4. **Meetings and events** — rehumanizing meetings and adding happy hours, BBQs, etc.
5. **Training** — formal and consistent, never ad hoc.

6. **Carefrontations** — caring enough to confront and provide kind but direct feedback.

7. **Human skills development** — training on how to build healthy relationships.

1 COMMUNICATIONS

George Bernard Shaw wisely stated, "The single biggest problem in communication is the illusion that it has taken place." By far, the best tool we know for improving communications is two-step decision-making, which we covered in its own chapter. It is the simplest and most valuable way to improve communications. I cannot think of a single miscommunication in our company in the last few years that could not be tracked back to skipping over someone in step one or step two.

There are also great new technologies such as Slack and Workplace[5] that can effectively enhance communications. We'll talk a little more about these when we address how to eliminate classic Factory System meetings in favor of fewer, shorter DDM workgroup meetings.

Great communication involves full transparency. The more everyone knows about everything in the company, from financials to metrics, to new hires or pending big decisions, the more they are engaged. Input equals ownership, but input is only possible with transparency, and great communication is the tool of transparency.

Two-step decision-making should work in every corner of your company. If everyone is in the habit of simultaneously asking, "Who must carry this decision out?", and "Who else is impacted or affected?", effective communications skyrockets, and people will feel like you care again.

2 COACHING

When two thriving sister companies, Concentrus and VHA, made the decision to leave behind the Factory System hierarchy and adopt DDM workgroups, the founder, Vincent Huang, hired a coach to work regularly with the strategic leaders on the transition. It was a simple but insightful decision.

Coaching people to continue to grow in communication skills and relationships is another responsibility that generally falls to the manager, yet research shows most managers lack the desire, time, or skills to focus on it. Many bigger companies now hire people full-time to teach people to coach throughout the company. Studies show that the best focus for coaching is not actually on personal development, per se, but specifically on how to work together in teams.

3 MENTORING

Unlike communications and coaching, not enough has been written about the critical role mentoring plays in both onboarding new hires and building community in DDM workgroups. We have dedicated a chapter to onboarding and mentoring later in the book. Don't skip it — it's vital to rehumanizing the workplace.

4 HOW TO HOLD A MEETING (AND WHY)

Meetings are easily the biggest waste of time in any company. There are far too many, involving too many people, with very little group participation. In the Participation Age, it is critical that we redesign why and how we hold meetings. To that end, this massive waste of time, money, and energy also has its own chapter. While we think about reducing the number of meetings, we should think about adding BBQs, happy hours, free breakfast at work, and other relationship-building activities to bring community back to work.

5 TRAINING

Most training is ad hoc and not really training. Too often it is done by professional trainers when members of the team could do it better. See our chapters on four-step training and Freedom Mapping for the importance and simplicity of how teams can train each other.

6 CAREFRONTATIONS

In the Factory System organization, if I have a problem with Bob, my learned habit is to talk to the manager, who then must talk to Bob. At Crankset Group, we call that gossip. In a Participation Age company with no managers, members of DDM workgroups no longer have a co-dependent manager to handle the tough side of adulting at work. We must figure out how to care enough to confront for their benefit, not ours, with kindness and directness. Lane Rankin, founder of Illuminate Education, an extremely successful software company, dreamed up and instituted Carefrontations so DDM workgroups could learn to live in community together without managers.

The resulting privilege of DDM workgroups is that everyone gets their brain back and can make decisions as responsible adults again. Being an adult at work requires caring enough to confront, which most of us would rather avoid. We must stop being peacekeepers ("it wasn't a big thing") and learn how to be peacemakers who keep short accounts.

It is our experience that companies can develop this skill and that people really don't need a co-dependent mommy or daddy at work to handle their interpersonal relationships. There is a chapter devoted to this.

7 HUMAN SKILLS DEVELOPMENT

The Factory System divides skills into "hard skills" and "soft skills." Categorizing this way is convenient but inappropriate. The labels themselves teach us that the "soft skills" are fuzzy, hard to measure, and less tangible and, therefore, shouldn't be trifled with. "Hard skills" are more easily taught and measured: typing, writing, programming, welding, accounting, assembly, and so on. We focus on the hard skills because the soft ones seem too hard to measure and because we don't easily see their direct impact on production.

WorkTrends™ Global worker sample[6] discovered three remarkable results in companies where the primary focus is not on production but on human skills:

1. Work performance is 23 percent higher than in companies focused first on production.
2. Discretionary effort was 74 percent higher.
3. Intent to stay was 210 percent higher.

WorkTrends looked at creating productivity, happiness, and high retention. The list included a high level of trust, building relationships, meaningful work, recognition, empowerment and voice, belonging, purpose, and achievement. Threatening, cajoling, paying more, and emphasizing perks such as free lunches and ping pong tables didn't make the list.

The results of good human skills cannot be overemphasized in a work world where people now use their brains more than their bodies. "I'm too busy running this company" doesn't fly anymore. When strategic leaders focus on the human skills, the rest of the people take better care of the production process.

This Participation Age data encourages a new way of looking at hard and soft skills. We believe it is more helpful to see them as production skills and human skills. We must learn how to measure the human skills as well as the production skills because they have more impact on production than the production skills themselves.

Two people who are equally skilled at typing, writing, programming, welding, or accounting may produce very different results because of intangibles such as attitude, emotional intelligence, creativity, communication skills, and empathy. Emphasizing the human skills creates super-functioning DDM workgroups. In our chapter on incentives, we describe how to create utterly clear measurement to motivate people to fully develop both their human and production skills.

THE ESSENTIAL HUMAN SKILLS

Great organizations are focused on building relationships and developing both intuition and emotional intelligence. Participation Age organizations see the world essentially through the lens of people-to-people, not people-to-things. They understand that production is increased not by focusing on it but by focusing on the human skills within the DDM teams that equip them to maximize production.

The following are ten essential human skills that help create super-functioning DDM workgroups:

1. **Listening** — Taking the time to actively hear and evaluate fairly what someone else says.
2. **Trust** — Living in a world of abundance, not scarcity; assuming the best.
3. **Consistency** — Saying what I'll do; doing what I said — commitment to my word.
4. **Emotional intelligence** — Self and relationship awareness/management.
5. **Empathy** — What do others think and feel about themselves? How can I help them?
6. **Communications** — Two-step decision-making.
7. **Teamwork** — The desire to be interdependent, not independent or co-dependent.
8. **Adaptability/attitude/learning** — "How can I?" versus "I can't."

9. **Leadership** — Be/do/inspire/relate — everyone is a leader strategically, tactically, or both.
10. **Intuition/judgment** — "The highest form of human intelligence" (Albert Einstein).

No one person may possess all the listed skills, but in even the smallest team, there will likely be more of them present than in any one manager.

Emotional intelligence and empathy, also called emotional quotient (EQ), is perhaps the most ignored yet most important set of human skills. High EQ:

1. Creates better leaders[7].
2. Creates better performers — 90 percent of top performers have it, and 90 percent of bottom performers don't[8].
3. Accounts for 58 percent of a person's job performance. Of 33 variables, it was found to be the single strongest predictor of how someone will perform[9].
4. Increases personal income by an average of $29,000 per year[10].
5. Makes us happier[11].
6. Increases staff retention significantly[12].

Stunningly, average EQ outperforms high IQ 70 percent of the time, while average IQ outperforms average EQ only 20 percent of the time[13].

At Crankset Group, we test for emotional intelligence and empathy before looking at resumes or testing for production skills. The more strategic the leadership role, the more these human skills become the central hiring metric. Participation Age companies hire strategic leaders first for EQ and secondly for skills and experience.

LISTENING

Narcissism is, at its core, a dysfunction of listening[14]. Along with EQ, listening is at the top of the list of necessary human skills. Labels like narcissism aren't always helpful, but no one would disagree that the inability to listen well is going to create problems at work. Steven Covey's Habit Five from his book *Seven Habits of Highly Successful People* is "seek first to understand, not to be understood." He lays out a progression from a deep habit of not listening to a habit of deep listening. The parentheses are mine:

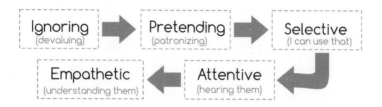

I appreciate this progression because it shows the interconnectedness of listening, emotional intelligence, and empathy, three core skills we all need to develop. The deep work of strategic leadership focuses on the human skills required to lead effectively.

INTERDEPENDENT PEOPLE

In the graph that follows, we see three basic ways people function at work. On the left edge, we have the classic rugged individualist. Some people in organizations, like salespeople, are taught to be rugged individualists and function outside of community. On the right edge are the co-dependent manager/reporters, which is how most people relate at work. Managers need people to command and control, and employees don't want to make decisions. Refocusing our reliance from managers to DDM workgroups brings us back to the middle, in balanced, healthy interdependence.

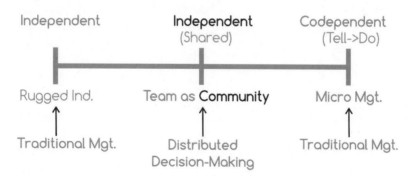

Interdependent adults know they can function on their own, but they also know that it would be foolish because there is so much more power to learn, grow, produce, encourage, motivate, and celebrate together. Healthy Participation Age organizations have no independent or co-dependent people and live solidly in the middle as a community of interdependent Stakeholder adults.

SUPER-FUNCTIONING DDM WORKGROUPS
High-functioning teams get things done better than individuals, but interdependent people in community get things done even better than high-functioning teams.

Creating community starts with a commitment to the seven formal community-building practices listed previously. It requires a shift from focusing on production to focusing on people, who then turn around to improve production. People first, then production. The rest of the book is devoted to the tools and practices that promote horizontal relationships over vertical ones, resulting in super-functioning DDM workgroups living in community at work.

THE NEXT ONE THING

1. Review the concept of interdependence versus the more normative independence and co-dependence (management). How could this apply to my organization?

_____

_____

2. What is the Next One Thing do we need to do to take our teams beyond high-functioning to full-blown community at work?

_____

_____

3. When will we start? _____/_____/_____

4. What are the first challenge that need to be addressed before we start?

_____

_____

RESOURCES

1   http://blogs.davita.com/stories/

2   https://www.researchgate.net/publication/200773258_Do_Friends_Perform_ Better_Than_Acquaintances_The_Interaction_of_Friendship_Conflict_and_Task

3   https://www.workforce.com/2015/12/20/a-great-place-to-work-takes-a-great-community/

4   https://medium.com/product-labs/5-culture-hacks-i-ve-learned-from-my-first-month-at-pivotal-labs-c17e99fded36

5   https://medium.com/@max.sather/slack-vs-facebook-workplace-1ae46aef77ea

6   https://www.globoforce.com/wp-content/uploads/2016/10/The_Employee_ Experience_Index.pdf

7   http://www.emeraldinsight.com/doi/abs/10.1108/02683940310511881

8   https://www.forbes.com/sites/travisbradberry/2014/01/09/emotional-intelligence/#62fe66551ac0

9   https://blog.crowdspring.com/2017/06/emotional-intelligence-entrepreneur-leadership

10   http://www.talentsmart.com/about/emotional-intelligence.php

11   https://www.sciencedirect.com/science/article/pii/S0191886917303884

12   http://www.sciencedirect.com/science/article/pii/S0001879105001260

13   https://blog.crowdspring.com/2017/06/emotional-intelligence-entrepreneur-leadership/

14   https://www.psychologytoday.com/us/blog/resolution-not-conflict/201210/are-you-narcissist-6-sure-signs-narcissism

CHAPTER NINE

Caring Enough to Confront　9

I f it weren't for people, my business would be perfect. Caring enough to confront, and confronting with care, is essential to building high-performing DDM workgroups living in community.

Interpersonal conflict is arguably the biggest challenge to address in any organization. At any given time, one-third of us are bugged about something someone is doing at work[1], and Accenture says a stunning 35 percent of people who quit do so to avoid confronting an interpersonal issue[2]. This is something we sometimes wish we could give back to a manager, except the data once again show that managers aren't much help with this issue either.

At least three of the five dysfunctions of a team, identified by Patrick Lencioni in his book of the same name, are directly related to not knowing how or not wanting to confront and resolve conflict: avoidance of accountability, fear of conflict, and absence of trust. The other two team dysfunctions are deeply affected by conflict: inattention to results and lack of commitment. The disengagement tax from conflict avoidance resulting in low productivity is staggering.

> **The disengagement tax from conflict avoidance resulting in low productivity is staggering.**

There are two ways to deal with an issue: now or later. "Never" falls under later, and as the free beer tomorrow sign reminds us, tomorrow, or later, never comes. Successful people do not live passively just hoping things work out. They understand the golden rule of business. As corny as you think it may sounds, all great organizations run on love as the basis for every decision, and love doesn't put off tough conversations.

Nearsoft developed their Art of Feedback workshop for new hires. Anabel Montiel says, "On their first day at Nearsoft, people usually go through some sort of culture shock. They enjoy having so much freedom, but at the same time, it confuses them. Most of our new joiners come from very traditional organizations in Mexico where they used to go to their boss for almost everything, like proposing an idea, complaining about someone, or asking for a raise. We find different ways to tell them that their confusion is very normal and also give them enough time, around six weeks, to assimilate the new set of mostly unwritten rules that come with this new culture."

"They learn through classes and with the help of a mentor about what they should do if they see a problem and have an idea to fix it. In this case, they are taught to create a leadership team and invite others to join them, or if they see an opportunity to grow an account, they should take the initiative and talk directly with the potential client without being intimidated, and if they see that someone on their team is struggling with something, we help them learn how to give honest feedback and offer their help. All these topics are part of the content of the onboarding, and the preparation that mentors have to go through before accompanying someone on their onboarding."

FOLLOWING ARE THREE GOOD RULES TO GOVERN CAREFRONTATIONS:
Rule #1: Seek the Other Person's Long-Term, Best Interests

Great business is about love. Stick with me here. This isn't woo-woo crap; this is hard-core success strategy. My working definition of love is more of an intended result than a definition. See if it works for you: Love always seeks the *long-term, best interest* of the one being loved. Read it a few times and let it sink into your view of business. Everything in a great organization depends on this definition: marketing, sales, production, leadership, customer service, and teamwork. The best way to keep customers is to seek their long-term, best interest, without exception. Never seek yours or even their short-term interest. Love runs everything in business, as in life, and if it doesn't, it eventually catches up with you.

That same principle applies to relationships inside your business. If we seek the long-term, best interests of everyone around us, and they do too, we have a solid foundation on which to build a great organization.

Why do we usually want to confront someone? Something they did bugs us, so we want to give them a piece of our mind, make them pay for their grievance against us, to emotionally throw up on them, or see if we can knock them down a peg or two. Whatever the reason, it usually has our own short-term interests at the center. We need to seek the long-term, best interests of that person by helping them see something that could help them live better at work and in the world around them.

THE SOLUTION — COMMUNITY AT WORK

Managers aren't the answer. Research says they avoid difficult conversations like the plague. Typically, any type of carefrontation, from morale-busting annual reviews to asking someone to step it up in how they dress, is handed off to human resources. Managers can find a dozen reasons to avoid talking — that person is too valuable to lose, he's funny, it's my boss's nephew, I hired her and I don't want them to think I'm wrong, I want everyone to like me, or I just don't want to cause waves.

While leaders lead with courage, managers manage by declaring policies. Instead of taking a walk with the one person who did something offensive, managers crank out a company-wide policy that belittles everyone's humanity via email, posted memo, or an all-hands meeting where no personal interaction has to occur. In an article about leading without managers, Ricardo Semler says, "We replaced all the nitpicking regulations with the rule of common sense and put our employees in the demanding position of using their own judgment[3]." Stakeholders are adults who are allowed and required to use judgment in Carefrontations.

In the Factory System organization, if Tim's attention to detail isn't what his teammate John needs from him, John reverts to being seven years old and tells the manager. The manager is then supposed to deal with the two of them like a mother defending the smaller child in the back seat of a car. That is what a mother is supposed to do, but not what two adults do. If I have an issue with someone else, I must be an adult and talk to him or her. If I don't, it isn't good for me or my co-worker, who may not even be aware of the offense.

We want all the privileges of adulthood without the responsibilities.

Who wouldn't? But adulthood doesn't work that way. If we want to be contributing and highly engaged adults, we must learn how to get along with other people for *their* benefit, not just our own. It is one of the many reasons that I believe great organizations hire first for emotional intelligence and empathy, not skills and experience. Strategic leaders should always be hired first for these things, but the hiring rule applies to all.

LEADER-LEADER APPLIES TO CAREFRONTATIONS

Remember the analogy where each person is a member of a soccer or hockey team? If there is a ball loose on the field and I can get to it first, it is my responsibility to grab it and then figure out later why it was loose or if anyone else should have been on it. It isn't helpful to affix blame or point fingers — do what needs to be done and then connect afterwards to review the process. The focus is on a blameless "why" (and how we fix it), not a blame-filled "who."

The loose ball analogy applies to personal relationships at work just as well. If you are the first one to notice that someone has made a coding error or responded to a customer incorrectly, you have the ball. You are the leader because you saw the issue first. Leaders, being proactive, grab the ball and do whatever they can to advance it. In this case, you would do whatever you can to help the person fix their mistake, for their long-term benefit and the benefit of the whole company, avoiding the perverse pleasure of merely calling out someone else's mistake.

This isn't optional, and it isn't personality specific. As one introvert shared with me, both introverts and extroverts need to learn how to confront uncomfortable situations. Nobody gets a pass. We may not like the hard work of being an adult at work, but we all must do it for the sake of everyone around us.

Typically, managers are the worst at this. Managers should never be allowed to foist their interpersonal issues off to someone in HR, nor should they be allowed to emotionally vent at others for their own satisfaction. We need coaches or advisers to teach us how to talk transparently to someone else for their benefit.

Appster is a fast-growing app development company with hundreds of developers on three continents. I interviewed the co-leaders and a dozen staff around the world for an Inc. article on being a Participation Age company. Without prompting, the majority of the staff I interviewed in Australia, India, and the United States commented on how open and transparent their relationships were and how necessary it was for all of them to take responsibility to give great feedback. A few of them said, "There is no room for being highly insecure here. If you can't take constructive feedback given for your own benefit, you won't last here."

If we are seeking the long-term, best interest of everyone in the company, we will help them learn how to give and take great, constructive feedback, or we will help them find another company where they can be supervised. This isn't harsh in any way. It is loving them more than anyone possibly ever has. Being an adult isn't easy, but it's a whole package. Being able to share with each other in love is part of the package.

Rule #2: Adults Are Peacemakers, Not Peacekeepers

Another driving principle of Carefrontations is the need to make the peace, not keep it. Often, under the guise of keeping the peace, we are avoiding potential conflict that cries out for a satisfactory resolution. Our inaction isn't for the sake of the other person; it's self-protective. We pretend it's for the other person with statements like, "It's not that big of a deal. I should just let it go," or "I don't want to cause unnecessary friction," or my favorite, "I don't want to hurt their feelings." All these are cover for, "I don't feel like adulting today. Please don't make me adult."

The reality is I don't have their long-term, best interests at heart, or I would take the few minutes to talk with them and be done with it. Peacemakers understand that dealing with issues as they arise keeps them small, keeps the slate clean, and builds an environment of trust where no one is waiting to be blindsided by someone blowing up at them. Peacemakers have small border skirmishes. Peacekeepers end up in world wars because they avoid the small, daily opportunities to resolve things. Peacemaking is not optional. It's part of being an adult at work and is a core business practice of healthy organizations. Everyone needs to learn to do it — no exceptions.

If I'm not part of the problem or the solution but just a convenient ear for you to air your grievance, it's gossip.

Rule #3: The No-Gossip Rule

Another core principle of

Carefrontations is the no-gossip rule. Rather than talking to the person I'm having trouble with, it's easier to blow off steam with someone who sits and listens or even agrees, but this accomplishes nothing except widening the circle of grievance. In a Mission-centered organization, gossip is never acceptable. In a Factory System hierarchy, gossip is normalized by going to the manager instead of to the other person.

If you approach me to talk about someone else being rude or inefficient, you're approaching the wrong person. If I'm not part of the problem or the solution but just a convenient ear for you to air your grievance, it's gossip.

THE END OF GOSSIP

Here are two quick steps to take that can stop gossip instantly and aid in building a caring culture of honest, transparent, community at work. It is built on peacemaking through Carefrontations.

First, take the responsibility to handle the conflict away from anyone who is not involved. Ultimately, this means taking it away from managers and HR, but it isn't as radical as it sounds. The Morning Star Company (4,000-plus associates) has been working this way for decades. If you have a problem with someone, you have the ball, and you need to go directly to that person and talk it through — no intermediaries, no managers. Participation Age organizations of every size function this way. No arbitrating mommies or daddies, just two adults working it out.

Second, make it the responsibility of every single Stakeholder not to listen to gossip from anyone. It must be treated as a serious violation of community at work. If someone begins to share with me, I have the responsibility to ask, "Am I part of the problem or solution?" If not, I need to stop them and take the conversation in a different direction.

> "Tom, thanks for thinking of me, but it doesn't appear that I'm either part of the problem or part of the solution, but now that you've involved me, I am part of the solution. Here's the solution I propose: 1) please go talk to Bob (role play with me if you want), 2) let's decide together when that will happen, and 3) come share with me afterward how it went so I can support you (and support you for having actually done it)."

If we made this a hard and fast practice in responding to gossip, it would quickly disappear in the workplace. Everyone would understand that if I want to simply vent, others are going to tell me to go talk to the relevant person for their benefit, and they're going to support me in doing it. I might as well skip the gossip step and just go talk to Bob.

TRAIN ME HOW TO CAREFRONT

In rare instances, someone, let's call her Daisy, might feel wholly inadequate to approach a fellow team member with his problem even though she wants to help. Daisy needs to know that she must approach her co-worker Bob with an unemotional delivery of the facts, characterized by appropriate words of support for him. In this scenario, Daisy already decided she must talk to Bob and simply needs some help learning how to do it. Training others how to carefront is legitimate and necessary, but make sure it doesn't degenerate into gossip.

FOR THEIR BENEFIT, NOT MINE

Learning how to share for their benefit and not for my own satisfaction is central to good Carefrontations, but it's not something we're used to doing. Society has taught us to blow up at people on the phone, on the road, and in person to defend our own territory and put others in their place. That is not love. It is narcissism. Let's learn how to do it for their benefit, and we then benefit, too.

A couple decades ago, I read The Power of Purpose by Peter Temes. In it, he describes three tiers of thinking that help us learn how to carefront appropriately. Tier III involves the empathy required to carefront — how do others think and feel about themselves, and how can I help them with that?

What if I invested all my energy in simply discovering what the other person is thinking and feeling? How could I help push them forward in some small way? By default, it also means that while I'm doing that, I do not consider my own needs or even how the other person might perceive me because of my desire to help. Tier III is the fully empathetic adult living to serve and make others better, regardless of the impact it has on me in the short term. Tier III causes me to develop this powerful question for myself:

Am I willing to love, even if as a result, I might not be liked?

Empathy is the number one driver of job performance, and getting people involved (Distributed Decision-making), is number two, but empathy is the second to last competency of managers; only 40 percent of managers even have it. Some people on a DDM workgroup, though, may have it in spades and can help the rest of us learn it.

Tier III empathy motivates me to leave myself behind and put myself in their shoes for their benefit. Remember some of the excuses above for not interacting well:

1. "It's not that big of a deal. I should just let it go."
2. "I don't want to cause unnecessary friction."
3. "I don't want to hurt their feelings."

For most of us, these sound unselfish and focused on protecting the other person, but they are self-serving and designed to protect the self. Do we love the people around us at work? We can demonstrate that by being willing to love, even if for a moment we are not liked for it. Living in community requires that we all become adult Stakeholders, genuinely seeking the best for those around us. The Nash Equilibrium gaming principle[4] has been broadly adopted in many disciplines because it shows how decisions that are good for the individual can be terrible for the group, that the best result is achieved by looking out not only for my own interests but also for the interests of others. Let's talk about the nuts and bolts of how to do it.

Before the Carefrontation

Review these seven steps to peacemaking:

1. **Where?** For a difficult conversation, pick a neutral location, not your office, and never discuss difficult things over food. That is not the neutral setting we think it is.
2. **Motive?** Do you want them to respond and change, or do you want to squash them? Get excited about how this conversation could help that person grow, but postpone the meeting until you can speak without undue emotion.
3. **Clarity?** Be clear about the issue and stay focused. Choose one thing and don't be steered in a different direction by the conversation. Successful people confront one thing at a time. Pick your Carefrontations carefully.
4. **Listening?** Don't assume. Ask questions and be prepared to hear a completely different view of the situation. Active listening might change your whole perspective and response.
5. **Your responsibility?** Did you play a part in causing the issue,

or is your responsibility simply to be outside eyes, providing a different perspective? Take the blame for your own part.

6. **Fear?** Understand that putting it off to be liked now is probably going to make it a bigger deal later. Remember, love always seeks the long-term best interest of the one being loved.

7. **Continue/repair?** Do your best to share the issue in a way that allows you both to leave the conversation with dignity and able to continue talking in the future. Nobody is supposed to win or lose. We're all supposed to grow.

BEFORE YOU RESPOND

This is tough, but whenever possible, avoid the initial knee-jerk reaction, which is the opposite of serving their long-term, best interests. Besides creating tension and division, it also makes it more difficult for them to hear me later. I still struggle with this, but I am getting better at apologizing quickly when I lose control. Since most of us struggle with giving appropriate responses at times, a quick apology is usually met with forgiveness, and I've found that by making a habit of apologizing, my tendency to jump in with a defensive response is commensurately curbed.

Wait to carefront someone until you can get your own emotion out of it, or at least under control. When I'm emotional, it's a signal to me that I'm not ready to talk to the other person because they might feel attacked rather than safe and encouraged. Focus on what would help them. It's not entirely selfless; I am highly motivated to help someone get something figured out so that it doesn't impact me again, as well as so they can grow.

Measure the impact of the issue. The smaller the impact, the less of an issue we need to make of it. We never ignore it, but we don't blow things out of proportion, either. "Learn to live above offense," as my friend John Heenan says. That's a great mindset. Stop thinking so much about how everything impacts you and start asking more about how others are thinking and feeling. It's very adult — it's just not easy.

During the Carefrontation
1) Seek to Understand

As we said in the chapter on community at work, Stephen Covey's fifth habit is the first step in Carefrontations because it makes us empathetic:

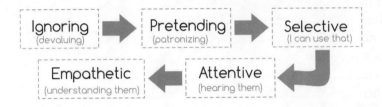

My friend Matt Perez, co-founder of Nearsoft says, "There's no bad apples, just bad barrels." The overwhelming majority of the time it's one of the many things in the "barrel" of our organization that is making the person respond like a bad apple. Edward Deming helped us understand that before we condemn the person we need to look at everything else first: values, vision, mission, leadership, training, communications, infrastructure, tools, and support. Let's seek first to understand how all that we are doing plays into how that person is responding.

2) The Blameless Why

Prioritize support over blame. Go for the blameless why, not the blame-filled who. Why could this have happened — process, training, infrastructure, lack of communications. As Deming suggests, it is rarely just a "who." Look at all the possible "whys". If there is nothing there, then it's a "ho." Discover the "who" last and deal with the "whys" first.

3) Focus on the Facts

...and maybe how they affected *you*, but...

   a.   Always   start   your   conversations   with
        "I"   (three   fingers   pointed   back   at   me)
        "*I* think I observed, I wonder..."
   b.   "The **_metrics_** show...", not "You did x"
   c.   "The **_customer_** said...", not "The customer was mad" (don't interpret)
   d.   "Your **_teammate_** appeared confused...", not "was confused" – you don't know
   e.   "It made **_me_** feel (mad, sad, glad, afraid) ..." not, "I felt this about you."

4) Find Common Ground — Include Yourself

One of the more powerful and helpful ways I have found over the years to have a difficult conversation is to first figure out what you and the other person agree on. Then, follow up by giving an example of how you came to the same conclusion. When people see that they are not alone, and you are willing to admit to your own foibles, it goes a long way toward having a constructive conversation versus an adversarial one. Don't be afraid to say, "I've had to learn the same thing — here's when I went to that life seminar…"

5) Reinforce and Reassure

"You've got this."

"You can learn this skill. Ask Bob. He struggled too and might be able to give you some pointers."

"You're such an important member of our team, and this will make you even more so."

"Thanks for being so willing to be here, learn and grow. Not everyone is willing to keep growing!"

People raise themselves to our lowest expectations of them. Assume the best for their future and communicate it to them. They'll walk away with more clarity about what they got wrong, they'll know it was important, and they will take action.

After the Carefrontation

1. Offer mentorship — I (or someone who is the expert) is willing to help on a formal/informal basis. If the situation is complex and requires training or mentoring, meet regularly until no longer necessary.
2. Set a course of positive action.
3. What one to three things need to happen to make this work in the future?
4. Set a date.
5. By when should these three things be accomplished (can be three separate dates)?
6. Follow up, reinforce, reassure — The carefronter(s) should put a note in their calendar to follow up and make sure the relationship is good, questions are resolved, etc. Be a friend!

WHAT IF SOMEONE DOESN'T RESPOND?

Not everyone is going to get it on the first attempt. We can be having a bad day or week, and it might take some time to see that something has to change. If someone isn't receptive to a loving, gentle one-to-one conversation, you can't just let it go and say, "I tried." Trying is not the objective. If people are not functioning at their highest and best, we all have a responsibility to persevere in helping them get there as quickly as possible.

FOUR-STEP ESCALATION

STEP ONE — Be an adult and talk personally first for their long-term, best interests.

Did you get resistance? Try step two.

STEP TWO — Two or three of you, depending on the impact of the issue, talk with the person together to mediate and provide a consensus that this needs to happen. Sometimes it's better to avoid going all at once, or it can look like ganging up.

Still getting resistance?

STEP THREE — formal mediation. Agree on either a single mediator that both parties trust or on a panel of three (never an even number — no ties) to come to a decision together. After everyone has had their say, the parties agree to embrace the final decision.

Not on board?

STEP FOUR — An arbitrator or panel decides the next action, which could go as far as dismissal.

The Morning Star Company, with 600 permanent staff and almost 4,000 seasonal staff, has no managers but instead runs on self-organizing teams. As such, they have a formal commitment to their version of Carefrontations, as do many other organizations like our own. Though it's rarely necessary, their fourth step is to take the problem to a team or person designated as the arbitrator. In our company, we have had one issue get to step four in the last couple years. If you have a trusting culture, step four is needed only as a rare last-ditch option.

While you can still see "management" at play here, it's not about managing people but managing the process (Manage stuff. Lead people). Without managers, we still have a formal path for resolution. In our experience, it is a much tighter, more defensible process than depending on one appointed person to hire, fire, and to arbitrate personnel issues.

Carefrontation Escalation

1. One2One - Be an adult, talk personally first. Resistance?

2. One2Few - 2-3 people who agree - again, will love

3. Formal Mediation - Small group or single mediator facilitates

4. Arbitrator/Panel - We had our say, embrace & support, or?

Carefrontations are not ancillary to the "real" business and cannot be sloughed off onto an HR department of people specialists while the rest of us get on with the "real" business. There is too much clear research showing that Carefrontations must be everyone's primary responsibility because when relationships break down, the business suffers. We need to ensure we're all learning how to carefront as a common, daily way of supporting each other in the community.

THE NEXT ONE THING

1. What Next One Thing do we need to do to implement or increase everyone's ability to practice kind, direct Carefrontations?

_____

_____

_____

2. When will we start? _____/_____/_____

3. What are the one or two challenges that need to be addressed before we start?

_____

_____

RESOURCES

1   http://www.psychometrics.com/wp-content/uploads/2015/04/conflictstudy_09.pdf

2   https://www.accenture.com/us-en

3   https://jeremiahjosey.wordpress.com/2011/08/25/managing-without-managers-ricardo-semler/

4   https://www.economist.com/the-economist-explains/2016/09/06/what-is-the-nash-equilibrium-and-why-does-it-matter

CHAPTER TEN

Freedom Mapping

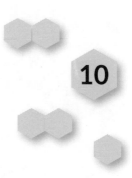

10

> *"Most of what we call management consists of making it difficult for people to get their jobs done."*
>
> —PETER DRUCKER

A Participation Age company has clear objectives, agreed upon processes, shared metrics, and well-defined roles and responsibilities for each function. Freedom mapping brings utter clarity to all of these things and can also be used to determine performance, incentives, and corrective actions. It is one of the most practical ways to encourage horizontal relationships over vertical ones.

Freedom mapping uses some recognizable process mapping conventions but with one very important distinction: maps are built first for finding each person's highest and best contribution to the process, not for the sake of defining the process. In the act of finding everyone's highest and best, the process is even more well defined.

We use Freedom Mapping as one of the three legs of our Stakeholder reference guide. We (and many other Participation Age companies) don't have traditional employee manuals. We use a much more personalized approach that builds around a detailed offer letter, Commitment Letters, and the DDM workgroup's freedom map. We discuss offer letters and Commitment Letters in other chapters.

The Three Legs of the Stakeholder Reference Guide

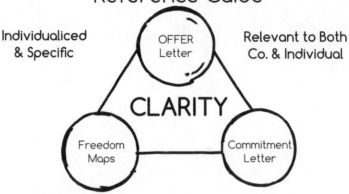

Individualiced & Specific

OFFER Letter

Relevant to Both Co. & Individual

CLARITY

Freedom Maps

Commitment Letter

INPUT EQUALS OWNERSHIP

If you search the Internet for "process mapping" or any similar topics, you find that the focus is usually on the process itself, and it is assumed that the people conform to the process. This is a Factory System approach that continues to re-create people as extensions of machines. You see this vividly in the programmer's blog post at the opening of this book. He learned to leave his best self in the car because the process only included the part of him that did the programming. These sorts of enslaving processes are developed and foisted onto others by the archetypical heroic genius who demands loyalty without input "because I'm the boss, that's why."

DDM workgroups practice two-step decision-making for Freedom Mapping. Processes are developed by those who will run them in collaboration with those who are impacted. The team decides who should be responsible for which steps in the process, and each person's part must be clearly designated. Those who must carry out the decision should develop the process (with input from those who are impacted) because when an amazing heroic genius at the top develops it and dumps it on those below, there is no ownership.

WRITTEN AND CURRENT

If your processes aren't both written and current, you're playing Russian roulette with a wide range of critical business deliverables internally and with your end customer. When DDM workgroups develop freedom maps for their very few important processes, a consistent customer experience is ensured, and internal ownership and engagement is guaranteed. In this chapter, we show how Freedom Mapping moves everyone into activities that are the highest and best use of their time and talents.

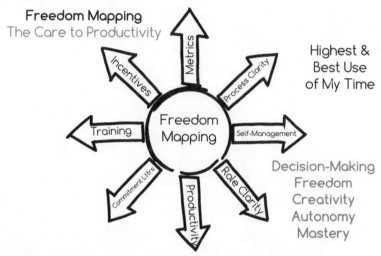

Freedom Mapping
The Care to Productivity

Metrics
Incentives
Process Clarity
Training
Freedom Mapping
Self-Management
Commitment Lttrs
Productivity
Role Clarity

Highest &
Best Use
of My Time

Decision-Making
Freedom
Creativity
Autonomy
Mastery

FREEDOM MAPPING CREATES CONSISTENCY

Occasionally, Mom would tell me in the morning before school that we were having hamburgers for dinner. One night, I found chicken on the table instead. I was disappointed by the switch, which is silly because I like chicken just as much, but because of the unmet expectation, I became an irrational, unhappy customer.

Remember that the number one asset and practice of a leader is consistency. It is true for any organization. We say what we'll deliver, then we deliver what we said. Freedom mapping ensures consistency without mounds of paperwork, shelves of binders, or lots of indecipherable arrows and boxes. Most often, process mapping is only understood by the heroic genius who created it. Freedom mapping is intentionally simplified (but not simplistic) to keep the focus on developing a great process. Process mapping is usually done by experts. Freedom mapping can be easily accomplished by those who run the process, thereby owning the result.

NO MORE JOB DESCRIPTIONS

Good freedom maps can replace the irritating vestige of the Factory System called job descriptions. These seemingly innocuous documents create clear boundaries that define what a person can and cannot do, and when the job description limits their ability to act, the motivated person is deterred from making the positive impact they otherwise could. Job descriptions encourage child-like, reactive behavior and relieve us from being true citizens of the organizational community around us.

"That's not my job" is a statement that would get any one of us fired at Crankset Group. The mission is our job, and we all do whatever we can to accomplish it. Yes, we all have clear roles and responsibilities described in our freedom maps, but that does not absolve us from proactively attempting to help elsewhere when we see a figurative ball loose on the field anywhere in the company.

Job descriptions, on the other hand, teach us to measure our performance relative to our own tasks in our own little cubicle, with no ownership of the world around us. They create a vertically defined world illustrated by the cube wall, where someone lobs something over for me to stamp before I lob it over the next wall for whatever purpose "I don't know and don't care." Job descriptions allow us to go home at night thinking we did a great job because everything on our list was done, even though we have no clue how those things interacted with the rest of the world around us or whether we as a team helped accomplish the mission of the company.

A simple freedom map communicates something entirely different than a job description. It helps all of us think systemically about how our piece of the puzzle interacts with all the others.

A HORIZONTAL, CONNECTED VIEW OF MY WORK

One of the greatest impacts of Freedom Mapping is that Stakeholders begin to view the world horizontally rather than vertically. As we shared previously, every tool presented in this book is designed to help turn our work world from a vertical orientation of bosses, departments, and promotions to a horizontal orientation on interdependent community, the mission, and results.

In the first day or so at their new position, a Stakeholder should see the freedom map developed by their DDM workgroup, as well as a second one that shows how the whole company functions together in what we call our macro map. If someone walks a new person through the macro map on their first day, in five minutes, that person should know at least three things:

1. What we do as a company, as a whole.
2. How I fit into that big picture.
3. Why what I do is so critical to the success of everyone around me.

EMPHASIS ON ROLES, RESPONSIBILITIES, AND FUNCTIONS

Participation Age companies emphasize functions, not departments, and roles and responsibilities, not job descriptions. This is not semantics but a very real and important distinction. A department has physical boundaries. Everyone knows exactly who is in and who is out. In math, this is called a bounded set — the set of all apples or the "sales" department. We like to do the same for jobs — give them very clear boundaries so people know exactly what to do and what not to do, but this segmentation is a throwback to the factories and is unhelpful in a knowledge economy.

We love clarity, even when it does not help us accomplish the mission: Bob is in the sales department. Jenna is in the marketing department. Got it. Bob has seven things listed on his job description. If the does those seven things, he's good. If he does anything beyond that, it may not be recognized, or worse yet, he could get reprimanded for stepping out of his role, but what if Bob's primary role and responsibility was sales, but he was also doing a few marketing things that he's really good at, and vice versa for Jenna? In math terms, this is a "fuzzy set"; the set of all red apples (when do they get to be called red, when they are less than 50 percent green or yellow, or...?). At what point does the marketing or sales department get to claim Bob or Jenna as "theirs"?

In a departmental setting, with people crossing boundaries, we now introduce the nagging, power-based question of who "owns" these people. Both departments would prefer that the other just keep their nose out of "our" business, but if that can't be accomplished, both departments want to claim ownership of that person for budgeting, salary, and occasionally just plain bragging rights purposes. The Factory System created matrix relationships to attempt to deal with this issue, but over time, this has proven to be unnecessary complexity and more lipstick on the pig. There is a better, easier, and more elegant way to deal with complex adaptations of a system.

If the strategic leaders own departments with utterly clear boundaries, it is human nature to guard the boundaries from what appears to be intrusion, but what if the leaders all owned the same result together, accomplishing the organizational mission, and were committed to using the varying activities of a business or "functions" to accomplish that one result? What if we focused on being mission centered and simply used the function of marketing or sales to help us accomplish that mission? In a Participation Age organization, nobody's loyalty is to the function of sales or marketing. We're all just using those functions to serve and accomplish the mission. Our loyalty is to the mission, and anything and anybody that can help us accomplish the mission through some sales or marketing activity, we're glad to have them.

This doesn't suggest chaos or anarchy. It simply defuses the boundaries and opens up the question, "Could Jenna or Bob do something that is traditionally a sales or marketing function that would help accomplish the mission?" If so, and the leaders and teams agree it would serve the mission, those functions become part of their roles and responsibilities. Jenna and Bob's "job descriptions" are first and foremost to accomplish the mission, and if they can see ways to do so, they work with their DDM workgroups to make that happen.

Job descriptions get in the way or this mindset because they focus us on a limited set of things we are presently do, and they have a long history of boxing people in and creating boundaries in the same way departments guard functions. A properly drawn freedom map for the sales function simply has Jenna showing up now in one of those functions, and Bob shows up on the marketing map somewhere. Roles and responsibilities are crystal clear via the freedom maps, which emphasize using a function to serve the mission.

Jenna doesn't need a personal job description because everything she does shows up on a freedom map for all to see, and as she grows and develops, her role and responsibilities change, and the maps continue to reflect very clearly and precisely what she is responsible for — all without departments or job descriptions. This emphasis on a function map versus a job description creates a culture of possibilities, not limitations, and continues to develop the humanity of everyone at work.

From the get-go, they are not seeing a Dilbertized, segmented job description but an integrated, interdependent role that makes them part of something much bigger than themselves. We're not featuring org charts but rather how someone can light up the world around them with their gifts, talent, skills, initiative, and contribution. In the first fifteen to thirty minutes of connecting with their new company, a new hire can acquire an entirely different view of work.

We would suggest that in the interview process you share a couple of important freedom maps to see how people react to them. It will give you insight into whether you are hiring someone who thinks like an employee (vertically) or as a Stakeholder (horizontally).

Another benefit of a simple freedom map is that it emphasizes to the new person (and to anyone who needs reminding), that our focus is not on bosses, departments, or promotions but on helping each other accomplish the mission, regardless of our function. I'm not told I'm in the marketing department. Instead, the map shows a marketing function that only exists to serve us in accomplishing the mission. The mission is the emphasis. Marketing is only a means to an end, and the only boss that shows up on the marketing freedom map is the intended result for marketing, which is tied directly to accomplishing the company's mission.

A subtle emphasis change in Freedom Mapping replaces certain Factory System words with Participation Age terms:

Department	becomes	Function
Job description	becomes	Responsibilities
Titles	becomes	Roles
Promotions	becomes	Taking initiative

See Addendum One, Words That Matter, for a list of unhelpful Factory System terminology and suggested replacements. This isn't semantics. It is a tectonic shift in the way people view work and their relationship to it. The DDM model is a new operating system in an emerging work world that replaces the Factory System model, and it requires a new set of terminology to describe it.

RESULT OVER PROCESS

The only reason a process should exist is to bring about the intended result, yet too often we lose sight of this and begin to worship the process instead. There is another distinction between leadership and management. Managers tend to focus on process, while leaders are obsessed with the result and can change the process as needed to get the intended result. In a leader-leader organization where everyone leads, a DDM workgroup needs to be taught to tweak the process along the way so that it is always focused on the result. The intended result should be prominently stated on every freedom map.

THE SIMPLICITY OF FREEDOM MAPPING

A simple rule of thumb: no map, including the macro map of the entire business model, should take up more than one side of a piece of printed paper, and it's cheating to use small fonts and tiny boxes. We've helped companies draw scores of these maps and have learned that the most helpful macro and micro maps never have more than twenty to thirty steps for each map. I'm not saying they should never be more complex, but do everything you can to minimize the steps that properly describe your unique process.

There are three levels of Freedom Mapping: the macro map, the micro map, and process descriptions.

Freedom Mapping Levels

Important note: Process descriptions are *only* used to support steps in the micro maps. A macro map *never* needs any process descriptions behind the steps.

THE MACRO PROCESS: DO IT FIRST!

A macro map is a map of the customer experience all the way from their first exposure to you (advertising, marketing) through production, delivery, and customer satisfaction analysis, including a drip system for staying in touch. It is a broad stroke overview of your company that any new Stakeholder can understand in five to ten minutes of training.

I can't emphasize this enough. Don't skip the macro map and dive into detailed micro maps of subprocesses. Discipline yourself to first develop a macro map for the entire company. Do this from the perspective of your customer. What is the customer experience from the very first thing we do to reach out to them (advertising, marketing) to the last thing they continue to experience with us (ongoing customer relationship)?

Here's an example of a macro map pf a real software company with about 200 developers:

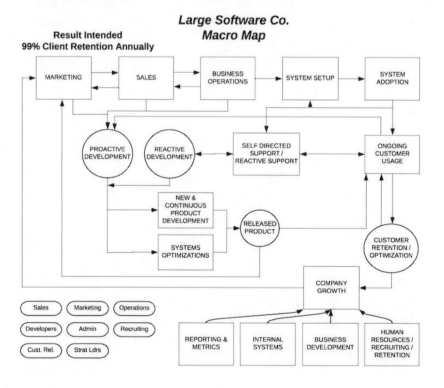

As you can see by the example, it is very broad and strategic, lacking in detail, what some might call high-level. If your macro process has more than twenty to thirty boxes in it, you're probably showing too much detail. Keep it simple (have I said that yet?). You can also see that the intended result is clearly stated at the top. At the bottom is a legend of champions who own and monitor the steps. Don't put names of people here but designate each person by the color of the box. This makes the roles and responsibilities of each champion clear, while also representing them all in one place to emphasize a horizontal orientation of company-wide DDM teamwork rather than departments.

By the way, when the specific company depicted in the above macro map dipped below 99 percent annual client retention, they all went into four-alarm fire mode. When you set high standards, lower ones no longer suffice.

Here's one more macro map of a commercial cleaning company with a few hundred Stakeholders.

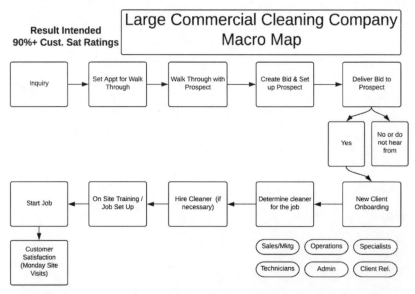

You can see on this simple, real-life example of a macro map how people fit in the company. Whether you were being hired to clean or to run operations, you would know by the colors in each box exactly how you fit and how your work interlinks with everyone else's roles and responsibilities.

A MACRO MAP FOR THE SALES TEAM

A good macro map demonstrates to clients how you will perform their work. Rather than, "Trust us, we're good", your macro map helps them see how you will work with them and what deliverables you need from them. This customer version also turns a top-down client-vendor relationship into a horizontal partnership where you both agree together on the process, and both have deliverables that are necessary for success.

ONLY A VERY FEW MAPS TO START!

To get started, just map the most "mission-critical" processes, and, again, keep it simple. One of the biggest problems with process mapping is that we go nuts by mapping every minute process, losing the important ones in the mountain of paper that results, so keep it simple. Having built many businesses, I can share from experience that there are only two conditions under which you should map any process to begin with (backfill later):

1. The process is already broken.
2. The process is working but is 100 percent guaranteed to break (it's in somebody's head, or we've been lucky).

That's it — under no other circumstances should you map a process first. I realize this is counter to everything the MBA programs and legions of process mapping consultants have taught you, but my practical experience is:

When we capture everything, we do nothing.

Why do we need to map a process? First, to allow and require the team to be Stakeholders and bring the humanity back into work, and secondly, because mapping ensures that we're running a better process for the end result. A function of strategic leadership is to keep the big picture in view and avoid the need to build endless freedom maps. To begin with, let's stick to the above two conditions, and if, down the road somewhere the team can't help themselves and wants to map something else, we need to ask a lot of hard questions to make sure there is alignment between desire and need.

NINE SIMPLE STEPS TO BUILD A FREEDOM MAP

We use Lucid Chart[1] to build our maps because it allows us to link documents, videos, PDFs, etc., to specific steps, which keeps the maps very high level and simple and provides all the detail needed to complete each step. Many companies find they have one or two people who just love processes and developing these maps, so those specialists make the maps in Lucid Chart or some other software for the DDM workgroups.

Step One: Result Intended
To build a macro map, ask two questions:
1. *What is the result we intend to get for our customer?* It could be a derivative of your mission statement, but make sure it is measurable.
2. *What is the process of delivering our product/service to the customer?* The macro map outlines the customer experience from advertising through customer service.

Keep your macro map high level and, again, resist the temptation to create detailed micro maps until you've done this work first. The macro map informs which micro maps to build, and it lends the most critical understanding of your business. You may be surprised at how many ships were passing in the night before your team built this map showing the whole company process.

For micro maps, start with three questions:
1. Who is handing off to us? (Unless you are the advertising function, there is probably someone in front of you who is handing something off to you).
2. What is the result intended for this process?
3. What function do we hand off to? (That will likely determine the last step in your process, the hand off to the next function.)

Step Two: Write Down Each Major Step in the Macro Process
A freedom map is quite simple for a DDM workgroup to produce. What is the very first thing, what are the major steps in the middle, and what is the very last thing in the process? These define the length and

---
1   http://lucidchart.com

breadth of the freedom map. Here's an example from one of our businesses that produces workshops for founders and company leaders to refer to as you read:

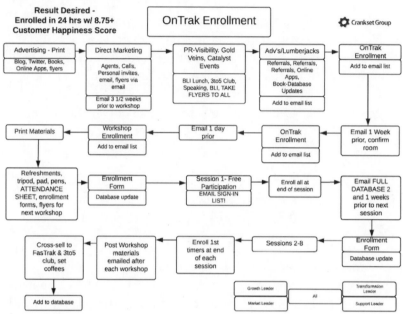

To begin, start at the bottom of a sheet of paper and answer, "What is the very last thing in the process?" Write that down. Because we've done this a lot, I can guess that what you write down may not actually be the last thing, but we can fix it later.

After you've written down the last thing, ask yourself what happens right before that, and keep going until there is nothing else that happens in front. Many times, we tend to map out only the production part of the process. Don't forget things such as advertising or marketing, putting the check in the bank, sending a thank-you note, or other similar things on either side of operations. Refer to the sample but know that it is not representative of the best map—there is no such thing. Just try to capture your process and map it in a way that works best for you.

Why do it backwards? Good proofreaders read a piece backwards because it slows them down, and they catch more that way. You are so familiar with your processes that you are more likely to skip major steps if you do it from beginning to end. It's not a big thing, but it will help you to be more thorough.

Stay Broad

Only put steps in the process that cannot be included in a broader step. For example, if you were a chair maker, you might be tempted to describe each step you take in making a chair. However, this map is not the place for such detail. Just create a step called "make chair" and move on. You can create a subprocess for how to make the chair later that is valuable for training the actual maker. The macro process, which entails everything from advertising, marketing, and promotion to public relations can be rolled into one step called marketing.

Exceptions

One of the many benefits of Freedom Mapping is that it can and does highlight the parts of your processes that need the most attention, either because you've not trained for them well, they are difficult, or they are extremely important.

Have the Stakeholders Do It Separately

Get some of your key Stakeholders to each take a stab at the macro process on their own, then come together and compare. There will likely be quite a delta between what you think your organization does and what they think it does. This can create some great discussion around aligning the actual reality with mere hopes. It may turn out to be the most revealing and productive meeting you've had in years.

Map the Present, Not the Future

Don't map the future first, map the reality—find out what you're really doing before you decide what you want it to look like in the future. It's important to face the music now, and it will be a great encouragement later when you can see where you were.

Yes, It's That Simple

The people who have paid us to teach them how to freedom map regularly ask us if this is all there is to it, and the answer is yes, at least for now. There are some other steps we'll cover later, but all of them are just as simple. Keep reading and you'll see the huge impact Freedom Mapping has on any size of organization.

Step Three: A Couple Iterations

The team might need to meet a few times to clarify the freedom map, but don't overdo it. There is no such thing as perfect. You want to shoot for "good for now." As you run the process, you can tweak it. Planning never creates movement; movement creates the plan. Commit to no more than three iterations, then move on. Nothing is set in stone; you can always make it better later.

Planning doesn't create movement. Movement creates the plan.

Step Four: Number the Steps

Number each step in the process; they will be used as reference points. This is important because after you publish these for everyone to access (yes, everyone), they may want to know who to go to in order to discuss Step 6 in the procurement process, etc. Referencing the number facilitates easy access for every party involved in a discussion.

Step Five: Champions Volunteer (organic leadership)

Somatic learning becomes important here, which involves learning not just with our minds but with our senses, perceptions, and mind-body action and reaction. A lot of research shows that when we involve our bodies in learning, we learn better and embrace things more deeply, with more commitment. We recommend a somatic experience such as the one that follows for assigning champions. Doug Kirkpatrick, who advises companies on how to grow self-managed teams, is particularly good at this.

Once you get this far (I've seen the first four steps completed in an hour or less), put all the steps on separate 4 x 6 sticky notes and put them on a wall where everyone can see them. Have someone ask the question, "Who sees a step they think they would like to champion?"

A champion (or steward or other description) is defined as someone who is good at a particular step and volunteers to lead and encourages others in the process. Remember, a leader does not necessarily perform the work (or do it all themselves). A leader ensures the work is done well. I might volunteer to champion a step that fourteen other people in the call center also perform, but I think I could serve others by making sure that we all do it well.

When someone volunteers, they walk up to the wall and grab the sticky note, but before they sit down, someone asks a second question: "Do we all agree that Jenna would be a great champion of this step?" If the answer is yes, the DDM workgroup has volunteered to follow Jenna as their leader. If they think Jenna would be better at something else, it's time to be kind and direct, suggesting another step for Jenna. (It could be that many steps get handled by team members volunteering other people for them.)

As with all Universally Distributed Leadership, this isn't about equal distribution. It shouldn't be a round robin where every person gets asked to pull a sticky note from the wall. After a step gets taken, the first question should be just as generic as before, "Who sees a step they think they would like to champion?" Based on gifting, talents, skills, and experience, on a theoretical team of five people and a process with fifteen steps, Jenna could end up championing ten steps while Bob takes three, Quinn, two, and the other two people take none at all.

It's not a contest, and there are no winners and losers. It's all just information to think about. It could be that the two people who decided not to champion anything are just really good at running the process, so they lead by doing (the four traits of leadership — be, do, inspire, relate). They may be great friends, mentors, or communicators, which weren't items on that particular map. Just get everyone into the highest and best use of their time and talents, and watch the engagement shoot up.

Step Six: Color the Boxes
Using different colors, have your Stakeholders color each box based on who oversees that step. Again, it's best to use roles or functions to describe who owns the step (developer vs. "Tina"), so when Tina moves on to another role in the company, the map doesn't have to be changed for the next developer who takes over.

Step Seven: Metrics
At this point, we should review the process to determine what metrics help ensure we are getting the intended result. These usually fall into three categories:
1. Timeliness — how fast are we building a chair?
2. Quality — how well is the chair being built? (quality control at various stages)
3. Happiness — how happy are our customers? (internal, external

or both)

Great processes achieve all three of these on the way to arriving at the intended result. These three metrics also lay the foundation for results-based incentives to replace the worn-out concept of bonuses (discussed in a later chapter).

Step Eight: Commitment Letter

Now we've got a finished process created by the DDM workgroup that brings people into the highest and best use of their time and talents. It's never perfect and it's never finished — see below for how to keep freedom maps relevant, but there is another important step here — committing to the process.

We discuss the central importance of Commitment Letters in a future chapter, but the concept is simple. To give us clarity on what we decided together we will do, and in order to override old, entrenched habits, we need ceremony, rituals, and practices to force the old out and replace it with a new habit. Each tool we commit to should be introduced with a ceremony and a commitment to the new process, principle, or practice.

Again, don't overdo it. A Commitment Letter for your freedom maps can be a couple paragraphs. The team (or volunteer) writes the basic letter, and individuals can add their own specifics to a copy they sign. As an example, Jenna might simply add a reference to the freedom map steps she is committing to champion. Later, each of these small Commitment Letters can be combined for a ceremony that helps us see we've all committed to the full spectrum of what it means to be a Stakeholder.

Step Nine: Publish the Map

Remember that full transparency is the best practice and a hallmark of a great Participation Age company. Having access to all the information about how the company runs is a prerequisite for team members to fully own the process.

The map for every function should be accessible in PDF form so that team members don't need to access it through specialized software. This way, if someone in marketing thinks there might be something going on in sales that inadvertently impacts him, he can easily review the sales freedom map(s), determine which step is the culprit, and identify which champion to contact about resolving it.

ADDING PROCESS DESCRIPTIONS

The last step in creating a freedom map, adding process descriptions, is intentionally left out of the formal nine-step process. Process descriptions are the nitty gritty and often extremely lengthy details that should be buried behind some steps in a process. There is a strong tendency for people who are creating a freedom map to immediately take a deep dive into the smallest details, instantly losing the forest for the trees.

Based on my experience, I suggest:

1. Only add process descriptions after the freedom map is fully completed (all nine steps).
2. Not every step needs process descriptions. At Crankset Group, some of our maps are thirteen years old, and only a very few have them at all. You might need more detail, or less.
3. Follow the same rules for adding process descriptions to a step that you used for building maps. Only add process descriptions to steps that are:
    a. Already broken, or
    b. Guaranteed to break.

Less is more, and you can always add more detail later. Get the maps done, then fuss with the process descriptions.

THE DEATH OF THE OPERATIONS MANUAL

Ops manuals, standard operating procedures (SOP)s, or whatever you call them are nothing but an impressive waste of time. I imagine that only the people who write them read them, and even fewer know how they apply to the real world of getting work done.

But if you have one, you've done a lot of hard work that can be useful. Chop it up into one-paragraph to three-page bytes that get attached to specific steps in your freedom maps, which people can read when it is critical to their work, team objectives, or incentive plan. A 150-page SOP can become 150 very short process descriptions behind 150 steps on fifteen different maps.

CLICKABLE PROCESS DESCRIPTIONS

As I mentioned in the beginning of the nine steps, the reason we like Lucid Chart (lucidchart.com) for building maps is that you can easily tie any document, video, PDF, form, picture, etc., to any step without having it clutter the freedom map. You simply click on a step and link the process description to it. A double-click on the specific step brings up all the documentation behind it, making it easy to edit and maintain. It is easy to revise right there, and your former 150-page SOP is up to date again in an instant.

POWERFUL USES OF YOUR MAPS

Besides laying the foundation for roles and responsibilities and clarifying the needed process, your freedom maps are useful for several other applications:

1. Transferring tactical decision-making from strategic leaders to tactical leaders.
2. Sales presentations. I know companies that have won contracts simply because they could show the client via their macro map how organized they were and how the process would run, giving them an edge on their competitors. A sales-oriented version of your macro map is a powerful tool.
3. Vendor management. If you have trouble getting things to and from your strategic partners, give them a version of your macro map that highlights what needs to be done, by when, and by whom. It can clear up any confusion.
4. Client management. The more complex your offering, the more you need this, for the same reasons you would use it for vendor management. It removes all the "he said, she said" twaddle that spins and deflects. Too often you risk being thrown under the bus by people at your client's company who aren't doing their jobs. A client management macro map is a great tool for reminding everybody the responsibilities, commitments, and timelines agreed to instead of pointing at people who defaulted.
5. Training and retraining (the restaffing tax). When you hire new people, don't throw a 125-page training manual at them. No one reads them. Show them your macro map and take five minutes to explain what the company does, pointing out the specific steps they are responsible for. People are visual, and a picture is worth a thousand-word training manual, so it can also be used for retraining people who are having difficulty doing their job well.

CHANGE THE PROCESS, KEEP THE PEOPLE!

When Krista Valentine joined us in 2010, we shared with her the measurable results we wanted and asked her to create her own micro maps, including the processes to make them happen. Her work on the maps defined who she became with us, a huge contributor who owns everything she does, including part ownership in the company.

A little over a year after she joined us, she remapped her work to show how the highest and best use of her time had evolved. The process happened organically over time as she grew into her responsibilities, motivating her to work harder toward refining the areas of work better left to others after that first year.

Very soon our growth had made the job too big for one person, so we hired Lauren, who loved doing the things Krista didn't like or do well. A year after she joined us, we had her remake her map, and a year after that we hired Donna, who loves doing the things Lauren wasn't good at or didn't like doing. As we've grown, we just keep iterating the process. Instead of shoe-horning people into a static job description, each "graduate" re-writes the freedom map, gradually placing everyone where they can best use their time and talents.

We've used Freedom Mapping in everything from call centers to legal assistant positions—anything to get people doing the what they are great at and enjoy. The result is always higher productivity and higher Stakeholder (employee) satisfaction and longevity.

When you write static processes and shoehorn people into them, you may find people leaving regularly. If, instead, you commit to getting everyone into the highest and best use of their time (the business owner's game), people stay with you because they can now make meaning, not just money.

Don't treat people like extensions of machines. Change the processes and keep the people, your most valuable asset.

KEEP THE PROCESSES ALIVE

At Crankset Group, we have team meetings at least twice a month. One person volunteers each time to bring a different freedom map to each meeting for review after we walk through our values, vision, and mission together (see the chapter on how to have a meeting). When presenting the map, the person asks two questions:

1. Is this still the result we want (we review the result intended)?

2. Is this still the process that gets us that result?

Sometimes these two simple questions are answered "yes" and "yes," and the review takes two minutes. Other times we have launched into a twenty-minute revision of some important changes that would have gone unnoticed without the review. This is another example of leaders beating the drum, gently and relentlessly, on the few things that are important.

You can also create a thirty-minute quarterly meeting with the owner of each process and have them present the updates, revisions, etc., to strategic leaders. It's a good idea for Stakeholders to stick the freedom maps on their walls and keep the process descriptions on their desks. Encourage them to check their work against them regularly and suggest any changes that need to be made to keep current. However you do it, make sure you have a scheduled, committed review process, or your process may soon be no process at all.

The "father of process improvement," W. Edwards Deming, said 85 percent of a worker's effectiveness is determined by the process he works within and only 15 percent by his own skill. How well defined are your processes? Get good processes in place.

THE NEXT ONE THING

1. Pick one to start with:
   a. Build a freedom map.
   b. Invite some people to build a map.
   c. Have them make a list of processes they think are broken or guaranteed to break.
   d. Build the first map with two-step input from both those who must carry it out and those who are impacted.
2. Ask who might want to become the Lucid Chart specialist (always good to have one person as the gatekeeper).
3. What will we do?

_____

_____

4. By when? ____/____/____

5. Who will support us to ensure we do it?

_____

_____

CHAPTER ELEVEN

Number: The Language of Business

11

Participation Age companies need to be transparent about their financials. In many of them, like Semco Partners, salaries and benefits are open to all. These companies understand that the more transparent you are with the numbers, the more people know how to participate in building a great company and how to share in the results. Input equals ownership, but input is only possible with full transparency. I can't help fix things if all you say is, "we lost money last month[1]."

Transparency on financials and production metrics indicate an organization's maturity as a Participation Age entity. Mature Participation Age organizations exhibit three healthy relationships to metrics:

1. Clarity on metrics tied to freedom maps.
2. Full financial transparency across the organization.
3. Ownership by the DDM workgroups through Distributed Decision-making.

UTTER CLARITY

Managed organizations rely too heavily on managers to know what the numbers should be. Clarity and ownership come about when teams develop their own metrics by collaborating, cooperating, and communicating with strategic leaders. No process should be developed without first defining:

1. The intended result — the most important metric(s) of any

---

1 https://www.ted.com/talks/ricardo_semler_how_to_run_a_company_with_almost_no_rules#t-476895

process.

2. Leading indicators of success — those few measurements during the process that indicate we are moving in the right direction. Handoffs from one person or team to another, or back and forth with the customer, involve timelines, quality, quantity, and/or happiness measurements that indicate the "health" of the process and help us to stay on track. See the chapter on results-based incentives.

3. Incentives around achieving or exceeding the intended result. It's important that incentives not be something additional to the already comfortable base salary and that missing the objective involves a downside that team members want to avoid. In short, incentives should be based in capitalism: risk/reward.

Numbers are the language of business and are both friend and ally of Participation Age DDM workgroups. They free us to rely on metrics rather than mercurial managers to gauge how things are going. A growing number of futurists forecast that advancements in data collection and reporting tools can contribute to making managers irrelevant. Full transparency and ease of access to any metric are giving DDM workgroups more tools for self-management.

FULL TRANSPARENCY

Business is a numbers game. The numbers are the scoreboard, yet I am amazed at how few organizations are clear on what numbers they are shooting for in marketing, sales, production, or even accounting, and in the rare cases when the numbers are understood, they tend to be held very close to the vest by a tiny fraction of Stakeholders, typically those who have the least ability to affect them.

The more transparent a company is with their numbers, the more ownership people have. When the numbers are agreed upon by both the strategic and tactical functions instead of being "announced" as a goal, everyone can own them. Horizontal relationships are once again prioritized over vertical ones.

Every person in the organization must develop and know their metrics intimately and then design processes to achieve them. It might be a good exercise to randomly stop teams in the middle of producing something or providing a service and ask them which numbers indicate to them that they are being successful. He who aims at nothing hits it every time. We don't want people blissfully shooting a gun off in the woods and calling it bear hunting when they don't even know if there is a bear in the woods or even what a bear looks like.

Semco requires every newly hired person to go through an accounting module so they can read a profit and loss statement and a balance sheet. These are published daily for everyone to check. The company's profit and loss statement and the team's local numbers become the scoreboard for how they are doing. Semco and others drive budgeting out to the edges of the organization, something which scares secretive organizations. Some with very well-established transparency even have salaries decided locally without approval from the strategic function. The more transparency you create, the more people take on the adult responsibilities of being full-fledged Stakeholders.

Pearson's law of productivity (first attributed to Thomas Monson in the 1960s) is very important to rehumanizing the workplace: *"When performance is measured, performance improves. When performance is measured and reported back, the rate of improvement accelerates."* Everyone needs to know both their own DDM workgroup numbers and the global organization's numbers and be committed to achieving both. Numbers transparency is just another facet of Distributed Decision-making, resulting in a level of ownership not seen in more covert organizations.

METRICS FIRST, PROCESS SECOND

Metrics should always precede the development of processes. You must know specifically what result you want from a process before designing it. This sounds obvious, yet I rarely see it happen this way. "We need to hire someone" is not an intended result because nobody should ever intend to hire someone. There should be a compelling reason for hiring someone that shows up in the metrics and timetables. Otherwise, we're back to aiming at nothing and hitting it every time.

Questions must be asked: Why do you want to hire? What numbers result from hiring — revenue, profit, cost reduction, production increase, etc.? How often is this discussed with prospective applicants, so they understand what to expect?

In the same vein, "We need to develop a customer service process" implies that having a customer service process is the intended result of the process. Instead, to the extent it's possible, we should predetermine the resultant increase in customer acquisition, customer retention, customer happiness, or other metrics with a timetable. These should all be expressed in verifiable numbers by counting things or surveying customers.

WHO DEVELOPS THE METRICS?

Two-step decision-making requires that whoever must carry out the decision should make it. Metrics are one of the more difficult decisions for management to release to DDM workgroups, but the reluctance is due to a misconception about Distributed Decision-making. Just because you have now granted power to the team to make a decision doesn't mean they can or should make it in a vacuum. Two-step decision-making requires the input and agreement of the strategic function any time that function is affected by the decision (step two). We collaborate, cooperate, and communicate together until we arrive at metrics that work for both the tactical and strategic functions.

THE FEW BIG ROCKS

On the strategic level, metrics get overly complex. We are addicted to things that are complicated, and as a result, some organizations are tracking numbers that don't even matter. When it comes to numbers, we follow the principle, "When you capture everything, you do nothing." There is a myriad of things we could track, but tracking them all obscures the very few things that matter.

Stephen Covey famously told of the speaker who filled a clear vase with big rocks and asked the audience if it was full. Then, he poured in pebbles and asked again, followed by sand, and finally water, at which point the vase was truly full. The point is that if he had started with water, sand, or pebbles, there would have been no room for the big rocks, but when you start with rocks, there is always room for pebbles, sand, and water.

Every organization has just one or two big rocks it should define each year. Those should be put into plans first and take priority over any others. Once we have defined the one or two big rocks, we can identify and watch the few numbers that help us achieve them. Dave Thomas, founder of Wendy's, famously had just one number come find him regularly — the number of buns sold. From that, he could extrapolate revenue, profit, and which products were sold along with the bun[2].

At Crankset Group, we keep it to one big rock for our two very separate and distinct initiatives, all run by different people who focus only on the one big rock. Even with that separation and narrow focus, we find it hard enough to stay on top of them. I have found that anything more than one or two big rocks with fully dedicated people and resources to each rock turns into another form of playing office.

If you don't have teams of people and resources to dedicate to separate initiatives, you should consider having only one or two big rocks each year for your main focus. When our company has focused on just one or two things, we have been more successful. When we attempted to accomplish multiple things, we usually lost focus and accomplished none of them.

PARTICIPATION AGE NUMBERS

Companies committed to Distributed Decision-making through Distributed Leadership are successful when the intended result is transparent and simple — not a lot of numbers to follow. Local teams should create intended results for every freedom map, which are prominently displayed next to the process itself. They should also know how their numbers fit in with the larger picture of building a great organization. "We lost money this month" is not transparency. Knowing how we lost it, where we lost it, and how much we lost allows everyone to play a part in fixing it.

Barry Wehmiller hit a down cycle in the Great Recession that could have been solved by eliminating 20 percent of the jobs, but instead, everyone agreed to staggered furloughs so no one would lose their jobs. Those who could afford it volunteered more time off to help those who would be more deeply impacted[3].

This kind of global cooperative community would never happen in most companies where numbers are only known by the few.

NUMBERS ARE CRITICAL

One of the myths of a Participation Age company is that they don't measure things — they just take care of people, and good things happen. This is not the case. Along with guard the values and champion the people, the third responsibility of a leader is to "pilot

2   https://chuckblakeman.com/2011/07/texts/leaders-are-reactive-not-proactive
3   https://www.trulyhumanleadership.com/?p=645

the results." Numbers are the scorecard of business. Don't ignore them, and especially don't hide them.

THE NEXT ONE THING

1. What Next One Thing do we need to do to create clear performance metrics for our DDM workgroups, built on transparency around the numbers?

_____

_____

_____

2. When will we start? _____/_____/_____

3. What are the one or two challenges that need to be addressed before we start?

_____

_____

_____

4. A lot of our processes seem to fall into the process description category, so we are
   a. Creating macro maps (calling them SOP) and,
   b. Work instructions (what we call a process description).

Measure one to three things!
"When we measure everything, we do nothing."

CHAPTER TWELVE

Catching People Doing Something Right

12

What is the number one performance motivator at work that is more than five times as important as things such as pay raises, more training, or promotions? Recognize me[1].

What is one behavior that is among the most difficult for managers? Recognizing people[2]. In fact, of the top ten things managers do worst, recognizing people is related to the top four and eight of all ten.

The data is consistent and stunning: A Harris survey recently revealed that an overwhelming 63 percent of American workers cited a lack of appreciation as the number one issue with their managers[3] and that 65 percent of people got no recognition at all over the last twelve months[4].How bad is that? For perspective, definitions of a political landslide range from 48 percent to 60 percent on the high end; 65 percent is a landslide loss for the position of manager[5].

Once again, we have unfairly piled yet another critical need, positive recognition, onto the back of the beleaguered manager along with everything else the lonely heroic genius must deliver. No position in business is more set up to fail by virtue of our expectations than that of manager. It's important to note that managers are rarely bad actors. The problem lies with the role of the manager.

If we are going to shift from vertical management to horizontal community, we must begin the process by engaging everyone in catching people doing something right. In this chapter, we discuss two tools that Crankset Group and many others use for peer recognition.

1. **Kudos** — recognizing people spontaneously for going above and beyond what they are normally expected to do. We develop a formal program to encourage this.
2. **Peer recognition surveys** — getting regular feedback via a

monthly or bi-monthly survey that team members share with each other. These replace one of the worst inventions of the Factory System, performance evaluations.

3. **Incentives** — using the surveys to establish results-based incentives in place of traditional bonuses.

As you reorganize horizontally around DDM workgroups, kudos are a terrific tool to begin with because it is popular, easy to implement, and brings value quickly, so we'll start there.

THE KUDOS SCARCITY EPIDEMIC

YOU'RE IN TROUBLE NOW, DUDE

"Salvador, the boss wants to see you right now."

If you are Salvador, what are you thinking? You suspect the worst. Why? Because by nature, we are more likely to criticize someone's mistake or failing than we are to commend them for doing something well. Managers excel at negative feedback because it is implied in their job description.

Studies over the last fifty years show that people who receive more positive comments than negative ones stay married longer, learn more in school, and, for our purposes, perform better at work, both individually and on teams[6]. While there is no magic number, there is a magic range and a simple principle — talk to others more about what they are do well than what they are challenged by. Positive recognition makes the difference between low- and high-performing individuals and teams.

Just a few more positive comments than negative ones can make a difference. One study showed lower performing teams receiving a ratio of 2.2 positives to one negative, and high-performing teams, just under three to one.

| LOW-PERFORMING TEAMS | 2.2 Positives to 1 Negative |
| HIGH-PERFORMING TEAMS | 2.9 Positives to 1 Negative |

The obvious takeaway is that a slight increase in praise, three positives to every negative, can make a huge difference in your team's performance. Other studies go as high as four or five to one. I suspect that at Crankset Group we may be at six to one, or more. We've found that catching people doing something right and emphasizing it publicly is the best corrective action and motivator for change.

One client confided in me a few years ago, "Do people really need that stuff? Isn't paying them well enough?" That's Industrial Age Factory System thinking. The studies on positive feedback all agree: when you treat people well at work, you make more money, and they stay longer.

IT ISN'T ALL SUNSHINE AND LOLLIPOPS

Twenty-first century parents and school systems shouldn't jump on these studies to confirm the need for participation trophies and other empty feedback that praises the act of merely showing up. People should be praised for doing or being something positive. This isn't "the power of positive thinking." While we all need positive feedback, we also need regular constructive feedback about how we can improve because we all have blind spots. It's a *ratio* of positive feedback and constructive criticism, not a blank check to "be nice" in the hope that people perform better.

The kind of praise matters. "You do good work" feedback is generally dismissed as generic and unhelpful in motivating me to want to work harder. Be specific in pointing out exactly what I did that you like.

THE HABIT OF CATCHING PEOPLE DOING SOMETHING RIGHT

The conclusion is this: Creating a culture that emphasizes catching people doing something right accounts for higher productivity, better individual and team performance, and a significant increase in staff retention.

The bell is ringing loudly on this subject—pay attention to your people. Allow and require them to be fully human at work in a positive environment, and they will take care of the business products and processes that result in quality, quantity, and customer happiness. It's the second responsibility of leadership—champion the people. When we champion the people, they will champion every aspect of the business.

WHY WE NEED PEER RECOGNITION

The research says we want it, but why do we need it?

1. It is a basic human and fundamental psychological need. Stakeholders who know they will receive recognition for going above and beyond have a strong incentive to do so[7].

2. We make more money — Gallup says increasing employee engagement investments such as peer recognition programs by 10 percent can increase profits (not just revenues) by up to $2,400 per employee each year[8].

3. Stakeholder retention — Organizations with effective recognition programs have 31 percent lower voluntary turnover than organizations with ineffective or nonexistent recognition. JetBlue revealed that for every 10 percent increase in people who were positively recognized, the company saw a 3 percent increase in retention and a 2 percent increase in engagement. That's a very strong return on investment.

4. Praise and commendation were rated the top motivators for performance, beating out other noncash and financial incentives, by most workers (67 percent).[9]

5. Recognition programs are one of the top three biggest factors in retention.[10]

6. Roughly 76 percent find peer praise highly motivating[11].

7. Peer-to-peer recognition is 35.7 percent more likely to have a positive impact on financial results than manager-only recognition[12].

Note especially those last two. People do appreciate positive feedback from leaders, but according to Gallup, people want to receive recognition daily. With a US manager to staff ratio of 1 to 10, it is just one more way we have set up managers to fail. A formal peer recognition system works better, since positive peer feedback can occur more regularly and is likely to be more genuine than that given by a manager who does it to fulfill part of his or her job description.

WHAT GOOD FEEDBACK LOOKS LIKE

Specific — Not, "Thanks for working hard, Jen," but something more like, "I'm really impressed with how you got the project done faster than expected, with a customer satisfaction rating above what we were shooting for. Awesome, thanks." If it's not specific, it's not meaningful or instructive about how to continue to be great.

Timely — Praise should be given as close to the performance as possible. We wouldn't wait until the quarterly meeting to tell someone they are programming something incorrectly. Catch people doing something right and have a formal system for informing them immediately.

Peer-to-Peer — Strategic leaders should have their own formalized way of beating the drum gently and relentlessly to recognize others, but remember, every arrow in the Participation Age quiver is designed to promote horizontal, peer-to-peer relationships even as the leaders manage the metrics, results, processes, roles, responsibilities and assets. A peer recognition program, besides being more effective than top-down praise, is one of the most appreciated ways to begin and continue the process.

Peer-Led — Too often we think we have great ideas for how we can make other people's lives better, so we impose our great idea on them, as well as the process behind it. By using open space leadership, you can create an opportunity for people to form a small team to lead the peer recognition initiative. Strategic leaders can provide resources, connections, examples from other companies, and even suggestions.

Formalized — Ad hoc recognition is important but so is having a formal process. Simple is best: give a certificate, a digital signature button, an actual button, a lighthearted gift attached to the theme of peer recognition, a gift card, or another appropriate item. The best combination might be immediate walk-by recognition with a fun token of appreciation, followed by more formal recognition at a monthly or quarterly meeting.

A SAMPLE KUDOS PROGRAM

Step by Step

It is important to have peers volunteer, develop, and lead the peer recognition program. The role of the strategic leader is to ensure it's working and to provide tools, ideas, and ongoing support (beat the drum, gently and relentlessly).

1. Share the vision for it via a town hall style meeting, email, or Slack. In-person is always better so people can see your resolve. Visit, **www.RehumanizingTheWorkplace.com/Kudos** for some sample communications and emails on rolling out a kudos program.

2. Keep the kudos leadership team to a maximum of three to five people. If more than that apply, take a quick anonymous vote (quicksurveys.com, surveymonkey.com, etc.)

3. A volunteer leader can convene the group and explain the idea. In sharing an open space leadership idea, the emphasis is always on the "Why," the potential desired results. Give the team the freedom to suggest how and agree together with strategic leadership on the intended result.

   a. Make it clear that strategic leaders do not run this but that the strategic leadership team will lean on the team members who volunteered to make this a big success and to keep momentum going.

   b. The strategic leaders should have the mindset that a viable, ongoing, and vibrant kudos program is not optional — beat the drum gently and relentlessly with the leaders of the kudos program. As with everything, if they see strategic leaders treating it as a priority, they will too.

4. Name it something that ties in with your values, vision, mission, or other unique messages inside your company. Google calls them gThanks. Zappos calls them WOWs. We call them Crankset Kudos.

5. Create some physical way of representing the kudo — a handwritten card, a coffee/restaurant card for $5, a grab bag of desk toys, etc.

6. Think about quarterly or other longer-term recognition and rewards for those who received the most kudos that quarter or year. Don't pre-announce rewards but mix it up and give something of value (money is the least memorable) to the top three kudos earners.

7. Ask the kudos leadership team to develop a reporting mechanism to measure how the program is going. Put up a bulletin board (electronic if possible). Talk about it in morning stand-ups, give quarterly awards to people who have given and received the most kudos. Keep it alive!

8. Avoid the use of the word "committee," as in kudos committee. Committees are not the intention here — true leadership is the emphasis.

The Process

Put kudos boxes in key locations (or electronic — physical kudos memos are the best but not always doable with remote Stakeholders). Here's one of our client's communiques to people on how they can participate:

1. Observe someone doing great work or be the beneficiary of someone going above and beyond the norm to help you. Kudos is *not* for doing what is expected but for being a nine or a ten. Eight is great, but it reflects doing what is expected. It doesn't get a kudos response.

2. If you've observed someone doing something worthy of a kudo, grab a kudos card (or email) and write down how they helped you, just a sentence or two.

3. Drop it in the kudos card box (or email it), then immediately email your team leader and their leader and let them know you've recognized that person.

4. A leader from the team or organization will grab that kudo out of the box and walk it to the person who received it *[ideally no more than a couple hours later]*, congratulate them, and recognize them for their work.

5. The kudo is then sent as an email to everyone *[someone appointed to manage this]* with a simple header – "You're great — here's why!", *[or something else]* so everyone at our company can recognize you, too.

We want to catch people doing something right, and it must start with the team members. Peers see who is doing exceptional work every day. Please take the time to recognize them so we can all celebrate their work with you.

Optional program:

1. Everyone receives one kudos bucks each month worth some cash value. Keep rewards small; it's the thought that counts.

2. They must give it away within thirty days, or it is no longer valid.

3. Suggestion — It can only be given to someone in your own function (i.e., sales, ops, marketing, etc.) once every three months.

4. Suggestion — It can only be given to the same person once every three to six months.

5. Anyone can receive as many kudos from everyone else as possible — no limit (we've seen them used to cover someone's car repair or medical expenses at times).

Catch someone doing something right today!

The following are good resources for using technology to manage a peer-led kudos program:

Motivosity — a peer recognition software[13].

Globoforce — another (I think maybe better or more widely used) peer recognition software[14].

Peer Recognition Surveys

Kudos and peer recognition surveys are sister tools for catching people doing something right. Peer recognition surveys can replace some traditional evaluation tools that are often used to catch people doing something wrong. It is important to present the surveys just like kudos, focusing on great behavior, not emphasizing deficiencies. People will work on their challenges when they are recognized more often for their great contribution. Let's dive into why peer recognition surveys are so helpful.

THE END OF ANNUAL REVIEWS

One of the worst tools to come out of the Factory System hierarchy is the annual review. For the last decade or so, there have been countless books and articles on how bad they are, how they reduce performance, and how there is a growing, justified call to ban them altogether.

I'm in the "ban them altogether" camp, but I also know that numbers are the language of business and knowing how to appropriately measure our performance makes us want to perform even better (Pearson's law). Ongoing research also shows that working with "stunning colleagues," as Netflix calls them, is one of the three things that make for happy, contented team members. Peer feedback is the best way for us to make sure we're all stunning.

Let's be clear about what we should ban. Banning the Factory System review is a wise move. Banning feedback is foolish because organizations with regular employee feedback systems have turnover rates 14.9 percent lower than organizations with no formal feedback system[15]. So, performing annual reviews badly, as we have for decades, is dumb, but giving up on them altogether is even dumber.

WHY WE HATE REVIEWS

Deloitte says only 6 percent of companies believe their performance reviews are worth the time!

1. 76 percent of staff do not feel heard during reviews[16].

2. 42 percent of companies don't do them at all[17].
3. Corporate Executive Board (CEB) found that 95 percent of managers don't like their performance management system.
4. 90 percent of HR heads believe reviews do not yield accurate information.
5. Most of the research on annual reviews came to the same two conclusions:
   a. We hate reviews.
   b. They reduce performance.

Research shows that 360 reviews don't fare much better[18]. They still happen in the context of a power-based, imposed hierarchy, and while they are more inclusive about feedback, they tend to happen only around promotions or corrective actions, usually without guidance on how to give feedback.

WHY ELECTRONIC PEER RECOGNITION SURVEYS?

Personally, I would love to have a live meeting each month for DDM workgroups to evaluate how each person is living out the agreed upon production and human metrics, but I have found that in this context, the loudest voices and strongest personalities dominate. In an anonymous, electronic survey, we all get an equal voice.

Some people object to being rated numerically because it can trigger a fight or flight response. Numbers are the powerful and revealing language of business, so we tend to want to avoid them like a doctor's diagnosis. Knowing how I stack up against a metric I agreed to can still be scary if I never want honest feedback, but this presupposes a system where somebody else, the manager, imposes the number to directly rank one individual against another.

PETER PIPER NEEDS THE NUMBERS

Seeing each other's numbers can also have the effect of making me want to emulate others who are doing great. A couple decades ago, we advised a pickle factory in New England where Peter had packed eight to twelve cases of pickles a day for decades. We brought in a few people who had no idea what others had done, released them from any processes the managers had imposed on how to pack pickles, and in a few weeks, they were packing sixteen to twenty-four cases of pickles per day — a 100 percent increase over decades of production.

We shared the numbers with everyone. Within a few more weeks, staff who had not been able to pack more than eight to twelve cases for a decade or longer were doing it too. Being able to see what others are capable of can be a powerful tool for those who want to grow and become adult Stakeholders at work. Numbers are only threatening to those who don't want the diagnosis for fear they may have to change something.

WORKING OUT THE KINKS

Team members may be apprehensive or negative about giving peer reviews. We had one client whose first survey responses contained a lot of vitriol, sniping, and backbiting with "the other guy" on the team. The open complaining revealed by the survey seemed to surprise the leaders, but when pushed, they reluctantly agreed it was there all along.

They had unknowingly developed a very passive-aggressive culture where no one was kind and direct, just people-pleasing, so when people finally got the chance to say what they really thought anonymously, they abused the peer recognition survey process by finally venting their pent-up emotions. None of it was about helping the next person; it was about feeling better after letting off steam.

Starting peer recognition surveys was the best decision the company made in years. For the first time, they had to squarely face a fundamental issue that had been a caustic undertone for years. Instead of quitting the survey process, they plunged in, learned how to use it constructively, and taught everyone how to give helpful feedback to one another. It took several months, but the survey results began to reflect a more positive tone and people picked up on the idea that reinforcing what people do well causes them to do more of it.

STUNNING STAKEHOLDERS ON A SCALE OF EIGHT TO TEN

In his book *The Ultimate Question 2.0*, Fred Reichheld gave measured meaning to what it means to have happy customers. People used to think that on a scale of one to ten, five was average, but people tend to grade on a curve. When someone gives you a five out of ten, you're not average. You're in deep trouble. There is little allegiance at all until you get ratings of eight or above, but when you get north of an eight, a potential client might choose you over others and may gladly refer you when their experience is equally happy.

Before Reichheld's research, companies who regularly got six to 7.9

aggregate scores from customers thought they were doing better than average, but it should have been like a four-alarm fire to them. Grading on a curve is human nature, and it tells us that nothing less than an eight is acceptable.

When we all know eight is the bottom, it reminds us that everyone needs to be a high performer every day. If you can start to accumulate a group of people who work at a 7.9 or an eight, the others either step up to the job or leave. Leaders don't need to wonder why they have some people functioning as threes and fours. They do need to find one person doing one thing at a 7.9, then another, and another. It builds on itself.

THE HEROIC JERK

The best example of a gradual erosion of standards is the function of the heroic jerk. Everybody wants them gone except the manager because they are great producers. Though they cause those around them to be less productive, it isn't as readily measurable as the production of the heroic jerk.

More importantly, what does it communicate to everyone? Even though the heroic independent may only be a three as a contributing team member, it is just fine as long as he personally produces like an eight or above. This reinforces the demoralizing idea that there is no point in acting well in community, since in reality, "it's everyone for themselves." On our Crankset Group peer recognition surveys, if someone gets an aggregate, anonymous peer score of a 7.9 or below on their ability to get along with others in community, we treat it seriously because human skills are as important as production skills.

THE THREE TO EIGHT TRAP

Highest common denominator teams are built around an eight to ten mindset, but if you look at the engagement, commitment, and performance of most companies, you can see that they are operating at the range of a three to an eight level. As we've mentioned, worker engagement has hovered around 30 percent for years, with nearly 70 percent of people just going through the motions at work.

When various companies discover that their low worker commitment numbers are a common denominator with other companies, they set a trap for themselves by saying, "What can we do? Everybody has the same problem." No, everybody doesn't. The companies we profile in this book are numerous happy exceptions across many industries and have been successful for too many decades for anyone to think they just have to live with a majority of acorns who never want to become oak trees.

HOW TO GIVE FEEDBACK

Giving great feedback must be taught. The general guideline is to avoid giving it when you're angry or just to make a point, win the argument, or stick it to the other guy. Feedback should be focused on the long-term, best interests of the other person.

The primary purpose of both kudos and peer recognition surveys is to provide positive reinforcement for the things people are already doing well, backfilling with an occasional constructive rating and comment on things they could improve. We need to take seriously the need to teach everyone who wants to be a Stakeholder how to give kind, direct, and other-centered feedback.

BUILDING A GOOD REVIEW SYSTEM

The following are good peer review practices:

1. **Self-regulation** — The teams, in collaboration with strategic leaders, develop a system of incentives and corrective actions to respond to the metrics, and they deliver these to each other without the need for HR or managers.

2. **Review as close to the performance as possible** — Annual reviews rarely review anything but the last few weeks of kissing up before the review. Our Crankset Group DDM workgroups do peer recognition surveys every other month. Some companies do them monthly. More frequent recognition, closer to the behavior, affords both positive motivation and the occasional opportunity for correction.

3. **No status ranking** —There isn't any need to compare people. Plenty of better metrics exist. Jack Welch's famous practice of firing the "bottom" 10 percent every year, dubbed "rank and yank" pitted people in rivalries, not teams, and could result in the dismissal of someone ranked in the top 10 percent for ten years but who had a bad year. It was also shortsighted because it kept people from developing long-term sales relationships that could have been valuable to GE. A couple years ago, GE finally relented and scrapped the whole mess, citing that

millennials want feedback more frequently, as if millennials are any different than anybody else.

4. **Three measures of performance** — We use three things to measure performance: 1) quality, 2) quantity, and 3) happiness (internal and external). Quality and quantity are production metrics. Happiness is a human metric. We use all three to catch people doing something right. We talk more about these metrics in the chapter on incentives.

5. **Agreed upon metrics** — Following the principle of input equals ownership, the teams design their own production and human metrics, with the support, input, and collaboration of strategic leaders (the metrics have to work for both the company and the teams.) Since they own the metrics, they are vested in beating their own game. Combining the human metrics with the production metrics keeps anyone from becoming the independent producer everyone dislikes, or the nice nonproducer who gets along with everyone and everything except the metrics.

6. **Achievable** — I should be reviewed only on things I can control. We don't rate someone on how well the company keeps its values or company profits. We rate each other based on our own personal contribution to those things: "On a scale of one to ten, how well did Chuck reflect the company value of community this month?"

7. **Transparency** — At Crankset Group, everybody's average survey scores for each question are open to all, since more transparency makes for a better company. Typically, people offer to help someone who is not doing well on a specific metric.

8. **Change it when it's no longer working** — Nothing should be set in stone. DDM workgroups should review their surveys at least annually, or whenever they have a question about whether they are helping us or not.

9. **Anonymous** — We only see the average score for each question, which keeps us from being distracted by trying to figure out who gave us the perfect ten or the "undeserved" seven. Manager reviews are the opinion of one person. When we combine multiple people's opinions, we are much more likely to achieve an accurate average view of performance. A great,

enjoyable read on the subject is *The Wisdom of Crowds,* by James Surowiecki. It will help you embrace the entire concept of DDM workgroups.

10. **For their good, not mine** — All comments must be shared with positive, go-forward language. Instead of, "You're never on time," say, "The team relies on you, so we need you here on time, and we're looking forward to that small adjustment." "You're terrible at relationships" becomes, "Please work on your relational skills; take advantage of the company resources on that and get open feedback from people you trust."

11. **Review the few** — I should only be giving feedback about those I work with regularly. On a team of twenty-five people, realistically, I might interact regularly with eight to ten others, so that becomes my DDM workgroup. Sometimes a strategic leader may show up on multiple surveys.

12. **Keep it short and high-level** — Resist the desire to rate on a micro level, such as how often someone says thank you, or how often they pick up the phone on the first ring. What is the over-arching, high-level question you could ask that would allow you to address a myriad of small things? One of the questions on our survey is, "On a scale of one to ten, how well does Chuck live in community?" That question allows others to review me based on how I function as a team member, how I function toward clients, whether I was rude last week, or if they saw me sharing in another team member's pain over a family issue.

13. **Give comments** — A good rule our team developed is that if we give anybody a number other than an eight, we need to leave a comment. Don't tell people they were a ten that month and not tell them how to reproduce that behavior next month, and don't leave me a seven ("eight is great," seven is a problem) and not share how I can improve — it doesn't help me.

14. **Review only the human metrics** — Measuring happiness, both internally on our team and externally toward our customers, is the meat and potatoes of a great peer recognition survey. The production metrics, on the other hand, are self-rating. If you make fifteen terrific chairs that don't need to be returned under warranty (quality and quantity), the numbers tell the story.

15. **Have them compiled outside the company** — This guarantees

anonymity. At Crankset Group, we know that the surveys are anonymous, and no one in any corner of the company has access to the raw data. We all get the same averaged responses.

16. **Review the team and company** — "On a scale of one to ten, how well did we function as a team this month?" This has been very revealing at times and created some great discussion, and it's a real source of celebration when we give ourselves a higher than normal average score.

LEADERSHIP SURVEYS

In addition to their regular peer recognition surveys, every six months, Semco also takes an anonymous survey about their tactical and strategic leaders. These determine whether the leaders continue in their positions or go back to production. Only when following the leader is voluntary can you know if you truly have a leader or just a manager. Once the survey results are reported, everyone knows they have had their say and are to get on board with the decision Semco's DDM workgroups have made[19].

The following is a screenshot of part of our survey, designed and developed together. Initially, I had an entirely different direction in mind, but I love what the team came up with instead. It takes under fifteen minutes for eight to ten team members to complete, including thoughtful comments.

Crankset Team Recognition Survey
* Required

Chuck Blakeman

Chuck Blakeman: Abundance*
Serving/Interested/Fun

	1	2	3	4	5	6	7	8	9	10	
So fired	O	O	O	O	O	O	O	O	O	O	Amazing!

Chuck Blakeman: Internal Community*

Here's a look at the results. We all see everyone's results, which helps us shoot higher together.

Chuck Blakeman			
	Average Score		
Abundance	9,375		
Internal Community	8,875		
External Community	9		
Clarity	9,25		
Conation	9		
Trust	9,75		
Kudos			

Unwavering in core competencies that keep us from getting distracted.
I really appreciate how there are no hidden agendas with Chuck, he really walks his walk and talks his talk. I appreciate his encourag.

OTHER TIPS

1. You can use KwikSurveys.com, Google Forms, SurveyMonkey. com, and other options for setting up a survey. Crankset Group can also manage a blind survey process for you. Stay away from the old performance review mindset. It should be more about:
   a. Catching people doing something right—first and foremost.
   b. Confirming what we are doing well.
   c. What we could be doing better, improving on our strengths.
2. Recognize and evaluate personal and team metrics only when doing peer surveys.
   a. Production metrics — Hard metrics such as revenue, profit, sales conversions, production, etc., should be left out of surveys.
   b. Human metrics are all we rate in the surveys — how well I live in community, lead individually, and uphold the values, vision, and mission of the organization. These are not easily quantified without a survey. An average of the team's input turns these soft metrics into a hard metric with a real number.
3. Creating the survey — those who fill it out should create it (input equals ownership), with input from strategic leaders. Use Slack.com or an in-person meeting to get input on what the surveys should cover. It's usually simpler for everyone to have the same survey in the company, but sometimes there are

good reasons to have it vary. Following are some of the types of human metrics you could measure:

   a. Individual performance — How well does Jenna perform and lead individually? One to three questions.

   b. Team Performance — How well does Jenna perform as a team member? One to two questions.

   c. Mission-centered performance — How well does Jenna uphold the values, vision, and mission of the entire organization? Usually one question.

   d. Rating other teams — Which one to two teams interact most with our team? One question for each team, not each individual. You can always praise specific individuals in the comments section below the rating.

   e. The company — How well does the company support our team? With a question this broad, you can recognize individual strategic leaders, systems, infrastructure, etc.

4. Ask as few questions as possible and keep them broad, which allows for a wide range of more specific comments. Going narrow requires more questions, making the surveys laborious. If ratings on the few general questions are not high, we can always dig in to find out why by asking people or with a one-time survey on a specific question.

USING THE SURVEYS

1. Option one — At first, they can just be information, so we get used to the idea of getting feedback from each other. Build trust and get people comfortable with the survey before doing anything substantial with it. In some cases, it could take a month or two of tweaking to get there.

2. Option two — If an atmosphere of trust already exists, you can move quickly to include any or all of the following. (Don't create uncertainty or fear. Introduce these in stages, depending on the existing trust level in the company):

   a. Training/retraining

   b. Incentives (along with any hard metrics from the freedom maps)

   c. Finding or verifying someone's highest and best use of their time and skills

    d. Dismissal

SAMPLE

CRANKSET GROUP PEER RECOGNITION SURVEYS
How We Use Them

Objective: Recognize and provide feedback for each other's ongoing contributions to Crankset and to our community. Our survey lays the groundwork for the expectations we have for each Crankset Group team member.

The primary use of the survey is to recognize people for their strengths and contributions. Much more rarely we use it to share areas of improvement. The surveys have caused us to go more directly to people with issues because we don't want to put them on the surveys for all to see. Surveys are a last-resort mechanism for getting someone's attention on an area for improvement.

What are Crankset Group's Metrics?
(Your team can create their own – these are just ours)

Note: We recommend using a one to ten scale. Roughly based on Fred Reichheld's net promoter score concept, we see an "eight" as the minimum, and anything less needs improvement. Eight is great. If you are an eight, we want you to be here your whole career. We don't have a "satisfactory" rating — there isn't such a thing. You're either doing well (eight or above), or you need to improve (7.9 or below).

7.9 IS A FOUR-ALARM FIRE

Therefore, for us, an average rating of 7.9 or below from the team is a four-alarm fire. We feel we need to get people back up above eight immediately. Otherwise, it's a sliding scale to the bottom. We invite and require each other to bring our best every day, never "okay" or "good enough." People have bad days or even bad weeks, and that is understandable, but an eight or above, as a regular effort and attitude, is the minimum requirement.

Anytime a strategic leader has expressed frustration with people being disengaged or not giving it their all, I ask them, "How do you think it has become acceptable that they perform as a four, five, six, or even seven?" Surprisingly, very few can answer that question. The reason is that the company, at some point, tolerated someone being a

7.9 because it was close enough. Somebody else noticed and decided to be a 7.9 in a different area, then someone was a 7.8, and off they went, in a race to the bottom.

When I speak at conferences, I'll ask, "What will definitely get someone dismissed from your company?" I get answers such as lying, cheating, stealing, simply not showing up for work (sometimes that even takes a few violations). Where are these human metrics on a scale of one to ten? They're all zeros or ones. Is this really our standard for performance, just to show up and all is fine? As Netflix puts it in their hiring information, "Adequate performance receives a generous severance package." You get what you tolerate. Put up with a 7.9, and you will soon have fours and fives working in your organization.

MEASURING ON A SCALE FROM ONE TO TEN

I didn't come up with the following. Our Crankset Group team did. They put themselves under this rating system based on catching people doing something right and occasionally using the surveys as a last resort to share things that need to be changed.

10 — Amazing! Congrats, you're perfect for a few minutes, but keep growing.

9 — Remarkable — for a few days or weeks, but never settle; keep growing.

8 — Eight is great. You're doing everything asked of you. Please stay for your whole career and keep improving!

7 — Refinement. An average rating of 7.9 or below for three periods in a row equals dismissal. Get immediate help from your team or others to get back above eight.

6 — Significant growth required. An average rating of 6.9 or below for two rating periods in a row equals dismissal. Get immediate help from your team or others to get back above eight.

5 through 1 — Never acceptable. An average of 5.9 or below on any one survey would be immediate dismissal.

We recommend the following rule: if you give someone anything other than an eight or a nine, you need to add a comment to say specifically why:

10 — "You're amazing because you stayed late this week and helped me when you could have just gone home. Thank you!"

7 —"Please work on step seven in your freedom map and on your

communications. Thank you!"

We've never let someone go because of a rating of 6.9 or below, but one person did lose their position because they were below an eight for a number of months in a row. He had an entire team working to help him and was very aware of his tenuous status over the months, but he still didn't make the effort to get back above an eight. By the way, this kind of dismissal with an extensive record of corrective action by an entire team holds up much better in a worker's compensation hearing than one manager deciding on their own to let someone go.

THE THINGS CRANKSETTERS RATE EACH OTHER ON

Our surveys directly reflect our company values because we decided them together. They cover the three main survey elements (individual performance, team performance, and company-wide allegiance).

1. On a scale of one to ten, how well did Sean live in abundance? (serving, giving, interested, fun)
2. On a scale of one to ten, how well did Sean live in *internal* community?
3. On a scale of one to ten, how well did Sean live in *external* community?
4. On a scale of one to ten, how well did Sean live in *clarity*? (communications, focus, results)
5. On a scale of one to ten, how well did Sean live in *conation*? (acting with resolve)
6. On a scale of one to ten, how well did Sean live in *trust*?
7. On a scale of one to ten, how well are we functioning as a *team*?
8. On a scale of one to ten, how well does the *company* support our team?

Our company is small enough that we don't have a question about how another team interacts with ours, but that is a great question when you have multiple teams interacting.

HOW WE USE THE SURVEYS

We use these for everything mentioned previously:

a. Training/retraining
b. Incentives (along with any hard metrics from the freedom maps)
c. Finding or verifying someone's highest and best use of their

time and skills

d. Dismissal

The focus is always on the positive, and even when we want something to improve, it's always presented in a positive light. Am I giving feedback so I feel better or so they can improve?

Not: "Stop being late."

Yes: "Our team is depending on you to be on time."

Not: "Your attention to detail is bad."

Yes: "Please work on your attention to detail."

COMPLETING THE SURVEY

1. The survey form is distributed, filled out, and then locked. No one sees anyone else's result.

2. When it's completed by everyone, an outside source tallies the responses and turns them into averages for each person.

3. Results are reported to everyone — we all see each other's average scores for each question.

   a. If little trust exists, you could start by showing me just my own ratings, but quickly, you should have an open, transparent system, not to shame people but to congratulate those doing great and encourage the rest to shoot for that.

   b. Remember, the focus is on "Catching people doing something right," backfilling with positive suggestions for improvement (no negative talk).

CRANKSET GROUP SURVEY SAMPLE

We put a few words below the listed value to remind us of what these values mean. You can do the same for each question. You can see that by keeping these questions very broad we have a lot of leeway as to how very specific we can get in leaving a comment for someone.

Crankset Team Recognition Survey
* Required

Chuck Blakeman

Chuck Blakeman: Abundance*
Serving/Interested/Fun

	1	2	3	4	5	6	7	8	9	10	
So fired	O	O	O	O	O	O	O	O	O	O	Amazing!

Chuck Blakeman: Internal Community*
Working with team

	1	2	3	4	5	6	7	8	9	10	
So fired	O	O	O	O	O	O	O	O	O	O	Amazing!

Chuck Blakeman: External Community*
Performance with client and vendors

	1	2	3	4	5	6	7	8	9	10	
So fired	O	O	O	O	O	O	O	O	O	O	Amazing!

Chuck Blakeman: Clarity*
Communications/Focus/ / /Receptive

	1	2	3	4	5	6	7	8	9	10	
So fired	O	O	O	O	O	O	O	O	O	O	Amazing!

Chuck Blakeman: Conation*
/   /   /

	1	2	3	4	5	6	7	8	9	10	
So fired	O	O	O	O	O	O	O	O	O	O	Amazing!

Chuck Blakeman: Trust*
Adult Behavior/Support/

	1	2	3	4	5	6	7	8	9	10	
So fired	O	O	O	O	O	O	O	O	O	O	Amazing!

Kudos for Chuck Blakeman

Your answer _____

  BACK   NEXT   ▬▬▬▬▬▬▬▬▬▬▬▬▬▬▬▬   22% complete

Sample of Individual Grade Average Response (Seen by All)

Chuck Blakeman

	Average Score		
Abundance	9,375		
Internal Community	8,875		
External Community	9		
Clarity	9,25		
Conation	9		
Trust	9,75		
Kudos			

Unwavering in core competencies that keep us from getting distracted.
I really appreciate how there are no hidden agendas with Chuck, he really walks his
walk and talks his talk. I appreciate his encourag.

HOW OFTEN SHOULD WE FILL THEM OUT?

Some companies with a lot of short-term projects do them twice a
month. Crankset Group does them every other month, which is as far
apart as we would recommend. If you do them less than bi-monthly,
you begin to forget things from six to eight weeks ago, and then you are
grading on only the most recent performance, a typical problem with
traditional annual performance reviews.

SOME THINGS TO DECIDE

1. What grading scale do we want to use (one through five, one
   through ten, A-F, etc.?) (Note: We like the one through ten
   system.)
2. What do the scores "mean" to us? How do we use them? This
   doesn't have to be decided right away — we can just use the
   surveys as "feedback" for a couple of iterations and get used
   to them, but within a couple months, they should be used for
   training, choosing leaders, incentives, and possibly for dismissal.

Some companies also use them to determine base pay.

3. Do we agree the teams should come up with their own questions?

4. Besides the questions to a) evaluate our own team, b) evaluate other teams, and c) evaluate the company, is there any other question we want the teams to rate?

5. How often will they do them? Don't go with too seldom. You can always back off, but it gives the surveys real emphasis to do them more often than less at first.

6. When do they need to be completed? Ex: Third Friday of the month by 3 p.m.?

7. Who will tally these to ensure they are anonymous? (someone outside the company, i.e., an accountant or bookkeeper, virtual admin, etc.). Crankset Group can do the tallying for a fee if needed.

8. To begin with, will people only see their own score, or will everyone see everyone's score? Eventually (within a month or so), everyone should see all average scores, but you can do this in stages. Note: people only receive averaged scores for each question. They don't see that one person gave them a nine, another gave a six, etc. They just see 8.7.

ENDING THOUGHTS

Feedback from others is a very sensitive process, so it may never feel completely comfortable. Remember, in the Participation Age model, we're not shooting for perfect, just better, and peer recognition surveys are proving to be a much better way of praising, recognizing, and giving honest feedback.

THE NEXT ONE THING

1. What Next One Thing do we need to do regarding kudos and peer recognition surveys?

_____

_____

2. When will we start? _____/_____/_____

3. What are one or two challenges that need to be addressed before we start?

_____

_____

_____

RESOURCES

1   https://www.greatplacetowork.com/resources/blog/creating-a-culture-of-recognition

2   https://www.businessinsider.com/the-worst-traits-your-boss-can-have-2017-8

3   http://www.businessinsider.com/employees-top-complaint-about-bosses-2015-10

4   https://www.amazon.com/How-Full-Is-Your-Bucket/dp/1595620036

5   https://www.thoughtco.com/definition-of-a-landslide-election-3367585

6   http://happierhuman.com/losada-ratio/

7   Gallup, 2013 State of the American Workplace

8   https://www.motivosity.com/articles/13-reasons-to-have-a-peer-to-peer-recognition-program.html

9   McKinsey Motivating People, Getting Beyond Money, 2009

10   https://www2.deloitte.com/ie/en/pages/deloitte-private/articles/recognition-programmes.html

11   https://badgeville.com/what-motivates-employees-today/

12   SHRM/Globoforce Employee Recognition Survey, 2012

13   https://www.motivosity.com/articles/13-reasons-to-have-a-peer-to-peer-recognition-program.html

14   https://www.globoforce.com/products/

15   http://blog.surveyanalytics.com/2014/02/top-5-infographics-of-week-employee.html

16   https://www.bamboohr.com/blog/performance-reviews-people/

17   https://www.bamboohr.com/blog/better-ways-to-manage-employee-performance-reviews-in-smbs/

18   https://www.nytimes.com/2016/02/28/jobs/360-reviews-often-lead-to-cruel-not-constructive-criticism.html

19   https://www.ted.com/talks/ricardo_semler_how_to_run_a_company_with_almost_no_rules#t-287238

CHAPTER THIRTEEN

How to Hold a Meeting

13

M anagers spend (not invest) around one-third of every week sitting in mindless meetings or, worse yet, holding them. For directors and VPs, it's up to a mind-boggling 50 percent of their week[1]. What do we think we accomplish by living a meeting-centered life? Surveys and research show:

Leaders believe at least 67 percent of all meetings are unproductive wastes of time and money.

92 percent of people multitask (play Candy Crush on their phone) during meetings.

The number one complaint in every company is a lack of communication. With all these senseless meetings, people still don't know what's going on!

It's all just stupefying. For the love of all things sensible, let's stop the meeting madness and let DDM workgroups get to work.

CUT MEETINGS BY 50 PERCENT

You won't miss a beat. Perhaps one of the most impactful things you can do because of reading this book is to:

Get an accurate accounting of how many hours per week/month people are in meetings.

Resolve to cut the number of meetings by a minimum of 50 percent in the next three months.

A 50 percent reduction in meetings for most companies would be brain-dead easy, and if done right, it would dramatically increase communications at the same time. Dropbox eliminated all recurring meetings for a two-week period to force people to reassess which ones

---

1   https://www.themuse.com/advice/how-much-time-do-we-spend-in-meetings-hint-its-scary

were necessary. There were fewer, shorter meetings after that[2].

MAKING MEETINGS OPTIONAL

There are 25 million meetings every day in the United States alone, and estimates are that they cost us $37 billion a year in lost productivity and that 15 percent of every organization's collective year is wasted in meetings. While giving a TEDx talk in 2014, I mentioned that in our company and some other Participation Age organizations, all meetings are optional. I asked the crowd to imagine, "How many unproductive meetings would go away if we made all meetings optional?" 2,900 people sent up a collective roar of cheers and whistles.

If you have the courage to do it, declare all meetings optional going forward. At our company, as well as Semco and others, there are no repercussions for not showing up. This is hard to do if your managers have the power to fire people, but it is enormously instructive for discovering who's leading and who's intrusively managing. Remember, leaders have followers, while managers only have reports who they can eliminate with the stroke of a pen. Make all meetings optional and see who has followers.

WHY MEETINGS ARE SO DESTRUCTIVE

Here are a few of the bigger reasons why meetings don't work:

1. We're winging it. We think that a bunch of people showing up in a room together to talk is a productive meeting. It's not. It's a recipe for wasted time and brain power. No agenda, no written action items, and no focus.
2. We may have a formal agenda, but we wander off or abandon it regularly.
3. We don't know what the result of the meeting should be. He who aims at nothing, hits it every time. The answer to "How was the meeting?" is too often, "Great, people were really engaged," or "Great, I got to talk the whole time, and people looked like they were listening."
4. Some heroic geniuses think meetings entitle them to take the stage, pontificate, dominate, and eliminate any discussion.
5. We use them to solve problems but should use them instead to bring the issues to the surface, assign champions and due dates,

---

2   http://money.com/money/4160139/collaboration-teamwork-lower-productivity

and move on. The champions, who are the problem solvers, can call their own meetings with the few people who actually need to be there.

6. They have no ending time. Simple human respect and courtesy requires that we give people both a beginning and ending time and stick to it. If you're feeling pressed near the close of a meeting, decide together which of the remaining items should be addressed, then table the others for the next meeting or deal with them on communication tools such as Slack.

STATUS OR SOLUTION? NEVER BOTH

To eliminate the problem of ineffective meetings:

1. Have two guiding principles for each regularly scheduled meeting:

   a. Have a clearly stated intended result. If it's a strategic leadership meeting, make sure it is covering strategic issues, not tactical ones, and that by the end everyone has a clear understanding of who is championing what action items and by when.

   b. Cover only the core issues that are bottlenecks right now and have them submitted in writing beforehand.

2. Is it a status meeting or solutions meeting? Decide which it is and don't mix the two.

   a. Status meeting — These regularly scheduled meetings are for general awareness and agreement on what is important right now. *Never solve problems in a status meeting.* It is seriously annoying when a few people dive in deeply to solve something while everyone else checks email. Be very deliberate not to solve problems during a status meeting. Instead, identify the issue, agree on a champion and accompanying details, and move on. Don't attempt to solve any problem that doesn't involve 100 percent of the people in the room. Call a solutions meeting later for that.

   b. Solutions meetings — These are rarely scheduled, not weekly occurrences. It may be a one-off meeting, or they may occur over the course of a few weeks or even months to get past a particular bottleneck (a software installation, moving to a new building, solving a nagging process issue, buying a copier, etc.) Solutions meetings should only involve people who are going to help solve the issue, plus whoever else is impacted and wants to give input. Those who attend can report back to the larger group during a status meeting as to the status of the solution, resources needed, timelines, etc.

HOW TO PREPARE FOR EFFECTIVE MEETINGS

Here are a few things we have learned over the last thirty-five years building twelve business in eight industries on four continents:

1. **Openly shared document** — Keep a single shared document that presents a running history of all the status or solution meetings on a shared drive that is accessible to all. Remember, participating and sharing are the two hallmarks of the Participation Age, and transparency is key to both. This document is a priceless tool to observe long-range patterns you won't see month to month otherwise, and it can reveal the heartbeat of each DDM workgroup without having to call a meeting.

2. **Everyone sets the agenda** — In our company, everyone is trained to add relevant issues to the agenda by pulling up the document and adding their name to the agenda item. This person then leads that part of the meeting. If enough of us feel the item isn't relevant to that meeting, we are kind and direct in moving past it.

3. **Respect everyone's commitment** — We hold to meeting start and stop times. Running late on either end should be the rare exception. Break the habit and show respect for people's time.

4. **Have a facilitator versus a leader** — A facilitator mindset says the meeting is not an audience with the pope, but it's an opportunity to get everyone involved. Rotate the role between people who have good facilitation skills and can keep things moving. Move away from the notion that whoever has been around the longest with the loudest voice should run things. The facilitator exists to move things along and get everyone else involved, not to dominate the meeting. They should be more like a referee—when it works well, people forget they are on the field.

5. **Result intended** — For any regularly scheduled status meeting

or one-off production meeting, there should be a clear intended result. If we can't determine how we know if the meeting is successful, we shouldn't hold it to begin with. Get this figured out up front.

HOW TO HOLD EFFECTIVE STATUS MEETINGS

After years of working at efficient use of time, we practice the following format for our meetings, especially our status meetings. Most teams need a weekly status meeting for an hour or less, but for us, strategic status meetings can be biweekly and likely lasts a little bit longer.

Strategic Status Meeting

The following describes our agenda for meetings that are more strategic in nature. Regular production meetings follow a little different process, outlined below this.

1. **Be human together first** — Meetings should primarily be about everyone connecting on a human level. Only then are we well positioned to attack the strategic or tactical issues before us. We see the deleterious effects of the Industrial Age Factory System in the notion that meetings are for attacking production issues, processes, and customer problems, with barely an acknowledgment of the people tasked with these items. We must be regularly reminded that when we take care of people, they will take of systemic issues. Only then are we well positioned to attack the strategic or tactical issues before us. Being human together can be as simple as going around and sharing how the last week went, our highlight or low light, focusing on one person's psychometric profile and how we can help get them into the highest and best use of their time, or reading a book together and using some of our meeting time to share what we're learning.

2. **Review vision, values, mission** — This exercise is important for creating the right context for any meeting and should only take a couple minutes. After we connect with one another for a few minutes, someone states our five values, and we are invited to give an example of how one or more of these were lived out since we last met, either by us, our customers, or in the bigger world around us. We do the same with both our vision and mission. This simple exercise beats the drum, gently and

relentlessly, on what is ultimately important and puts the issues listed below in the right perspective relative to our true north and our mission. People really value and appreciate this process.

3. **Review one freedom map** — In our status meetings, someone is responsible for bringing just one freedom map (see the chapter on those) for review. They ask two simple questions:

   a. "Is this still the result we want?" If so, then:

   b. "Is this still the process that will get us that result?" We review the map for any corrections and move on. Sometimes this takes sixty seconds of confirmation, and other times, it develops into a twenty-minute re-write of part of the process. We rotate all our freedom maps through this progression to ensure alignment with our agreed upon process.

4. **Review the big rock(s)** — We quickly review the one or two big things we want to crush this year. This helps us gain perspective on the more granular discussions to follow and reminds us to table things that won't help us get there. This, too, can be accomplished in a minute or two, although sometimes it sparks great strategic discussions that we would never have had without the intentional review.

5. **Review of results intended** — Each owner of ongoing intended results takes the floor to share updates about how he or she is going about crushing the big rock. We all ask questions, get clarity, see what obstacles or issues need to have a champion, assign them with a due date, and then move on to the next update. These reviews take up the bulk of a strategic status meeting

6. **Twelve/Three/One plan review** — We look again at this year's one or two big rocks to see our progress and be reminded that the clock is ticking. We look at what must be done in the next three months to chip away at them, and then we look at the current month to see what we can do to get the three-month objectives accomplished twelve-month, three-month, one-month. Lastly, we look at what we can do this week to accomplish the monthly objective. We start with the end in mind (Stephen Covey) and figure out how to eat the elephant one week at a time. See my book *Making Money is Killing Your Business* for how to develop

a simple two-page strategic plan to run your business.

7. **To-Dos** — One of the more important and helpful distinctions we've discovered over the years is the difference between what we call problems and obstacles. Only obstacles go on the two-page strategic plan. Problems are separated into a different spreadsheet or report we call "to-dos." You know you solved a problem when the business reverts to where it was before the problem occurred — nothing has changed. We have forty people. One quit, and we need to replace him—that's a problem. We replace him, and we're back to forty. Nothing has changed. Conversely, you have solved an obstacle when something small (or big) has materially changed in your business as a result. As an example, you have an eleven-step customer acquisition process. You decide to update it and include new steps, possibly eliminating some others. That kind of material change to the business belongs on the twelve/three/on strategic plan. If it isn't going to materially change your business, it's just a problem and belongs on the to-do list. With to-dos, as well as with obstacles, we agree together on a champion, due date, next step, and resources needed. These decisions free us to be disciplined about moving on rather than solving the problem during the current meeting. Solving to-dos tends to dominate meetings, pushing aside the longer term, really important strategic things that would help us avoid more problems, but because we put them in the context of being human together, reminding ourselves of how we're living out our values, vision, and mission, our big rocks, and our strategic obstacles, we find we get through them more quickly, and there are a lot fewer problems.

8. **Any new obstacles?** — Problems (to-dos) will come find us and should be added in between meetings. We must hunt down the obstacles. A simple way to see if a problem can be turned into an obstacle and permanently solved is to ask, "Why?" when addressing the problem. "Why did that person quit?" Solve the who, what, where, when, and how, and you are solving the problem. Solve the why, and you're solving the obstacle.

9. **BFOs** — We end our meetings by having everyone share a "blinding flash of the obvious." What is one thing they got

from the meeting that can help them going forward, whether at work or at home? Sometimes someone has an inspirational quote to send us off.

A key reminder — don't use status meetings to solve problems or obstacles. Just identify them, assign champions, due dates, next steps, and resources needed, and move on. Please also notice there is no place in any meeting for self-important people to pontificate, throw their weight around, give inspiring speeches, or tell people what to do. Everyone is a leader, and everyone brings different strengths to a meeting. Respect and utilize all those strengths by designing meetings that keep strong personalities or "experts" from taking over. A great agenda does just that. Our agenda also makes it easy to rotate who facilitates the meeting. We rotate that responsibility and still have a consistent meeting because the facilitator always follows the agenda.

Production Status Meeting

In a production meeting, the issues are generally more tactical. Start and stop on time and design a meeting that mitigates against strong personalities and experts taking over. If most people don't see themselves contributing, they punch out.

1. **Be human together first**
2. **Review vision, values, mission**
3. **Review one freedom map**
4. **Review the big rock(s)** — It's critical for tactical DDM workgroups to be reminded of how what they are doing fits into being mission centered.
5. **To-dos**
6. **Any new obstacles?** — Can we solve these, or do we need to send them to another tactical or strategic function to get resolved? Again, tactical to-dos should be added between meetings to keep from wasting time dredging them up during the meeting.
7. **BFOs**—Blinding flash of the obvious

Here's the simple format of our two-page strategic plan worksheet. Again, for a thorough understanding of how to build a strategic plan that runs your business on a daily basis, see my book *Making Money is Killing Your Business.*

Page One:

Our Principles/Values	
Our Vision	
Our Mission	
One- to Three-Year Strategies	(How we can lead based on our values, vision, and mission, and how we can make money based on our mission)

Page Two:

Twelve-Month Big Rocks:

Obstacle or Opportunity	Champion	Due Date

Three-Month Objectives to Accomplish the Big Rocks:

Obstacle or Opportunity	Champion	Due Date

One-Month Objectives to Accomplish the Big Rocks:

Obstacle or Opportunity	Champion	Due Date

To-Dos Worksheet:

Our format for the to-dos portion of our strategic and production status meetings

What is the Challenge?	Why is it a Challenge?	Champion	Due Date	Resources Needed	Update	Resolved Date

USING TECHNOLOGY TO CUT BACK ON MEETINGS

Slack.com and Workplace.com are two tools that are designed to help eliminate meetings. They do so by giving us an organized place to research, talk, and ask questions, so we can make great progress before a meeting ever happens. They provide a way to push issues so that the meeting length is reasonable. We no longer have to "table that thought" but can keep the discussion going in a relevant and organized way.

We use Slack.com for its simplicity and ease of use. We decided together as a company to make the switch from internal email (we still use email externally) to Slack in one day, and we gave ourselves three weeks to prep. We didn't miss a beat and were collectively surprised by how seamless the transition was. Now, we regularly use Slack in several ways: for virtual "meetings," to prepare before physical meetings, and to continue conversations after physical meetings have ended. I've heard from others that Workplace.com and similar tools work as well for them.

These kinds of inclusive technologies are highly supportive of Distributed Decision-making teams, two-step decision-making, and the whole concept of a Participation Age company where everyone is a leader. People can start topics with no manager involved, and everyone can see who is leading by who follows what ideas. Leadership emerges organically using these tools.

FREEDOM FROM MEETINGS

Let's stop monopolizing people's time and let's stop having meetings aimlessly week after week just because they are on the schedule. Meetings are the most tangible evidence of Stakeholder abuse by managers. We should relentlessly challenge the need for every meeting. Try making them all voluntary and see which ones still exist three months later. A full commitment to two-step decision-making will ensure that no meeting is ever missed that was essential.

THE NEXT ONE THING

1. What Next One Thing do we need to do rehumanize meetings (declare a moratorium on all meetings and see which ones matter, start every meeting by being human together, read a book together)?

_____

_____

_____

2. When will we start? ____/____/____

3. What are one or two challenges that need to be addressed before we start?

_____

_____

CHAPTER FOURTEEN

The Value of Commitment Letters

14

At the Morning Star Company, no one can tell anyone else what to do, so no one tries. People commit to their work through colleague letters of commitment. Everything is voluntary, yet the complex work of running a processing plant goes very smoothly. Everyone creates their own colleague letter of commitment by conversing with as many as ten other people who are affected by their work. This ensures that everyone gets the reports, communication, equipment, mentoring, vision, or conveyor belt they need to get the work done. The Commitment Letters highlight that Morning Star colleagues live in community, without bosses or managers, and are deeply committed to the consistency principle of leadership we talked about in an earlier chapter: we say what we're going to do, then we do what we said.

People change their habits slowly, not all at once. The best way to start is by introducing a ceremony, or reset, with new rituals that quickly become new practices. The bigger the desired change in habits, the bigger the ceremony or reset should be. Moving from a system built on creating vertical relationships to one built on horizontal relationships requires practical tools for the transition. Commitment letters provide one of the best.

In my history of building a dozen or so businesses, I concluded that consultants wasted a lot of our money, not deliberately but by default. Their typical approach is to arrive, present a three-inch binder with some new ideas, and then leave. I call this seagull management — you fly in, squawk a lot, crap all over the place, and fly out, leaving the mess behind. Since everybody continues to be busy dealing with old messes and old habits, within a short period of time, everyone reverts back to the lousy behaviors that inspired them to hire the consultant in the first place.

It took me years to figure out why things don't change. First, if people don't see the world differently after you present a new way of doing things, they don't change, and the challenge of breaking old habits is difficult but not insurmountable. Seagull management won't do it, but leaders beating the drum, gently, and relentlessly, can. The gentle drum beating should take two forms: ad hoc and formal.

Ad hoc — If we catch someone doing something right, stop the bus for fifteen seconds, recognize them, and move on. If we hear someone is confused about their new process, jump over and help train them if nobody else can do it. We should always have our antenna up to beat the drum gently and relentlessly in pursuit of the desired change.

Formal — We must develop formal rituals, practices, tools, methodologies or processes to replace the old habits with the new. According to displacement theory, or replacement therapy, it's the classic problem of how you get oil out of a glass glued to the counter — you pour water in. Most people aren't inclined to stop doing what has worked for them for years unless you convince them that the replacement action works better, requiring you to make a big deal of it at first. My communications 101 prof in college said, "If you want your audience to bleed, you have to hemorrhage." A bit gross but very descriptive. When you require big behavior changes from people, you must be dramatic and emphatic, and the more important it is, the bigger deal you make of it. Enter: the ceremony, which resets the old behaviors.

KICKING OFF A CHANGE

Life is full of ceremonies that signify big changes; baby showers, coming-of-age celebrations, graduations, and weddings are a few. Why do we make such a big deal out of these? Partly, it's because we want the people involved to know there are big changes afoot. It's graduation day — you will no longer be sleeping until noon and skipping afternoon classes on your way to the bar. You'll be getting up at 6 a.m. and giving it your all every weekday. A ceremony is the best way to kick off a change.

Making the transition from a top-down Factory System hierarchy to a Participation Age Mission-centered organization is not easy. When done well, it can take twelve to eighteen months or longer if you have no ceremonies to formalize the new direction. For each new practice, we should have a ceremony, introduce the new rituals, and agree together not to turn back. The bigger the change, the bigger the ceremony.

HONOR YOUR COMMITMENTS

Every well-functioning business says what it will do and then does what it said. When there is alignment and consistency between our declared intentions and our day-to-day actions, the magic happens. This consistency, the number one practice of the successful organization, is a primary feature of Commitment Letters.

The Morning Star Company does Commitment Letters very well. Chris founded the company on two guiding principles:

Use no force — an influence on our legal system and an argument for not having managers. People volunteer to work with each other, and, as a result, teams, teamwork, and leadership are organic.

Honor your commitments — one of the driving forces behind civil law and civil society. If we all agree that red means stop and green means go, things flow well. Every team member at The Morning Star Co. has a Commitment Letter called a CLOU, or colleague letter of understanding. This CLOU is reviewed and revised annually, and it expresses their commitment to the company and to other team members who are impacted by their work.

Commitment letters are also helpful to develop clarity about a process, about who owns what, and about the incentives and consequences of not keeping our commitments.

COMMITTING TO ONE PRACTICE AT A TIME

For a company that is making the switch from the Factory System hierarchy to a Mission-centered organization, putting one new practice in place at a time can help as new habits are adopted.

Celebrating each of the small steps established along the way helps seal our resolve to go a new direction. When we launch a new Participation Age practice, a ceremony to formalize our commitment is in order, and then another one later when we feel like we have fully embraced the new practice. It can be a lunch together, a happy hour, or even a ninety-minute workshop and discussion, but the more relational, the better. The ceremony reviews the new habit that has been successfully embraced and reminds us of the practices we agree to use to keep it alive. The centerpiece of the celebration ceremony can be a Commitment Letter, or CLOU as The Morning Star Co. calls them.

A DDM workgroup can create a separate Commitment Letter for each new tool or practice. By mutual agreement, someone can be designated to write the first draft, just as Thomas Jefferson did when he drafted the Declaration of Independence and then turned it over to Congress for tweaking, but everyone who signs the Commitment Letter should have input.

We recommend having one copy for the team, which everyone signs, and another for each team member. The signing ceremony has more impact if you relate the new tool or habit to the ceremony. For example, if you are celebrating the new use of kudos, have some people share some kudos, their thoughts about them, how they are used, and how it helps to make the company better.

Part of the benefit of doing these bite-sized Commitment Letters is a recognition that habits change slowly. As I mentioned in the chapter on DDM workgroups, you can't go into the office after reading this book, gather everyone together, and tell them, "This is a Participation Age company; you're now all Stakeholders who are committed to Distributed Decision-making, and I'll be on the golf course." Committing to each new tool separately, with a kickoff ceremony and an adoption celebration, emphasizes the intention for permanent change.

Here's an example of a short Commitment Letter around just one tool, a kudos program:

> ### Our Kudos Commitment
> January 15, 20XX
>
> Together as a team, we developed a program to recognize one another for going above and beyond our standard roles and responsibilities. We call it our Stakeholder kudos process, or our "skip" process for short. We developed a simple one-page guide that demonstrates how we will give kudos to each other and what that means to the giver, the receiver, and the team.
>
> I individually commit to 100 percent participation each month. If I do not give kudos, I should not expect to receive kudos. There is always someone who is going above and beyond, and it is my commitment to proactively look for and recognize at least one person

every month for giving it their all in some way.
Signed,
[Name]
Team keeps the original, and each individual keeps a copy.

Side note: the DDM workgroups of one client decided that participating in the quarterly incentives process was contingent upon participating in the kudos program each month. Sometimes teams come up with forms of capitalism that we would never dream up.

THE STAKEHOLDER COMMITMENT LETTER AND CEREMONY

When you feel you have most of the basics of a Mission-centered organization in place, put the short Commitment Letters together into one comprehensive Stakeholder Commitment Letter, and have a big ceremony or celebration about becoming Stakeholders in a Distributed Decision-making, Mission-centered organization.

You never fully "arrive," and the company's Participation Age practices will continue to evolve, but when your communications, business practices, and processes all reflect a basic understanding of what it means to be Mission-centered, living together in community as Stakeholders, put a stake in the ground and celebrate that milestone.

THE THREE LEVELS OF A GOOD COMMITMENT LETTER

Some smaller Commitment Letters and every comprehensive Stakeholder Commitment Letter can cover a personal commitment, one we make as a team, and even an organization-wide commitment. Get everyone involved in writing the company-wide piece, and get the team involved in the team piece as well as the individual one. Individuals can add anything to their personal section, with agreement from the team.

ONGOING USE OF COMMITMENT LETTERS

1. For annual review and revision. Having a "reset" ceremony annually to refresh commitments to one another is important.
2. As team members, we review each other's performance, along with offer letters and freedom maps.
3. To remind someone of a commitment they made on which they aren't delivering. Again, consistency is our most importance practice — Say what we'll do. Do what we say. Consistency is

the vehicle that builds trust, and inconsistency destroys it.

4. To clarify roles and responsibilities. Sometimes we may change up who does what on the freedom map processes, then tweak the letters to reflect that.

5. For correction — Great Commitment Letters have consequences as well as rewards written into them. If X is a commitment, what happens if I don't do X? Teams should draw a line in the sand at a very high bar — that we commit to bring it all every day and be an eight or better. If we fall below the line, the letter spells out how to correct it, within a given time period. (See the Miami Sedation letter that follows for a good example of rewards as well as consequence for dropping below a 7.9 on the peer recognition surveys.)

6. For new hires — Even in the process of interviewing, it is valuable to see the level of commitment required to be part of this organization, and upon being hired, they will be guided by a Commitment Letter to be signed after 90 days. This brings people in at a very high level of performance.

A SAMPLE STAKEHOLDER COMMITMENT LETTER

There is no one way to write Stakeholder Commitment Letters. Individual commitments can be combined, or the Commitment Letter team could write a cover letter for the smaller ones that ties them all together. The principles are:

1. Clarity of roles and responsibilities.
2. Clarity of commitments around tools and practices of all aspects of a Mission-centered organization, personal, team, and company-wide.
3. Clarity on how we interact with each other to reinforce our commitments (recognition, consequences, incentives, etc.).

Accomplish the principles any way that works for you. We recommend that the Stakeholder letter be as "generic" to the whole company and team as possible, with personal commitments being the one main variable. The following is one example:

MY AGREEMENT AND COMMITMENT
PREMIER DENTAL

November 28, 20XX

I am writing this Commitment Letter to myself, my team, and the entire practice, for two purposes:

1. To demonstrate my desire to help us all build a great practice together and be a great team, and to express my individual commitment to those goals, and

2. To clarify in writing how we can build that great practice and be that great team. Without written, clear objectives and measures, we can only talk about being committed. Our Commitment Letter gives us all individual clarity on exactly how we can go about contributing to those goals.

This letter expresses my deep commitment to our success and my personal agreement with how we will get there. It is very important for us to understand what we it is we agree to and then simply agree to do what we say we will do. This letter expresses my commitment and my agreement in detail. It doesn't express everything, but it hits some of the more important highlights of my agreement and makes it easier for me to see how we can get where we want to go as a practice.

My Personal Commitments

I embrace the processes we have developed and agree with the way they are expressed on our freedom map.

As a Stakeholder, I own my part in the macro freedom map that shows how Miami Sedation works as a whole practice. It is extremely important that I see my individual work and our team's work as part of the bigger picture of serving our patients and making Miami Sedation successful.

I also agree with and commit to the micro freedom map that shows how my individual team gets work done. I have committed to be the champion or guardian of specific steps on my team's micro freedom map and will take that responsibility seriously. It's not about me being successful. It's about me helping my teammates and our team to be successful, and I will do everything I can to make that happen.

I am the guardian of steps _____ on our freedom map.

   a) These steps are being done well by all of us.

b) The steps are relevant and continue to be necessary to deliver the desired results.

I personally commit to the following specific areas that support the overall team goals and freedom map(s). (If someone has an individual contribution they feel they can make that is above and beyond their role and responsibilities, they can express it here.)

Our Team Commitment

We commit as a team, to a monthly review of the freedom map, which could be anything from quickly agreeing together that it is good and relevant as it stands, or it needs modification to reflect the changing realities of our practice. If it needs modification, I commit to participating in making those changes as it fits my skills and talents to do so, and if I have any questions or issues with the map, I commit to immediately bringing those up with the team in order to resolve them.

Our Peer Recognition Survey — We commit together as a team to "catch people doing something right" regularly and to share our positive and constructive feedback with each other on an anonymous peer recognition survey every month. I will not receive an individual score from my peers but an average of all their scores. That average score will help me know exactly how I'm keeping all the commitments outlined in this Commitment Letter and will encourage me to always keep growing personally and getting better professionally.

Each of us on the team own individually, and as a team, that we will bring our best to work every day. Dr. Raymond Bane's office is a dental practice that is committed to working at the top and not just merely meeting the minimum. As a result, I also own the following company expectations for regular high performance. Missing the mark on any one of these could result in immediate dismissal:

1. Failing my commitment to our work week.
2. Attendance to our daily morning huddles on time.
3. Using company paid time as personal time.
4. Receiving an average of 7.9 or lower, three monthly surveys in a row.
5. Receiving an average of five or lower on any one survey.

It is important that we all understand together that the most valuable function of the surveys is to catch each other doing something right. We assume that everyone wants to "bring it all" every month and will look for ways to complement each other every month for going above and beyond our basic responsibilities.

To that end, we commit that "eight is great." If anyone is getting an "eight" on the survey, we have indicated to them by giving that average score as a team, that they are doing great — they are doing their job, fulfilling their commitments to the team and to the practice, and should feel proud of everything they are doing. If I get an 8.1 or higher, I understand that my peers are telling me I'm going above and beyond my specific responsibilities. Getting a nine or higher is rare and will be a special thing that should be celebrated by the team in a special way.

Getting a 7.9 or below is not punishment or an expression of any kind of hostility. It is an expression of love and concern and should result in an "all hands-on deck" response for the entire team to see how they can help that person get back above an "eight" the next month. We are a "highest common denominator" practice — all of us will bring everything we have, every day. We don't anticipate that anyone will get a 7.9 or below because of our deep commitment to each other and to the boss, our mission statement.

PERSONAL AND TEAM INCENTIVES

I own the metrics on our freedom map and the results desired, and I understand that a combination of these "hard metrics," plus the "soft metrics" of peer recognition surveys determines our incentive. In a separate document, we outline the specific incentives that are part of our practice. Money is only one of the seven things that incentive us — these are our "TERMS" of engagement, one of the keys to eliminating the disengagement tax:

Time
Experience/Education
Recognition/Relationships
Money and
Stuff

We document our TERMS of engagement and our incentives in that separate document. We prioritize team incentives above personal incentives because we want each of us to use our personal rock star abilities to make the team better, not to be "rugged individualists."

OUR KUDOS PROGRAM

I own that I will regularly "catch people doing something right" and recognize them formally through our kudos program. Kudos should not be used to just say someone else is doing their job well. That should be expected — it's a "base line" expectation that we all do our jobs well. The kudos program is another way of catching people doing something right that is above and beyond what they normally would do. I commit to regularly catching other people doing something right and recognizing them formally for going above and beyond.

Our team will produce the following overall result. This result will be written on the freedom map and will be reviewed monthly along with the freedom map.

As we run the process(es) outlined on our freedom map(s), we commit to the following results:

1. Open communication with other teams.
2. Specific freedom map results [put team actionable and measurable goals here] — What are the one or two very specific goals of each freedom map?

My Personal Commitment to Our Entire Practice

I commit to working to make our team and every other team in the practice successful and to demonstrate ownership of the company's needed overall results (revenue, profit, production, retention, living in community together, our values, great customer services). I will work hard to ensure the company has no "job silos" and that our focus is on the results we get together as a team.

MY COMMITMENT TO MIAMI SEDATION'S MISSION

At Dr. Raymond Bane's office, our mission is to make a positive difference in the lives of all our patients by offering the highest quality dental care in a private office atmosphere. By providing a team of professional, highly educated, honest, compassionate, and committed team, we aim to improve patient health, appearance, self-confidence, and overall quality of life.

This mission statement will be our team's boss. Everything we do on our team is for one purpose only, to fulfill the mission of this practice. I commit to mission statement as my boss.

MY COMMITMENT TO MIAMI SEDATION'S VISION

Our vision is to use dentistry to contribute to whole body health and total well-being. Our vision statement is our guiding light, our true north. We work for the mission statement (our boss), and our vision statement tells us the values we hold dear in accomplishing that mission statement. I commit to uphold the values expressed in our vision statement as m guiding light for how we accomplish our mission.

I personally commit to bring it all every day and doing everything I can to keep my agreements and commitments outlined in this letter, and to keep the other unwritten agreements that we have with each other that make us a great practice.

TEAM LEADER

By_____ Date:_____

STAKEHOLDER

By_____Date:_____

WHAT ABOUT NEW HIRES?

We don't have people sign a comprehensive Stakeholder Commitment Letter when they start. Most people are coming from a Factory System hierarchy and need time to adjust, so we give them the letter and let them know that if they think this is a good fit, we will all sign it after ninety days.

THE THREE LEGS OF THE STAKEHOLDER GUIDEBOOK

Along with the acceptance letter, and our freedom maps, the comprehensive Stakeholder Commitment Letter forms the third leg of our Stakeholder guidebook. This is distinct from an employee manual in that much of it is specific to each individual, not generic for the company at large. Stakeholders appreciate the clarity and respect it brings to each of them, so different from being an impersonal cog in a machine.

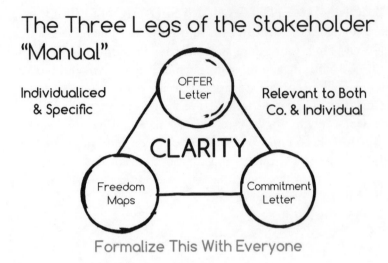

The Three Legs of the Stakeholder "Manual"

Individualiced & Specific

OFFER Letter

Relevant to Both Co. & Individual

CLARITY

Freedom Maps

Commitment Letter

Formalize This With Everyone

KEEP YOUR AGREEMENTS

This is simple, fundamental human respect for one another — say what I'll do, then do what I say. It is also at the heart of every successful business because it creates the consistency that is the foundation of all trust, both within Stakeholders internally and with your external customers. This simple principle has the most profound impact on your company. We must take it seriously and make personal, team and company-wide commitments, and faithfully executing them, a central theme of our organization.

THE NEXT ONE THING

1. What Next One Thing do we need to do ensure we all a) understand our commitments to each other and to the rest of the organization, and b) keep those commitments?

_____

_____

_____

2. When will we start? _____/_____/_____

3. What are one or two challenges that need to be addressed before we start?

_____

_____

_____

CHAPTER FIFTEEN

Results-Based Incentives, a Tectonic Shift

15

Most Semco Partner team members set their own salaries. This didn't happen overnight, but getting there demonstrates a deep commitment to results-based compensation over the familiar time-based Factory System approach. The thousands of Semco Stakeholders can go to any number of computer terminals to view the salary of every person in the organization, including the six co-leaders. They also see what the industry average is for their position and the salaries of others who do what they do at Semco. They then plug in a number which they feel represents their contribution, and a check for that amount starts showing up at their house[1].

That may seem like an invitation to chaos and anarchy, but remember, Semco team members do peer recognition surveys regularly, and each team is responsible for its own profit and loss. If your contribution isn't affirmed by your peers, the team may see you as a drag on their own ability to perform and make money and can vote you off the island. More often than not, Semco has to make upward adjustments to stay competitive with the rest of the industry.

I recently attended a fancy panel discussion on incentives and was surprised to have been teleported back to 1975. The first hour focused solely on monetary compensation as the means to retain great people. When I mentioned that there are a lot of other ways that have proven to work better than money, every panelist agreed, then quickly returned

---

1   https://www.ted.com/talks/ricardo_semler_how_to_run_a_company_with_almost_no_rules#t-287238

to the topic of money.

The Factory System pyramid scheme has missed the boat entirely on incentives in at least four big ways:

1. Time-based bonuses that largely ignore measured performance.
2. A focus on individual incentives instead of team incentives.
3. Assuming money is the big motivator.
4. Assuming results-based incentives are only for salespeople.

RESULTS-BASED INCENTIVES VERSUS TIME-BASED BONUSES

Before factories, the shoe cobbler was paid directly by his customers for how many shoes he made, how well he made them, and how satisfied his customers were. These three things form the basis for good incentives programs:

1. Quality — how well is the shoe made?
2. Quantity — how many did I make?
3. Happiness — how happy are my customers with both me and the shoes?

Outside of sales, most compensation has nothing directly to do with any of these three. The modern cobbler now gets paid for showing up for eight hours. Most compensation systems do little if anything to reward people for great performance. Remember the two hallmarks of the Participation Age—participation and sharing. People want to participate in building a great company, and they want to share in the results. How we create incentives for people in a Mission-centered organization is a tectonic shift from the Factory System bonus system still in place in most companies.

Great incentives programs promote participation, but most compensation still reflects a slavish adherence to the time clocks of the Factory System. I get a salary because I showed up for two weeks, and I get a bonus at the gracious whim of my manager because I'm on her good side right now, and I spent another year sitting in my chair. Compensation and personal engagement have no relationship under these circumstances. Who wants to play that game? Isn't there a better one?

Results-based incentives eliminate subjective, manager-centric bonuses that do nothing to motivate people to bring it all every day. Time-based bonuses are the antithesis of Distributed Decision-making and Distributed Leadership, and without those two fundamentals, you won't retain engaged people.

SALARY AND PERSONAL INCENTIVES OVER TEAM INCENTIVES

Time-based bonuses are the first egregious error of Factory System compensation and a focus on individual rewards over team incentives is the second. According to multiple sources, salaries have little impact on engagement. There is no capitalism at play here — nothing to shoot for, no game to play, no control over my destiny. Sit in the chair, do the minimum, and you will get paid. Hourly wages and salaries are the worst possible way to engage people, yet they are the default method by which almost everyone gets paid, even in the face of overwhelming research that says it shouldn't be so.

Individual incentives are better but not ideal. If someone is receiving a results-based incentive, it can increase their engagement and productivity by 22 percent, but the best way to motivate someone is by rewarding teams who achieve a goal together. Team incentives increase individual engagement by a up to 44 percent. Do you want individuals to work harder? Reward the team more than individuals[2].

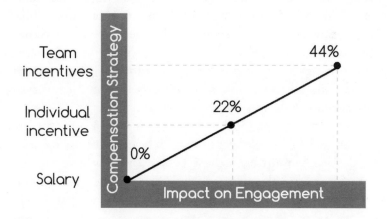

MONEY IS NOT THE BIG MOTIVATOR

Contrary to Factory System thinking about incentives, money is not the best motivator to retain great talent. The reality is this: an issue over

2   https://theirf.org/research/incentives-motivation-and-workplace-performance-research-and-best-practices/147/

money may cause someone to leave, but offering more rarely convinces someone to stay. If you pay less than what a similar position elsewhere would command, people will leave, but if you try to bribe them to stay by paying more, the best Stakeholders will still exit, leaving you with the unmotivated and disengaged who are willing to work in a lousy business simply because it overpays.

In the early 1990s, I worked for a caustic company that had a turnover rate of 65 percent per year. I was making $59,000, and when I gave notice to go to a company that would pay me $75,000 to do the same thing, they immediately offered me $90,000, well over the going rate. I said no on the spot. Staying in that mangled, top-down, Jekyll and Hyde mess was not worth an extra $15,000 a year. In the company I moved to, where my humanity was incorporated into the culture and I was able to use my brain again, I soon owned a 10 percent stake.

There are at least seven ways to reward people, which we expand on later. If you're paying an industry rate, the other six are more motivating than money. We'll cover them below.

ASSUMING INCENTIVES ARE FOR SALESPEOPLE

The fourth major misconception of Factory System compensation is to assume that incentives are only for salespeople. In fact, results-based compensation is historically the only way most people got paid.

Throughout history, it is estimated that somewhere between 80 to 90 percent of all free people owned their own businesses — farmer, cobbler, blacksmith, etc. People apprenticed with owners so they could learn the craft and eventually open their own business. It was the rare individual who worked for someone their whole lives.

The Factory System is inherently unpopular. For over seventy-five years after the first factories were built, 90 percent of the workers were under the age of fourteen because people saw how unattractive the pay structure and work environment were. It took decades to force the cobbler out of business and into the factory. We want a personal stake in how we live our lives.

There is some negativity surrounding the idea of "pay for performance," as though it were some kind of new, untested trick, or a scheme to oppress workers. Nothing could be farther from the truth, since results-based incentives give everyone the ability to take significantly more control of their financial destiny, but the undoing of the Factory System requires people who are invested in their work and are rewarded accordingly, so we have to be patient in the process.

When Alan Wyngarden owned his mortgage company, his loan processor was making $55,000 a year and had been processing eight to ten mortgages a month, which at the time was the national standard for a loan processor. He decided he wanted to institute results-based pay.

To do so, he offered to drop her salary from $55,000 to $25,000 and give her incentives based on how many mortgages she did each month, how accurate they were, and how satisfied the clients were (quality, quantity, and happiness). She declined, but he was patient and showed her a parallel spreadsheet each month revealing what she would have made under the new deal. Six months later, she finally took the small risk to jump to results-based pay, processed twenty-two to thirty loans a month, and saw her salary jump within a year to $125,000. She has solved efficiency issues that no manager in the entire mortgage industry had, and Alan said his clients were even happier than before.

Results-based compensation isn't just for a small mortgage company. Haier Corporation has 75,000 people dispersed into 4,000 DDM workgroups of ten to fifteen people each. Every team is responsible for its own profit and loss, and no team is required to use the services of another team if they feel they can get them outside the company at a better rate or competency. Teams come into existence or dissolve as needed. Results-based incentives reflect simple capitalism in its best form.

Not every move to results-based incentives is so dramatic as these two examples, but all of them demonstrate the opportunity to engage people at uncommon levels.

WHAT MOTIVATES PEOPLE?

There has been a lot of noise recently about people not being motivated by money. While money isn't the only motivator, it is definitely one of them. If 3M had paid the millions in royalties Spencer Silver and Art Fry deserved—they're the guys who, through a fluke, invented the sticky note— how many more people at 3M would have been motivated to keep their eye out to invent something out of nothing, too? A Starbucks card and an "attaboy," while 3M runs off with hundreds of millions doesn't usually cut it.

Remember, it's about both participation and sharing. If you don't share, they won't participate. If I bring dramatically more value to the bottom line than the guy sitting beside me, and we both get a 2.3 percent pay raise and the same size "bonus" for having sat in the chair for another year, where is the motivation to excel? How does that measure and honor excellence for me?

A hypocritical business practice today focuses on increasing my "engagement" through intrinsic motivators without increasing the actual money, or extrinsic motivator, that should come with my increased engagement. Complex business problems rarely get solved by pure altruism. If I'm working just to make the other guy rich, the intrinsic motivators won't take me very far by themselves.

Harvard Business School's V. G. Narayanan, discussing the LSE findings in a Harvard Business Review article, said that, "Effective incentive systems should focus on effective organizational learning and growth, process improvements, and customer-related metrics and milestones," and went on to support results-based incentives, saying, "Below market salaries, coupled with aggressive incentive pay linked to individual performance, is likely to attract self-motivated entrepreneurial individuals[3]."

We want to attract entrepreneurial minded individuals, whom we call Stakeholders, to every position in the company.

What is the basis for good incentives programs in the Participation Age? Invite me to fully participate (the intrinsic, fuzzy-feeling motivators), and also invite me to share in the results-based rewards (the extrinsic motivators). When everyone in the company is a capitalist, capitalism works. When only the guys at the top benefit, it isn't capitalism, just industrialism — using other people for my benefit. In that scenario, tortured attempts at increasing my engagement are just more lipstick on the pig.

TERMS OF ENGAGEMENT

There are at least seven major incentives that cause people to get out of bed and run to work.

---

3   https://www.management-issues.com/news/5640/performance-related-pay-doesnt-encourage-performance/

Results-Based Incentives

SEVEN TERMS
of Engagement

(T) ⟶ Time

(E) ⟶ Experience/Education

(R) ⟶ Recognition/Relationships

(M) ⟶ Money

(S) ⟶ Stuff

Money is only one of the seven, and if someone is getting paid similarly to the industry standard, pay falls to the bottom as the least compelling reason to stay. As I said earlier, people may leave an otherwise good culture if the pay is too low, but you can't pay great people enough to stay in a bad one. Decades of research shows that paying close attention to the other six non-monetary incentives is the key to keeping someone for decades. They are all related to the idea of community at work.

Semco, with a few thousand people in several industries and professions, has had annual turnover in the 1 to 2 percent range for decades. Wegmans turnover is in the 4 percent range in an industry where 39 percent or higher a year is the norm. W. L. Gore, The Morning Star Co., and many more have a strikingly lower turnover then others in their industry because they work hard at the other six incentives that create community at work.

TIME IS THE NEW MONEY

The industrial mindset of trading time for money is ingrained in our psyche as normative when, in fact, it is a new and unnatural thing in the history of man.

I still shake my head at the report of two women a couple years ago who worked in the same department at a large company and had babies at nearly the same time. Together, they offered to split the hours, each working twenty hours a week to fill one forty-hour-a-week position. There was nothing about the job that couldn't accommodate this, but the company said no. Their only reasoning — they needed full-time people. They had two experienced, committed, and well-trained people who wanted to work forty hours between them, at a higher sense of commitment, but the company went out and hired total strangers instead.

Where and when we work is also still tied to the Factory System. Work has both a place and a time assigned to it, and if you are not at that place at that time, it is assumed you are not working. Ricardo Semler made the bold move of eliminating shift work in his factories and leaving it up to individual DDM workgroups to decide when they should work. Production has remained at industry standards ever since. He understands that in the Participation Age, with the exception of some retail and other work, time and place can be left up to adult Stakeholders. Semler says, "9-5 workdays will disappear. We will work fewer days and weekdays, and weekends will no longer exist[4]."

When we instituted unlimited vacation and flexible work hours over a decade ago, two things happened:

People got more done in less time — they were more productive.

They took less vacation — we actually had to institute a vacation fund and pay people $1,500 a year to go on vacation. Their teams vote on whether it was truly a vacation, and if not, they don't get the $1,500 and must try again.

This shouldn't be surprising. When you treat people like adults, they take on the positive and the negative attributes of ownership. Owners have trouble walking away from their businesses, so we make it enticing to learn how to do so regularly. It should be said here that with every move in the direction of giving people freedom and responsibility to make decisions, the responsibility has weighed on them every bit as much as the freedom. People truly want to participate in building a great organization, and they also want to share in the rewards of doing so. If you are concerned about people taking advantage of that freedom, this is an issue of leadership and the kind of culture you have created. It is not an issue with 98 percent of your people, but rather the way they have been trained to relate to you. It requires you to change how you view and treat them, and as responsible adults, they will respond accordingly.

---

4   https://www.virgin.com/richard-branson/way-we-all-work-going-change

EXPERIENCE AND EDUCATION

An experience can be anything from watching a video together and discussing it as a team, to happy hour, to sending someone to a spa for a weekend. If you give someone $500 to go to a spa, the research shows they are not likely to remember where the money came from for long, but if the company pays for it up front, they will remember the kindness for years.

Lyric Turner, founder of Red House, took her entire team of seventeen people on a four-day cruise a couple years ago. Some of them had never been away from their home city. It was a trip of a lifetime for many of them. There were no expectations about spending time as a group, but she was amazed at how much everyone stuck together, how it melted boundaries between functions, and created a bond across the company.

Wegmans Grocers has been known to fill up a 737 with people from existing store locations to fly them to a city where they were opening a new store, just to get their input. No one forgets those trips, nor the message behind them — your opinion matters.

Education is also a great incentive, an experience all its own. On multiple occasions, some of our Stakeholders at Crankset Group have received training, sometimes expensive and time-consuming, on things that have nothing to do with their existing positions. We feel it created loyalty and made them more committed to the roles and responsibilities they already had. Sometimes people take advantage of our abundance mindset, but we'd rather get burned occasionally than miss out on opportunities to build loyalty with committed Stakeholders.

RECOGNITION AND RELATIONSHIPS

Recognition is a powerful incentive. As covered in our section on kudos (re-read it for more on this), praise and commendation were rated the top motivator for performance by 67 percent of workers, beating out other noncash and financial incentives[5]. If you don't have a formal peer-to-peer kudos/recognition system, you are undermining Distributed Decision-making and making it harder for people to fully engage in the success of your company.

As we shared in the chapter on community at work, relationships

---

5   https://www.mckinsey.com/business-functions/organization/our-insights/motivating-people-getting-beyond-money

are the most subtle, powerful incentive of all.

MONEY

If compensation is lower than the industry, people may leave. If it is comparable, and you have a great culture built on community work, it will be hard for others to recruit them away. If your work environment is dehumanizing, only the very unmotivated who have no interest in making an impact will stay, even if you pay above the industry average. More on money later in this chapter.

STUFF

Give someone $250 to buy a watch, and they won't remember where the money came from. Give them a watch, and they'll never forget. If you want more regard for where the money originated, give a bicycle, an iPad, a watch, or even a $10 gift card. All of them create more memories than cash.

As with all incentives, be sure you're giving people something they want. In a recent keynote address, a woman recounted to me recently that she had been given the Steak of the Month Club subscription. That's great, except she is a vegan. Too often, we dream up incentives without bothering to ask people if they are appropriate.

Levels of Incentives

We see three different levels of incentives:

1. Individual
2. Team incentives
3. Organization-wide

As shown previously, salaries do little to increase engagement, but individual incentives increase engagement by up to 22 percent, and team incentives increase engagement by up to 44 percent.

Company-wide incentives, whether monetary or other, when properly constructed can function with the same effect as team incentives. Broiler King makes great BBQ grills. A few years ago, they decided to take their already great quality to another level by rewarding everyone equally with a financial incentive for every BBQ that shipped without quality issues, but for every one that came back under warranty, they took the cost of repair, parts, labor, and shipping out of the pot. They put an electronic scoreboard to show both the additions and subtractions to the pot. Very quickly their already minimal defects went to near zero. People who had been doing a great job were now taking even better care of inventory, construction, shipping, and everything related to building a great grill. Broiler King invited everyone to be a capitalist.

Team incentives are equally powerful. At Spodak Dental Group, Craig Spodak and Erica Pusillo work with the production teams to create team goals. They are incentivized with team rewards that include different combinations of the seven TERMS of Engagement — time off, experiences, education, recognition, relationships, money, and/or stuff. The teams decide the reward system in collaboration with those impacted in the rest of the company (two-step decision-making), and as a result, they regularly achieve or beat their goals.

Turning separate teams, even within a single facility, into their own profit/loss centers establishes a great baseline for good incentives programs. Mortenson Dental Group, with over 150 locations, instituted an incentive that is specific to each location. If that location exceeds their own revenue and profit goals, they all go as a team for a four-day vacation at an all-inclusive Caribbean resort. The strategic leaders at Mortenson are rooting for all their business locations to be there at once, taking over a resort. That's a great capitalist incentive based on an providing an experience, not directly on monetary payouts.

We also believe people should be incentivized individually as well as on the team. These are classically easier for companies to create because there is a history of doing it with salespeople, but it is also part of the problem. The rest of us outside of sales have been without them for so long that a majority would reject them right now as destabilizing and confusing. Mindy Jordan doesn't feel that way.

Red House teams, The Spodak teams, each Mortenson Dental Group location — all have some tangible, significant measure of control over their financial destiny. If you want people to experience autonomy and meaning at work, you must invite them to be capitalists, not just altruists. Altruism hopes for participation but does not share. Bonuses share, but there is a disconnect between participation and any specific result. A Participation Age company motivates by clearly connecting the reward with the result.

If your company is small, a combination of individual and team incentives is usually enough. Sometimes the team is the whole company of twelve people. As you grow, a third layer can be added for company-wide incentives, but it should also tie back to performance. Annual bonuses decided upon by bosses based on tenure are not an incentive, just a part of an Industrial Age hangover.

PRODUCTION METRICS VERSUS HUMAN METRICS

In the chapter on metrics, we introduced a new mindset and practice around the former labels of hard and soft metrics. They are more rightly described as production metrics and human metrics and should be factored into any incentive program. Our bias, based on compelling research, is that measuring and incentivizing on the human metrics is even more important than production incentives.

WHICH MONETARY INCENTIVES ARE BETTER?

As shared previously, good monetary incentives are built on a combination of quality, quantity, and happiness. We apply these three to both repetitive work that does not require a lot of creativity, as well as to complex problem-solving. The following are different types of monetary incentives with differing applications.

Quota — Sometimes also called piece-rate, quotas are the best motivators as long as they also account for quality and happiness, not just quantity. Quotas can be coupled with incentivizing above the quota using the piece-rate model that follows, as we did with the pickle factory. This is great capitalism, especially when the incentive includes the whole team working together in community.

Tournament — Turning work into a game, or "gamification," has become a big motivator. It can be anything from a fun competition with nothing more than bragging rights to a big prize or cash payout. Incentivize team over individual and pit people against a metric, not against each other; otherwise, you create unhealthy motivations to "win" by making sure somebody else loses. Tournament incentives can lower production if people are pitted against others and think they have no chance of winning. Done right, they can be great incentives for getting people started on a new product or reenergizing an existing one.

Fixed-Fate — These are by far the worst motivators. Wages, salaries, and predictable bonuses — anything tied to sitting in the chair for another month, quarter, or year are not incentives but expectations. I get my annual bonus if I still exist a year later. This is one of the reasons Netflix says, "Adequate performance receives a generous severance package." We shouldn't create compensation plans around just showing up and being adequate.

FINANCIAL EDUCATION AND TRANSPARENCY ARE IMPORTANT

If you're going to invite people to be capitalists, you need to educate them on how to read simple profit and loss statements and balance sheets. Many Participation Age companies make it part of the onboarding process to teach people this skill and review it annually. We've said before that input equals ownership, but so does transparency. If I can't see how my incentive is working or how the profit structure plays out for me, I'm not incentivized to follow it.

Alan Wyngarden's five assisted living centers mentioned earlier all function separately as team-based cost centers. They all know the 12 percent basic profit required to keep things running, which stays in the kitty. For profits above that, they have a simple profit-sharing plan with Alan that is a combination of tiers of profit above 12 percent, based on surveys received from the resident's families.

Applewood Our House
Monetary Incentives Programm

Sharing % of profits, based on

ⓐ base (12%?) profit   ⓑ patient surveys 0-100%

90% = 25% (profits above base)
92% = 50% (profits above base)
94% = 75% (profits above base)
96% = 100% (profits above base)

Everyone at Applewood Our House has full access to the financials and is watching not just the cost of bacon but the comfort and happiness of the residents and their families (quantity, quality, and happiness).

THE MEASURE OF A GOOD INCENTIVE PROGRAM

If you have an incentive program, the best measure is regular feedback and adjustment to make sure it is working. If it's new, there are five good tests to determine if your incentive program works.

1. Design it with those who will receive it — more on this later, but always start here.

2. Keep it simple and easy to measure — If it's not easy to understand the game, people may find it frustrating. A complex program, or one that is too difficult to attain, can be just as bad or even worse than none at all. Participants may feel you're just pretending to be nice since they can't figure out how you are using them productively. Keep it simple to understand and easy to measure.

3. Directly connect it to results — Results-based incentives are a tectonic shift from the time-based bonuses of the Industrial Age Factory System model most companies still employ.

4. Make timely payments — If you are rewarding results that happened three months or even eleven months ago, nobody will see the correlation. Pay people as quickly as you can for performance. Cashflow can mitigate against doing it monthly, but keep a monthly scorecard that outlines exactly what you get at the end of the quarter, or rarely, annually.

5. Reward making meaning, not making money — Incentives should be tied to things that are not just a quid pro quo for the product or service alone. This is why it is so important to measure the human skills, how people live and work in community, and how well they are upholding the values, vision, and mission of the organization. We should not be incentivized to be heroic jerks and produce at the expense of the world around us, including our teammates.

6. Reward community and teamwork, not just individual performance. Motivate people to use some of their time, energy, and skills to make others on the team better, increasing personal engagement. Reward community as the holy grail because when people build relationships, the team always performs better than if they just coalesced around a specific task.

BITE-SIZED INCENTIVES

Some of the best incentives are simple. Here's a few examples from various companies:

Type of Incentive	Description	Benefit
TIME	Cranksetters also have no set work hours.	Remember, time is the new money. Get your work done, and we don't care where you are or when you are.
EDUCATION	Scores of companies do a good job offering paid education, even for things outside the job requirements.	Loyalty, especially when paying for education beyond their present responsibilities.
EXPERIENCE	Total Health Dental Care, with many locations in Oakland, CA, has regular happy hours sponsored by the practice.	Helps build community, a level above team, which causes teams to get the task done better.
RECOGNITION	Peer-driven kudos programs — see the section on kudos.	Peer-to-peer kudos is 35.7 percent more likely to have a positive impact on financial results than manager-only recognition[6].
RELATIONSHIPS	At the beginning of every meeting, we are first human together, all checking in on how we're doing or hearing about someone's adventure, reviewing their strengths profile, etc.	Teams organize around task; community organizes around relationships and gets the task done better.
MONEY	So many ways, see throughout this section	Participation and sharing. Engagement is not a process; it is a result of turning everyone into a capitalist.
STUFF	On the days the front desk people at Spodak Dental Group have a fully confirmed schedule (patient has responded), the next day they treat themselves to a round of coffee or bagels.	The bagel is both stuff and an experience. Gamification can revolve around winning an iPad, a coffee card, a bicycle.

6   SHRM/Globoforce Employee Recognition Survey, 2012

There are so many other examples of the above abound, but you get the idea. Good incentives are as much intangible as tangible, as much intrinsic as extrinsic.

THE BIGGEST INCENTIVE

The biggest incentive of all is the core practice encouraged by this book — Distributed Decision-making through Distributed Leadership. I get my brain back when I am allowed and required to make decisions. Absolutely nothing motivates people more to be productive and engaged than making decisions they must carry out.

Google and other software companies are famous for their seemingly cool culture, but for most of them, it's a surprising façade. Most Silicon Valley giants are designed around the antiquated Factory System pyramid scheme, devoid of the best incentives. As the famous Netflix slide show supports, a great culture is not created from free lunches, blue jeans, campus bicycles, glitzy buildings, on-campus sports, or even working from home. These are not culture. They are perks and can be used to bribe people to stay in a culture where they have no say in their destiny.

Playing ping pong at work doesn't humanize me. The ability to make decisions that affect my life does. From my experience in working with some of the largest, seemingly cool software companies on Earth, when it comes to decision-making, it might as well be 1890. People with broad responsibility over hundreds to thousands of people have told me how they foisted goal after goal on people, changing product paths, processes, teammates, and even career paths of people without so much as a conversation with those who had to live with their decisions, and then they wondered why people didn't own the decisions or were unhappy. Input equals ownership.

In many of these companies, the compensation packages are enormous, and the free lunches are great, and it's a good thing because the culture in many of them is terrible. The pervasive fear among managers I have talked with (there are very few leaders) is that people may jump to the next company for a few dollars more, which they do all the time. Why? Because compensation and ping pong are the only games being played by most of them. These popular technology giants are mired in Factory System organizational thinking, and they have not learned the lesson that money may cause someone to leave, but you can't pay them enough to stay.

Many so-called modern and forward-thinking companies are attempting to use perks as a cover for a lousy culture just to retain people, but the seven incentives are hollow if they are not founded on the principle of Distributed Decision-making. It's just more lipstick on the pig.

HOW TO INCENTIVIZE PEOPLE

Along with the principles and practices outlined previously, first ask your people what motivates them, and then get them involved in designing the incentive program.

Remember, managers tell. Leaders ask. I had one client who excitedly told me all about the great new incentive plan he had designed for his team members (it truly was good). He planned to roll it out after our call, but I threw a wrench into the works by simply asking, "Did they have a hand in designing this program?" He said no, and when I asked why, he replied, "Because I'm afraid they might come up with something I can't do that would hurt the organization." Two of his strategic leaders were with him on the call, and both in unison said, "If it's going to hurt the company, tell them that." Great point.

Distributed decision-making isn't chaos and anarchy. It is built on:
1. Communication
2. Collaboration
3. Cooperation

These result in interdependent community, not rugged individualism. Using two-step decision-making, the strategic and tactical functions work together so that everyone impacted is involved, and the final decision is made by those must carry it out.

If people come up with something wild, it should be talked through until it works for both the Stakeholders and the company. My client agreed to this, and the team decided on something remarkably similar to what he was going to mandate, but since they helped create it, the ownership was remarkably higher than if he had just dictated it.

YOU CAN'T LOSE BY ASKING

No matter what you ask about, you will win. If you get a response that exceeds your expectations, you can let go of yours and work with theirs. If there is a delta between what you feel works for the company and what they want, start negotiating, not telling. By asking instead of telling, you learn their perspective. If you tell, they will just nod their heads, and you'll miss hearing the concerns they think you need to address. Any goals you set *for* them instead of *with* them are destined to be ignored or patronized.

During an engagement with a giant software company, I had a director tell me his boss had decided that last year's revenue of $5 billion for their business group was great but that the goal this year would be $21 billion. The director told the managers, the managers told the staff, and the managers couldn't figure out why people still wanted to talk through this. The backchannel gossip was that the frontline people were just laughing at the goal with zero buy-in to make it happen. This is what happens when input doesn't equal ownership. Only personal input builds ownership. Ask people what motivates them, and then work with them to build incentives around those things.

WHO DESIGNS THE INCENTIVE?

First, ask what motivates them. Second, have them design it by communicating, collaborating, and cooperating with everyone who is affected. If you don't understand their idea or think it might hurt the company, turn all the statements in your head into questions (see the chapter on Universally Distributed Leadership), and ask them to look at the impact of their idea things outside their tactical world. Context is one of the main values of strategic leadership.

THIS IS AN EXPERIMENT

Third, present it as an experiment that invites everyone's input for fine-tuning. Be transparent and say, "We want you to design an incentive program. We'll help you as needed, and it will be an experiment until we see how it works for both the Stakeholders and the company." One of the beautiful things about Participation Age leadership versus Factory System management is that I no longer have to be the smartest person in the room. Now there is a room full of smart people who can work together toward building a better solution than I could have conceived on my own. Review it after the first, third, and sixth month, then every year.

AN INCENTIVES TEAM

Lastly, put the incentives in the hands of a team of Stakeholders nominated by their peers and approved by strategic leaders of the company. The Stakeholders oversee the program, while strategic leaders function as advisers, mentors, sounding boards, and champions for the benefit of the company as well as the Stakeholders — two-step decision-making. Incentives help to build horizontal relationships to replace vertical ones.

THE COMBINATIONS ARE NEARLY ENDLESS

There are seven TERMS of engagement, three levels of incentives (individual, team, and organization), and a myriad of possible production and human metrics to choose from. You can go almost any direction with incentives. It can seem daunting to tackle, but start out by having the newly elected incentives team decide on some bite-sized, easy incentives first, then expand from there. Incentivize the weaker performing metrics first, focusing on quality, quantity, and happiness together. If you leave any of these out, you are likely introducing questionable motivations that can weaken the incentive.

A final word—some incentives programs can be difficult to set up, and spreadsheet wizards can help, but when it comes to running them, simple, clear, timely, and result-based incentives lay a great foundation for building a Participation Age organization.

Let's move away from the worn-out and subjective bonus system not linked to results and instead get our DDM workgroups to build results-based incentives that motivate all of us. Community creates the magic.

THE NEXT ONE THING

1. Bonuses versus Incentives — What Next One Thing do we need to help us replace time-based bonuses with result-based incentives.

_____

_____

2. When will we start? ____/____/____

3. What are one or two challenges that need to be addressed before we start?

_____

_____

CHAPTER SIXTEEN

Four-Step Training   16

I n the Participation Age, training others and getting out of the way is one of the most highly valued skills a tactical or strategic leader can exhibit. We advised one well-known software company that in order to rejuvenate their innovative roots, they should identify people who are good at training others and giving others the credit and make positive examples of them. We were told that wouldn't work because the company specifically looked for people who could make things happen themselves and become well-known heros in their own right.

The Factory System promoted heroic activists with big personalities and amazing personal talents and skills. In the growing complexity and fast-changing nature of the Participation Age, individuals cannot have enough personal talent, knowledge, or skill to keep up with the ongoing need for adaptation. The best strategy for staying relevant in a complex, changing world is to focus leadership across the organization on the need to train others, share their knowledge, and get out of the way to encourage teams of people to learn, grow, and innovate together.

We traditionally understand the need to train people to do their job, but it is not common to see managers training others to do what they can do so that the former manager can become a true leader and focus on guarding the values, championing the people, and piloting the results. Participation Age training focuses on full sharing of knowledge and skills so that the trainer at some point is no longer necessary, not just as a trainer but also as a manager.

There are two types of training: the kind we're familiar with that gets somebody up to speed on a skill, and the kind that equips them to become a future Stakeholder and make localized decisions. Most people coming from traditional work environments need time and focused attention to achieve the transition to making localized decisions again at work as DDM workgroups.

SKILL TRAINING

Most training isn't. It can go one of two tracks — either a new hire who is following some impatient heroic genius around like a lost puppy, or they are getting thrown into the deep end until they figure out how to swim. Training should be simpler and more effective.

Our chapter on Freedom Mapping is the key to great training. When you have your core processes mapped on one side of a piece of paper, anyone can use it for training. Without maps, we default to the heroic genius or sink/swim training.

Both the trainer and the trainee should have a digital or physical copy of the freedom map, following it step-by-step. Using the map slows down trainers who do things intuitively and ensures deliberate training in a linear, logical fashion. As the trainee uses the map as a reference point for their work, they begin to envision it in their heads as well. Countless clients have extolled the virtue of training from a freedom map as the best way to ensure a consistent experience to those inside and outside the company.

Great training is a simple but not easy, four-step process:
Step One — You do
Step Two — You do/they watch
Step Three — You watch/they do
Step Four — They do/you mentor ("I'm over here if you need me.")

Training Progression From DOING through LEADING to Mentoring

Progression	Leader	Stakeholder
Step 1	DO	
Step 2	DO	WATCH (be trained - learn)
Step 3	WATCH	DO
Step 4	- (mentor)	DO

When accompanied by freedom maps and the corresponding

process descriptions, training a new person can be accomplished in a fraction of the time with better results, and it has the added benefit of communicating that someone cares enough about people here to make sure they get what they need to be successful. There is only upside to a focused, intentional, ongoing training regimen.

STAKEHOLDER TRAINING (LEARNING TO MAKE DECISIONS AGAIN)

Remember, everyone is a leader, some strategic and some tactical, and still others who work in both ways. In terms of their value, anyone who touches your company as a vendor, customer, temp, or permanent hire has a vested interest as a Stakeholder. The following training focuses on the permanent hire and semipermanent outsourced support, but it does not differentiate based on the number of hours worked. It is an Industrial Age mindset that people who work forty hours are more valuable than people who work twenty. You should invest equal effort to get everyone to be a Stakeholder.

Stakeholder training follows the same four-step model; we just change the face of it to help them reach level four, as opposed to merely being skilled at a position. The first three levels are familiar territory with some Factory System organizations. We can only declare ourselves leaders and Stakeholders when we get to level four.

STEP	MGR/LDR FUNCTION	EMPLOYEE IDENTIFIES PROBLEMS	EMPLOYEE IDENTIFIES SOLUTIONS?	EMPLOYEE / STAKEHOLDER FUNCTION
1	SUPERVISOR	N	N	EMPLOYEE
2	MANAGER	Y	N	EMPLOYEE
3	DIRECTOR	Y	Y but only identify/suggest	CLASSIC "GOOD" EMPLOYEE
4	LEADER	N	Y can implement w/out need to "approval"	STAKEHOLDER

Level One — This is the most basic level of manager-employee relationship. An employee not only can't formulate solutions, they don't even know when there is a problem. When that is the case, there is no way to function effectively in their position, so most companies only get people through level one to level two.

Level Two — At this level, a good employee can recognize when they have a problem, but in a heavily imposed hierarchy, they know better than to come up with a solution. Some managers need one of those "take-a-number" machines outside their office to handle this level of co-dependency. A good leader instead teaches people to develop solutions. Learning happens by imitating what the leader does. It's a good practice to agree together on how many times someone will observe the leader while learning a process. Otherwise, it can move from training to co-dependency.

Level Three — If you have any experience managing, you've probably said something like this, "Don't bring me your problems, Bring me three solutions." That's great management because now you have the employee doing your work for you, but you still get to decide which decision you'll take credit for. Most organizations expect managers to get people to this level, but it is still co-dependence.

Level Four — At this level everything changes. The employee becomes a tactical Stakeholder-leader, and the manager becomes a strategic Stakeholder-leader. The approach is now to make a powerful, radical statement, "Tanya, on this particular issue, I don't think you need to bring me three solutions. Just tell me what you intend to do, and I'll ask some questions." Or, at its best, "Tanya, you're fully trained on these kinds of decisions. Going forward, implement them and just let me know afterward how it all turned out." The strategic leader is still in the loop and can step it back to level three for more training when necessary.

There is no timeline for the four levels, and a Stakeholder may be functioning at more than one level at once depending on the various decisions they make. The point is to practice Distributed Decision-making; training versus telling, co-dependence versus interdependent collaboration.

Remember, the art of leadership is knowing how few decisions the leader needs to make. Strategic leaders should think of themselves as walking around with a mirror while everyone else has laser pointers. She should encourage the pointers to bounce back to the person, their team, or other resources, not to her. Jack Dorsey, CEO of Twitter and

Square says, "When I am making decisions, I am not leading." Making decisions is a failure of leadership and the core practice of co-dependent management.

Managers tell. Leaders ask. The training version is: Managers solve, decide, and tell. Leaders train by asking and then get out of the way.

THE NEXT ONE THING

1. What Next One Thing can help us bring everyone up to level four where we're all leaders, and we're all Stakeholders?

_____

_____

_____

2. When will we start? ____/____/____

3. What are one or two challenges that need to be addressed before we start?

_____

_____

_____

CHAPTER SEVENTEEN

Reverse Hiring

17

One of the most crippling legacies of the Factory System hierarchy is the way we hire. It is fundamentally broken and is a central reason why companies struggle to build great cultures full of highly engaged people.

The Industrial Age treated people as extensions of machines. The Factory System did not want the whole person at work, just the part that could run the machine. At work, they made money. At home, they could do and be something meaningful.

The "work to make money" mentality informs everything we have done in hiring for over a century, so it is no mystery why we lack the people we want in our organization. The process we use is not compatible with finding and hiring great people.

If we are going to move into the emerging work world of the Participation Age, we must relearn everything we've been taught about how to hire. It's not hard, and the process and benefits are enormous.

At the core of great hiring in the Participation Age are great values, vision, mission, leadership, and, in general, great culture. A great hiring process does not compensate for an archaic, top-down company culture, which results in a revolving door of people coming and going. Everybody wants a silver bullet that brings them great people. I deliberately put this section on hiring at the end of the book because the silver bullet is not the hiring process — it's Distributed Decision-making, Universally Distributed Leadership, and DDM workgroups.

If you already committed to DDM workgroups of self-managed adult Stakeholders, then the mechanics of Reverse Hiring can yield great people through a reliable process. Finding the right people to bring into your great culture will be hit and miss, otherwise. Let's cover the principles.

ABUNDANCE HIRING

Throughout this process, you will observe a different mindset than what is currently pervasive. Most companies are desperately trying to attract great talent, bending over backwards to get them to sign on the dotted line, while ignoring the whole idea of culture match. If your culture is bad, the classic desperation hiring process is your only option.

When Semco made the switch from the Factory System to a Participation Age DDM workgroup model, they were flooded with applicants soon after they put the word out. As a Participation Age company, you will be seen as the employer of choice, and people should be climbing the walls to get in.

This requires a world view of abundance. There are always enough customers, the economy is always growing, and there are great people looking for us. We just need to do the work to make the match happen. We have found some of our great unicorns (we only hire unicorns) in periods of full employment when it was supposed to be hard to find people. When great people are looking for something better, desperation hiring assumes a scarcity model that is reflected in the entire process.

Reverse Hiring Principles

1) Hire first for beliefs and culture

Never hire first for skills or experience. Test for beliefs and culture before you ever see a resume or name to keep bias out of it. More on this in the hiring priories and the eleven-step hiring process follows.

2) Resumes are nearly useless

We call them obituaries because they are usually an embellished version of what someone used to do and do not reveal the full, unvarnished story. The applicant might even believe their obituary; after all, very few of us have a highly accurate self-assessment.

Many companies are no longer even looking at resumes. Pivotal Labs, who hires programmers first for emotional intelligence, pays an applicant to come in and program for a few hours with a couple different people. They then decide whether the applicant should come back to program with five different people over five days. Those people get together to confirm a) this person works well in community (emotional intelligence and empathy), and 2) they have the demonstrated skills to do the job. No resume needed.

3) No Direct Referrals from Friends

This one might surprise you, but it works really well. When we take direct referrals, it introduces all sorts of bias and politics. We can end up trying to shoe-horn people into positions that really don't fit them or doing courtesy interviews that waste the time of both parties. We've had people close to us who wanted to lobby for a friend but have insisted that they be put into the same blind process as everyone else. In some cases, they emerged as the person we hired, but in most cases, they were not.

It is well known that referrals are more likely to perform better and be better cultural fits than non-referrals. This process doesn't interfere with that phenomenon, but it strengthens it by removing bias and politics. We have regularly seen a referred candidate get the position. If they are the right candidate, they don't need the name of someone else at the company attached to them throughout the process but will shine on their merits, and if they are the wrong candidate, this process makes it much easier for the referring team member to accept, as they understand the process was as blind as possible.

4) Unique Interview Process for Every Job

This is very different and extremely effective. For over a century, we've sat across a desk from people interviewing for everything from phone sales to CEO and asked them if their "obituary" (resume) is true. When they said yes, we hired them. How dumb is that? It's grossly irresponsible.

Someone being hired to do phone sales should be interviewed on the phone — see if they can sell themselves to you or sell an actual product/service. An admin should be given documents to repair, schedules to figure out. A boiler tech should be presented with an actual problem in the boiler, etc. This is all about demonstrated skills — again, see the hiring priorities that follow.

5) Focus on the Result Intended

The first thing we need to decide is why we want to hire someone. It is not "we need a salesperson" or even "to increase sales." There should always specific, accurate metrics involved — increase sales by what percentage, profit margin will be x, size of client is x, average revenue per client is x, etc. When we employ Stephen Covey's idea of carefully defining the metrics and talents we need, we can then design the right interview.

Adventure Dental in Vancouver, WA, needed two more dental assistants for their pediatric dental practice. The ability to deal with odd situations, to think quickly, to project creativity and childlike playfulness were all important traits in the job description. The final eight or so applicants were asked to arrive simultaneously and were told to stay together in the lobby. The staff were able to observe their personal responses to this unusual interview procedure. The candidates were then given five minutes to make a balloon animal, while the staff watched how they each reacted to being together and how they responded to the balloon animal idea. Two women in particular found the exercise to be a lot of fun, but they also saw some other people struggling, so they stopped making their own animals and started helping others. Guess who got the job? That's the kind of stuff that never shows up on resumes.

Hiring Priorities

The five principles mentioned are fleshed out in our hiring priorities that follow. We call this Reverse Hiring because the things the Factory System hierarchy taught us to focus on are at the bottom of the list, and things that most hiring processes ignore are at the top. Violate these priorities at your own peril.

1) and 2) — Hire First and Second for Business Beliefs and Culture

As we stated earlier in the book, you don't create culture. You simply live out what you believe one decision at a time, and the accumulation of those decisions is your culture. Knowing what we believe, writing it down, and living in full alignment are the core practices of a Participation Age company.

Our first priority is to see if the person we're hiring is in full alignment with what we believe as a company. A lot of HR people are squeamish about testing for culture because they have seen people use the excuse, "They are not a culture fit" for many forms of discrimination. That is simply a misunderstanding of culture, not a reason to shy away from testing for it.

Business beliefs don't include sex, race, religion, sexual orientation, or any other thing we think of as "cultural" when describing society in general. We test specifically for business beliefs to determine a great culture fit. We are asking ourselves, "What do they believe about":

1. Business — why does business exist?
   a. To add value? To make money? To crush competition?
2. Work — why does work exist?
   a. To make money? To make meaning? To survive? As a separate thing from the rest of me? As an integrated part of who I am?
3. People?
   a. Do they think people are generally stupid and lazy, smart and motivated, living in scarcity/abundance, want to participate versus be reactive?
4. Leadership?
   a. Do people need to be managed by command, control, fear, and intimidation, or do they need leaders who use vision, motivation, influence, serving, clarity, asking questions?
5. Success?
   a. Making money, making meaning, clawing my way to the top, promotions versus results.
6. Competition
   a. Crush others (scarcity), there is plenty for everyone (abundance)

There are other things you can watch for to determine if someone is a culture fit, but you get the idea. These are things that directly impact their alignment with your values, vision, and mission, and they have nothing to do with the color of their hair or how tall they are. In our eleven hiring steps, we show you that most people are eliminated at step one, which is our test for culture. If they are not a culture fit, we never even ask for their resumes.

3) Hire Third for Innate Talents

These are the things you can't teach or are beyond your focus to do so: things such as being detail oriented, a sense of urgency, silver-tongued, patient, kind, emotionally intelligent, empathetic, highly motivated, self-managed, problem-solver, etc. You can teach skills, but if someone doesn't have a great artistic eye, teaching them to use a paint brush and a canvas is a waste of time.

If someone makes it past our beliefs/culture test, we test for talents next, again, without having seen a resume.

4) Hire Fourth for *Demonstrated* Skills

This is so important. With rare exceptions, you still don't need to see a resume yet. Never hire someone to do something you haven't had them do before you hire them. Get a reality check on the skills they claim to possess. If they are missing, it is a big yellow to red flag. Either they made things up, or they don't have a sane self-assessment. Both are big trouble.

5) Hire Last for Experience, Including Education
In some licensed and certified positions, you still need to confirm their experience or education. Since you've already tested for demonstrated skills, experience or education can sometimes be irrelevant. The exception — always check references but not like you've been taught — more on that later.

You can see why we call this Reverse Hiring:
1) and 2) Beliefs/culture
3) Talents
4) Demonstrated skills
5) Experience/education

In traditional hiring, how do we do it? Just the opposite — we hire for experience, education, and skills and almost never bother to look at talents, culture, or beliefs. Is it any wonder we have people who aren't excited about our mission and who clearly don't fit?

OUR ELEVEN-STEP HIRING PROCESS

We developed this in the trenches over many years and have taught it to a lot of companies who consistently give us the feedback that their hiring process was revolutionized, enabling them to get the unicorns they had always hoped for. Everyone we hire goes through this process. You will see that one of the overt intentions here is to get as little information as possible early on that doesn't apply to the position. Bias is a very big problem in hiring, and we want to avoid any of the common biases as far into the process as possible.

Some people may look at this process and say it is too involved or takes too much time, but you get back what you invest. You may spend as much or more time with some of these people as you do your spouse, and hopefully you took that vetting process seriously, too. As Peter Drucker said, "Hire slowly, fire fast." Most companies do just the opposite. We're here to tell you that hiring slowly works, and it is pure genius.

MENTOR FIRST

Before we start the actual hiring process, we like to get the mentor in place for whoever will be hired. We get a volunteer, or someone nominates a mentor who agrees to the role. See the section on mentoring earlier in the book.

RESULT INTENDED

The other pre-work is to determine, with metrics, exactly the result you intend from hiring this person. You get what you intend, not what you hope for. You can then design the "demonstrated skills" part of the process. This focus on an intended result makes every hiring process different, especially the demonstrated skills step.

STEP ONE — WRITE THE AD

This critical step might be the one that gets the least attention, but it is the most important. I had a billionaire once tell me he has never seen a good ad that was longer than one paragraph. I told him I had never seen a good one that was less than a few pages (that was one of our minor disagreements). Our shortest ad is six pages, single spaced, before we flow it into the advertising medium. We have one that is thirteen pages. The exception to this would be when hiring highly strategic leaders from outside the organization, who are almost never hired through an ad on the Internet, anyway.

We stumbled into this practice. We got snarky one time and just decided to create a really long ad that told everything about us: our culture, beliefs, values, vision, mission, products, history, culture, work hours (flexible), vacation policy (unlimited), promotion process (you'll never be promoted but can make more money faster than with promotions), awards, dreams — everything. We decided whoever we're hiring should have just as much of a passion for interviewing us to see if we are a fit as we have for interviewing them.

Two great things happened as a result that continue to this day. First, the number of applicants plummeted from a few hundred for an ad to sometimes as few as ten. We would have to place the ad twice or three times just to get fifteen to twenty people to choose from. We were nervous at first but found out what accidental geniuses we were later when we realized what was happening.

We sometimes refer to this process with the title, "How to Get People to Quit Before You Hire Them" because we learned that the people who weren't a fit were quitting the process right out of the gate, and the few who we wanted to interview were still there. It soon became obvious why. The Factory System taught people to look for a job, not for meaningful work. If you are looking for a job instead of work, you won't work to get the position. Anyone slinging resumes at ads with no need for meaning in their employment took one look at this ad and punched out. It was just too much work to apply.

Stakeholders who want to make meaning have a different view of the world than employees who only want to make money. Quite a few people, after we hired them, said when they read the ad on their phones, they dropped whatever they were doing, ran home, and applied because, "This position is *me*, and this company is the company I've been looking for." When we hire, we typically get very few candidates — the cream rises to the top without the milk, and we usually have two or three great choices to flip a coin over at the end. Other companies who are aware of our hiring practices sit like vultures on a wire to pick off one of the finalists we couldn't hire.

To keep the book from being any longer, we've posted a few ads here for you to check out. All of them have been used to hire amazing people.

STEP TWO — PLACE THE AD

Where you place the ad can be unimportant if you have friends. When we need to hire, we post it on social media, notify our clients, and email a lot of people (who are okay with that). In every case, we tell our friends something like, "If you have someone you think is a fit, please don't send them directly to us, but give them the URL to the ad. We want everyone to have the same fair opportunity through our blind process. If the person you want to recommend is the best for the position, they will shine through."

Through this blind process, we hired Kyle Matthews, the son of close friends of ours when we lived back east twenty years ago. They could have just pulled the, "we're close friends" card, but they alerted Kyle, who went through the process. When we were down to ten or so candidates and finally read their resumes, I laughed and let the process go forward. The team had already identified him as the leading candidate, and he got the job. Two points here — 1) you can place the ad anywhere if it's just a URL people are pointed toward, and 2) keep the process blind as long as you can to avoid bias.

STEP THREE — REVIEW CULTURE QUESTION RESPONSES

Because we want people to work to get the job, and depending on the level of attention to detail we are advertising for, we bury something like this in the middle of the ad, "Please don't send us your resume, we don't need to see it yet. Just briefly answer the following seven questions and email them to HireMe@CranksetGroup.com. We'll get back to you with next steps."

If it's a low-detail job, we might make the above more obvious, but either way, we are looking for people who will do some work to get the position and who are excited enough about what they read about us to want to write something in response. If we were hiring a boiler tech, we would make it clear we just want a couple sentences for each question, but we would still want responses to those questions without a resume to start.

When we see resumes in the responses, we just delete the email. If they can't follow the most basic instructions in the ad, it doesn't bode well for their future with us, especially if we're looking for a detail-oriented person. We also don't want to open the resume and be biased to try to shoe-horn someone in because their "obituary" is amazing.

A team of two to three people give a rating on a scale of one to five, combine those, put them on a spreadsheet, and push the viable candidates forward to the next step. The others are notified — it's just common courtesy. Contact us at Grow@CranksetGroup.com for examples of the spreadsheet.

STEP FOUR — TEST FOR THE INNATE ATTRIBUTES

Skills can be taught, but the innate things such as emotional intelligences, empathy, and talent are things you don't have time to teach. If you're looking for someone who is highly detailed with a sense of urgency and a great ability to communicate, these are not easily developed. Based on the position, we test for different things, but everyone needs to score very well on emotional intelligence and empathy. (This is not universally necessary for some companies that have different needs. One large software company has a fantastic program for actively finding and hiring people on the Asperger's/autism spectrum. Every company is a snowflake).

There are a lot of tests for emotional intelligence, empathy, and talent, including ones that tell not only what people are good at but what truly energizes them. The team rates the responses, puts them on the spreadsheet, moves those forward they agree on, and informs the others they are no longer being considered.

STEP FIVE — TEST FOR SKILLS AND EXPERIENCE

The manager sits across the desk, stares at the resume/obituary, and comments, "It says here you're good at spreadsheets. Are you good at spreadsheets?" The applicant replies, "I'm great at spreadsheets," to which the manager responds, "Great, that's exactly what we're looking for — you're hired!" Sitting across a desk and talking about skills is a common, unhelpful part of Factory System desperation hiring. Whatever you are hiring for, have them do it before you hire them. For things like documents, spreadsheets, presentations, etc., we'll agree with the applicant on a time limit and have them return the completed assignment. The team again rates the responses, records them on the spreadsheet, and pushes people forward or informs the others.

STEP SIX — SHORT INTERVIEW

Even if you have only four to ten people to consider at this point, you're likely to have several unicorns to choose from. Remember that the majority who responded to your ad have a Stakeholder's view of the world and want work, not just a job.

We do short initial interviews for most positions, between ten and fifteen minutes. By this step in the process, you already have a strong bias toward your top two to three candidates. A short interview is just meant to give both you and them a quick opportunity to see if a thorough interview process is warranted. In a traditional forty-five-minute interview, either you or the candidate might know in the first few minutes that this isn't a fit, but you both pretend to stay interested and slog through the process.

We have three to six questions (depending on the position), and we invite the candidate to ask any questions they have, but we keep it short. We might also bring all the candidates in at once if the position calls for someone who can take over a room and be calm and relational in tense situations. We ask everyone the very same questions, which helps us compare the candidates fairly.

STEP SEVEN — FINAL INTERVIEWS

At this stage, you should be down to no more than three candidates. Ask them to set aside a larger chunk of time to come in and interview with everyone who will be working with them or be impacted by their work (two-step decision-making). If it's a position where they need to be able to work with a group of people all at once, bring in a group to meet them and see how they handle the situation. Again, every hiring process is unique depending on the intended result.

STEP EIGHT — FEEDBACK

Throughout the process, the hiring team of two to three people has been accumulating ratings for each candidate on a spreadsheet. The process can take two to three weeks or longer, and we want to be able to remember, with data, how someone's early interactions were received. We want to guard against one of us having a bad day and tossing someone out subjectively. The input from the spreadsheet and from everyone who interviewed the final candidates (rated on a scale of one to five) is used to guide the final decision. Part of the final scoring is an "intuition" score, "What does your gut tell you about hiring this person"? The subjective side becomes important near the end after you have as much information as possible.

STEP NINE — ASK FOR SALARY REQUIREMENTS

We do not believe in salary ranges. That is a Factory System flaw. If Jenna produces twice what Denise produces, she should make twice as much — results-based incentives. To that end, we rarely (ever?) put a salary range in an ad. Instead, it may say something like, "We don't have salary ranges because even in an identical position, two people may make vastly different contributions.

We pay people based on their contribution, and we look forward to talking to you about your value and agreeing on a salary that reflects that." In the pickle factory, we talked about in the chapter on incentives, line workers made anything from $12 per hour to $24 per hour or more, and nobody complained. It was all based on production. We hired one person at $39,000 a year who received a pay raise almost every month, and within twelve months, she was making $60,000. We had someone else who made the same things for the first two years she worked with us. Both were well compensated with results-based pay.

Leaving out salary requirements is just one more way we use to vet people. Throughout the entire process, you should be alert to whether someone views the world as a Stakeholder or as an employee. How often and how early they want to talk about things such as benefits, vacation time, 401ks, salary, and other classic employee-mindset topics tells us a lot about how they view work. We want people consumed with questions about our culture, beliefs, values, team, people, and their ability to function like adults at work.

It is important to mention that our benefits and compensation are always at or well above the industry standards because we hire people who bring great value. Netflix discovered that in procedural work their best hires are two times more productive than the average, and in creative work requiring more decision-making, the best hires are ten times more productive than the average. In the face of these facts, salary ranges make no sense. We should pay people for their contribution. It's what free people experienced for thousands of years before we built factories.

STEP TEN — CONTACT THREE REFERENCES

We don't call references until we're down to the last two to three people we would like to hire, and if we can't come to an agreement on salary terms, it makes no sense to contact references any sooner. The Keller Williams Realty process requires a conversation with a minimum of three people who know the candidate. Don't just talk to the reference the candidate gave you. Ask that person for someone to talk to, and then ask that person for the same. The first referral might have been highly prepared by the candidate. The others may give you the unvarnished story.

STEP ELEVEN — MAKE AN OFFER

We keep both or all three final candidates in the process until we have a signed offer from our first choice. If for whatever reason we can't get them across the finish line, the second person doesn't feel like second best because they've already been notified they're not getting the job, and they aren't sloppy seconds. It's usually a tossup between the last few candidates.

WE'LL NEVER DO THIS

Does this sound like a lot of work? First, it's not as much as it sounds, but yes, it takes a lot more energy and usually a little more time than we put into desperation hiring, but there are at least three solid reasons why you should have a system like this to hire people:

1. To protect your culture — Each person you add either strengthens your values, vision, and mission or takes away from them. The impact of the wrong person is one of the most underrated problems in business. If you love your culture, you want to protect it with a very thorough hiring process.

2. You get what you intend, not what you hope for — Stop hoping you'll find great people. Intend to hire only unicorns. You shouldn't have a few rock stars who stick out — everyone should be a unicorn. Netflix defines culture as comprised of "stunning colleagues." Everyone should be an eight and above, no exceptions.

3. Retention — People who are vetted thoroughly and hired well stay longer. The restaffing tax is one of the biggest hidden costs in any organization. When your retention is ten times higher than your competitors, as it is with companies such as Wegmans, Semco, ours, and many others, profitability skyrockets, as does production.

BECOME THE EMPLOYER OF CHOICE

Are you chasing people? Stop looking for the employee of choice and become the employer of choice. Participation Age companies have attractive, built-in advantages because they are mission centered. Remember, the Participation Age has two hallmarks: participation and sharing. When you create a company where people get both, they come running. You're no longer chasing them; they're chasing you. It's not even a fair fight.

Good Interviewing Questions to Reveal Emotional Intelligence (or Lack)

Who inspires you and why? (empathetic figures, heroic figures, domineering figures, etc.)

If you were starting a company tomorrow, what would be its top three values?

What feedback do you have on our values, vision, and mission statements? (What passion do these bring up in that person?)

What do you think of our hiring process? (Do they like the relational focus, or do they default to talking about the skills and task part?)

Where did your best friends come from? (any from work?) It takes a while for people to build relationships, and being able to do so is a sign of solid emotional intelligence, Alvarez says. "[A lasting friendship] tells you that relationships and caring about people are important to the person."

What would you like to keep learning the most about?

Is there something you could teach me in the next minute or two? Anything, just help me learn…. (see how they respond — blushing, can't/won't do it, or jump right in, enjoy teaching you, good at it, etc.)

What are the top three things you think make you successful? (technical skills? conceptual/strategic skills? relationship skills?)

THE NEXT ONE THING

1. What Next One Thing will help us replace standard Factory System hiring practices with a Participation Age hiring system based first on values, beliefs, and talents and secondarily on skills, experience, and education?

2. When will we start? ____/____/____

3. What are one or two challenges that need to be addressed before we start?

CHAPTER EIGHTEEN

Onboarding and Mentoring Stakeholders

18

What really drives great performance?

It isn't skills, clear objectives and responsibilities, free lunches, ping pong tables, or flexible work schedules. Research has concluded that the number one driver of performance is having someone to talk to who listens and responds with empathy[1]. Once again, we see the need for community at work and a primary emphasis on people first, production second.

What is the second biggest driver? Encouraging people to be involved in decision-making. In 2012, Zhang Ruimin, the CEO of Haier, reorganized the massive corporation around three simple concepts, one of which is entrepreneurial employees. People were taught that they can no longer be passive workers, which is what Haier defines as an employee. Going forward, they must be active partners—Stakeholders in the company. To that end, they are regularly encouraged to be innovative and entrepreneurial, to help create their own destiny[2].

Leadership skills which involve listening and encouraging others are the major driver of job performance. Perks such as free lunches and on-campus volleyball, which we regularly mistake for culture, don't even make the list. Neither does management or anything related to top-down hierarchy.

Mentoring, while equally important, is addressed even less by harried and overburdened managers. According to Korn Ferry Institute leadership development researcher Robert Eichinger, the ability to "grow talent" is ranked last out of 67 competencies for managers, despite decades of investment in talent development systems. In other words, on average, managers are worse at developing their employees than at anything else they do[3]. Mentoring is different from coaching. It is more about making sure someone gets the clarity, processes, training, guidance, and advocacy they need. The mentor may not directly provide these but ensures the trainee gets them from someone. They are the go-to person to facilitate whatever is needed.

Fifty percent of companies have a retention program[4]. My guess is that few of them include mentoring but are focused more on compensation, promotions, and other long-term career development.

WHEN MENTORING SHOULD HAPPEN

Mentoring should coincide with hiring. At Crankset Group, we have a fully developed mentoring process that begins with someone volunteering to mentor the new person who is hired.

Most companies have no formal onboarding process, which is tragic. *Harvard Business Review* writer Diane Coutu edited a study showing that the initial few minutes of interaction can affect how a group operates throughout its entire life[5]. If someone is not introduced to their new setting with intention, direction, and a commitment to relationship, it could affect how the team functions for years to come.

Because starting a new job can entail a sort of cultural shock, Nearsoft starts mentoring people the day they are hired. The new hires enjoy the freedom, but at the same time, it can be disorienting. They used to go to their boss for almost everything, whether it was to propose an idea, complain about someone, or ask for a raise. Nearsoft is patient, knowing the full transition can take six weeks to many months. Through classes and with the help of a trained mentor, the new hires learn what to do if they see a problem, have an idea to put forward, or need to give a teammate honest feedback.

One Nearsoftian software developer took it as a personal challenge to design a program where interns would go through phases to get hired, including feedback from Nearsoft clients who would be the recipients of the new hire's work. He called this initiative The Nearsoft Academy and worked very hard to make it a reality. With the help of others, the Academy is now an important source of new talent for the company, and its creator is fully dedicated to the process. He saw an opportunity to do what he liked that also met a business need for Nearsoft and made it happen. He faced challenges, but resistance from leaders wasn't one of them.

When we begin the process of onboarding someone, we think of issuing an employee manual to help someone find accounting, find their desk, find the bathroom, learn their processes, and become effective as quickly as possible. While these are all necessary, none of them help you retain great people because what they really need to know most is that they have friends here.

A friend is the number one need of a new hire, someone with whom they can feel safe to say, "I don't get how this process works, I'm confused," or "Why does Bob respond that way?" or "How can I succeed here?"

Onboarding should never be about the task first but about the relationship. People interested in joining a golf club, dinner club, church, or bicycle club typically make a decision to stay or not within a few preliminary visits. If they find someone who welcomes them, listens, and responds with empathy, they stay.

The same Gallup research says that listening and responding with empathy is the second lowest proficiency in manager's skills. In other words, there is a complete disconnect between what is most important for people and what we do.

By default, by virtue of being called a manager, the manager is set up to fail. As we discussed in the Universally Distributed Leadership chapter, the Factory System manager has so many conflicting requirements that only a rare heroic genius can make it work. We have set up the entire workplace to fail by requiring one person to be all things to all people.

GENIUS HEROES NEED NOT APPLY

Deeply entrenched in the worn-out Factory System hierarchical mindset, Jim Clifton at Gallup says the solution is to hire better managers, which is like wishing for ongoing tropical rain in a desert. Almost no one can live up to the unreasonable expectations of a managerial position. The answer isn't one superhuman but Distributed Decision-making through distributive leadership.

Find people who are good listeners, regardless of their specific job in your company, and help them form a leadership team of mentors who are fantastic at welcoming people, making them feel at home, and assuring that they develop a short list of things a mentor would need to be successful.

This doesn't mean the onboarding mentor has to provide

everything. That would merely be switching an absurdly comprehensive responsibility from a formal manager to a formal mentor. A mentor is a leader; they don't have to be the one doing. They just make sure the list gets completed.

THE ROLE OF MENTOR

In his landmark 1967 paper on the lattice organization, Bill Gore outlined one of the few key roles he felt every organization needed, that of mentor (also called sponsor at Gore). He saw the role of mentor as a way to: a) engage in a one-on-one relationship and b) focus on the development and growth of the associate[6]. The sponsor/mentor was to offer the associate:

1. Encouragement
2. Guidance on principles and practices
3. Feedback on performance
4. Help in securing resources
5. Advocacy for the associate in compensation discussions
6. Guidance in personal development planning
7. Role model behavior

A mentor's first responsibility is to listen empathetically and, as part of that, to ensure the new Stakeholder is finding their way around the company with regard to the mission, to accounting, to a clear understanding of their role and responsibilities, and all the other things that come with a new job. The mentor doesn't have to provide these directly but is their champion, taking the new person where they need to go to get them. A mentor embraces the three responsibilities of leadership: guard the values, champion the people, and pilot the results. The mentor is the early champion of the new person and pilots the results of getting the person onboarded well.

A mentor who is not part of any reporting structure is helpful because people are much more likely to open up, be vulnerable, and ask for help from someone they aren't concerned about impressing in order to keep their job. The mentor provides a pressure valve for them, a safe person to go to with all the important questions that come with a new job, new team, and new responsibilities.

THE MENTOR'S GUIDE

The mentor's guide covers the important resources, tools, and other things the new person needs. Remember, the mentor doesn't have to do all these things; they are just responsible to champion that person's onboarding and pilot the results. They have a checklist to help them champion the person's onboarding and pilot the results.

Any new Stakeholder needs great coaching on our values, vision, and mission (responsibility one of leadership — guard the values). The mentor may choose to give this responsibility to someone else.

Your mentor's guide should represent a hierarchy of what is most important. What the mentor shares as critically important, persistently, is what the new hire also focuses on.

When there were just a very few of us at Crankset Group, we didn't need a specific program to bring on the next person. We all just pitched in, but by the time there were eight or ten of us, we formalized a mentoring process for everyone who joined us. We all want to think we'll make sure the new person is brought on well, but the old adage is true: when everyone is responsible, no one is responsible.

Our formalized process follows as an example. If you don't have a freedom map or similar document that is regularly used to onboard, mentoring is unlikely to be a priority.

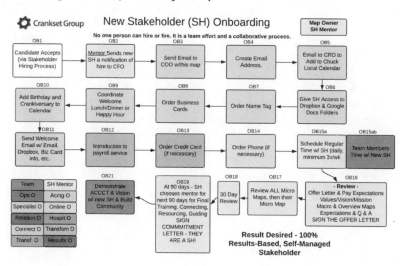

THE MECHANICS OF MENTORING

When the new description for a job is put out, ask for a volunteer to mentor the person who is hired. The volunteer can use the above freedom map as a guide, along with the mentor's guide and the

Stakeholder's journal, which we talk about later in this chapter.

The First Month — We ask the mentor to meet formally with the new person three times the first week (i.e., every other day) but to check in daily and then to meet formally once a week for the next three weeks, while continuing to check in informally. It can be as simple as a fifteen-minute coffee or a full lunch, whatever is needed.

First Things First — We always want the new Stakeholder to gain as much understanding of the values, vision, and mission as possible in the first day or two because what we emphasize is what they will focus on. If you start by emphasizing where accounting is and how to get paid, they will see that as most important.

In the first couple days, we also want them to have a thorough fifteen- to thirty-minute review of our macro process — what the whole organization does to serve our clients. This helps them to understand how they fit into something bigger than themselves or their own team, and it emphasizes the horizontal connectedness of everything we do. Reviewing the macro map and the idea of being mission centered are the first steps to reorient someone from a traditional top-down Factory System hierarchy to a network of teams in Distributed Decision-making.

Reviewing the micro map(s) of their personal and team responsibilities is the next step. Again, the mentor doesn't necessarily have to be the one sharing the values, vision, mission, macro or micro maps, but they need to ensure that someone does and that the Stakeholder grasps the importance of them to their daily life in the organization.

The Next Couple Months — After the first month, the two of them can review the progress made, as well as reviewing their relationship. The new Stakeholder might choose another mentor at this point. When someone is coming in with no friends, we assign a mentor, but during their first month, they might find someone they really click with, so the initial mentor can step back and transfer the relationship in that case.

The new or continuing mentor meets formally once a week for the following two months, so the new Stakeholder has had formal mentoring for their first three months. The meetings can continue if helpful, not to create co-dependence on the mentor but to continue to support the new Stakeholder in becoming a fully interdependent part of their team and the organization.

The following is our mentor's guide to help you develop your own._____

What to Cover with New Team Members

Our Crankset Group company culture, organization, relationships, and general business practices (transparency, incentives, surveys, etc.) are not common to most businesses. We need to do a great job of bringing every staff member on board by assuming nothing, seeing their experience through their eyes. We want them to by fully transitioned, comfortable, and in great relationships as quickly as possible.

The first responsibility of a mentor is to be a listener and to understand with empathy (put yourself in their shoes). We want the new person to know that someone is looking out for them, supporting them, and connecting them with the right people, resources, training, and processes. Along with developing your relationship with them, here is a list of important things to cover with a new hire.

Topic	How/Why to Cover	Date
First Day — The New Stakeholder Onboarding Map	The mentor of the new person should be familiar with the onboarding freedom map and follow it. Both the map and the mentor must be in "alignment" as to what is presented to the new Stakeholder.	
First Day — The Basics	Email address, name tag, business cards, birthday and Crankiversary in the calendar, payroll signup, credit card, system access (via 1Password to things like Dropbox and Google Sheets spreadsheet, other necessary systems for their work), computer setup; any other basics needed	
First Day — Key Introductions	Make sure the Stakeholder gets time with key people they will be working with via Zoom or in person. A lot of us don't work in the office, so building relationships could take longer. It is important to make people feel welcomed and to know who they are working with. Make it happen within the first three weeks.	
First Day — Macro Map	It is critical that they receive a copy of this overview of the entire Crankset Group organization. The mentor or someone else covers it with them to show the three aspects of our business, 1) 3to5 Clubs, 2) Crankset business advisory, and 3) Crankset online, and how those three interact with each other.	

First Day — Values, Vision, Mission	The mentor covers each of these with the new SH (or ensures someone else does) and shares how they perceive they are used to help us run our business. Every decision should be run through the values, vision, and mission to make sure the decision is helping us accomplish those things. Help the new person see how we "beat the drum, gently and relentlessly" on these in team meetings, our surveys, and informally with each other.
First Day if Possible — Micro Maps Directly Related to Their Role and Function	Note: The mentor may not be the one sharing these, but the mentor should make sure someone who is knowledgeable in the maps goes over them. The new SH receives a copy of their micro maps.
First Week if Possible — Welcome Lunch or Similar	During a team meeting or similar. Do the mentor intro to Stakeholder here, if it wasn't done as part of the hiring process.
First Week — Offer Letter	Acceptance letter — the acceptance letter forms one-third of a Cranksetter's "Stakeholder's guide." Go over each section with the new SH and make sure they have a grasp of what we're saying in each section. Have them sign an acceptance letter and keep a copy for themselves. This is more for the ceremony to recognize they are now part of us but also to confirm they have worked through this with someone. Make sure any questions the mentor can't answer are escalated to someone or get someone else to go through the full acceptance letter with them.
First Week — Mentoring Schedule	On the first day, the mentor should set up a weekly formal Q&A session with the SH. It should be completely open — no agenda, just coffee or lunch and "what questions do you have?" Anything is on the table. The new SH must feel safe to ask anything, and the mentor can also use this time to share things they have observed about how the new SH can speed up their own onboarding (ask more questions, get to know so-and-so, read this).

First Week — Intro to Participation Age Content	The mentor shouldn't have to explain our crazy company to someone. We have a growing library of videos for them to watch, as well as a spreadsheet with a ton of resources, blogs to read, recommended TED talks, videos, and books, etc. Recommend that the new Stakeholder do a two- to four-sentence summary on each video in a journal and accumulate these short summaries for themselves as well as for all of us. This is valuable for them to see and understand who we are and how to grow with us. It could also be fun for them to look back on a year or so later as a mini journal of their first few months here and see how they've grown.	
First Month — Ongoing Micro Map Training	The mentor ensures that someone (if it isn't them) is assigned to do intensive training with the new SH to get them fully up to speed in their roles, responsibilities, and results desired. This could take a few weeks to a few months, but it should include formal training on a scheduled daily basis, then a few times a week, then as needed.	
Ninety Days — Be a Friend; Then, They Decide Who to Go Forward With	Ask questions, listen, and rely heavily throughout the process on the question, "What are they feeling and thinking, and how can I help push them forward?" Listening and empathy (not co-dependence) are critical to them being be able to create attachments and build community at work at Crankset Group.	
First Six Months — Weekly Mentoring Continues (with First or New Mentor)	Ask questions, listen, and rely heavily throughout the process on the question, "What are they feeling and thinking, and how can I help push them forward?" Listening and empathy (not co-dependence) are critical to them being be able to create attachments and build community at work at Crankset Group.	

The mentor should remember that the list is not the main objective but that listening, being a friend, interacting about the intangible, relational things are what is most important. Questions like, "How are you doing?" and "What questions do have?" and "What part of the position gets you most excited/is holding you back?" are just as important as, "Do you understand your role, process, and intended results?"

THE STAKEHOLDER'S JOURNAL

The Stakeholder has another guide of sorts. Along with what they are learning through the mentor, they receive a Stakeholder's journal. You can create a simple folder and give them a blank journaling book as well — anything to emphasize the importance of playing an active part in their own onboarding.

The Stakeholder is encouraged to set a schedule for watching videos and reading from a suggested list of books, blogs, and articles and is asked to respond to them in a journal. Over the first few months, they should gain a grasp of the values, vision, mission, organizational structure (how we relate to one another), how we all lead, how our teams function, how to communicate (two-step decision-making), and many other vital relational practices. These videos and their journal become an important part of developing their foundation.

Depending on their position, there may also be skill and process-related videos and readings to perform. One of our dental practice clients in Chicago has developed an entire library of technical videos on everything from medical protocols to how to answer the phone with a new patient. These two kinds of videos, the business/relational side and the technical/skill side, become valuable ongoing resources for retraining. The journal becomes a great reminder of what they have learned.

Crankset Group Participation Age Videos to Watch
In Recommended Order

(Note: these are just examples of some of the resources Crankset Group provided to new Stakeholders at the writing of this book. It is an evolving set of resources and also includes things directly related to someone's specific role and function, not just those related to how we organize our community at work.)

The Stakeholder should be given a journal (digital or physical) or the following as a document, so they can record two to five sentences on each topic as they progress through them. What did they learn, and how does it apply to them and their position? This journal can be revisited in the future to remind them of how we live in community and how work gets done in a Participation Age organization.

Video Topic	Short Summary — What Did I Learn/How Does This Apply?	Date
The Participation Age Organization versus The Factory System Organization		

The Participation Age Organization — What It Looks Like When We're Done		
Leader-Leader How to Lead from Your Seat		
Distributed Decision-making (Also Covers Two-Step Decision-making)		
DDM Workgroups (Self-managed Teams)		
Kudos Program		
Teams As "Community"		
Carefrontations Part One of Two — Caring Enough to Confront		
Carefrontations Part Two of Two — Caring Enough to Confront		
Freedom Mapping for Teams		
Peer Recognition Surveys		
How to Hold A Meeting		
Why Beliefs Determine Our Organizational Destiny		
Incentives Programs		
Commitment Letters		
Self-Managed Vacation		
How to Promote Yourself		
?		

A summary of a mentor's responsibilities might include things like:

1. **Sounding board** — Being a sounding board and routing agent. "How are you doing?", etc., and, "Let me connect you with someone who can answer that."

2. **Intros and admin** — Make sure the mentee is connecting with the right people concerning email, business cards, payroll paperwork, 401(k), etc. The mentor makes sure it's all being addressed and getting done.

3. **Values, vision, mission emphasis** — This can be done by a video or by a presentation of the mentor or someone else.

4. **Freedom maps** — Have the mentor share the macro map in the first days or so (or get a strategic leader to do it). The maps

give them the best overview of how they fit in logistically.

5. **Culture or "how we work"** — Crankset Group has a list of videos and other resources for new hires. The mentor should encourage the hire to write a short recap of what they learned and discuss it with someone.

6. **Training** — The mentor may or may not do the training, but they ensure it gets done by the right person.

FIRST IMPRESSIONS ARE EVERYTHING

Traditionally, we have not paid much attention to how we onboard people. There is too much left to chance, and by default, we communicate to the new Stakeholder that they are either on their own, or worse, that we really don't care the much about them. As Diane Coutu's research shows, even the first few minutes matter for years to come.

Let's onboard people deliberately, with a focus on the relationship, listening, empathy, and with a formal plan to communicate the things that matter most: our values, vision, mission, and how we relate and work together. It's the least we can do if we want to build community at work and expect people to be fully engaged, deeply committed Stakeholders who stay for a very long time.

THE NEXT ONE THING

1. What Next One Thing do we need to do to build a great mentoring program? Remember, the first few minutes someone is with your organization has a lasting impact on the productivity of both that individual and the team they join. A well-implemented mentoring process could be one of your most important new Participation Age practices.

_____

_____

_____

2. When will we start? _____/_____/_____

3. What are one or two challenges that need to be addressed before we start?

_____

_____

RESOURCES

1 http://www.ddiworld.com/DDI/media/trend-research/hirezleadership-findings/hirezleadership_is-empathy-boss_finding_ddi.pdf?ext=.pdf

2 https://corporate-rebels.com/haier/

3 https://www.strategy-business.com/article/00275?gko=c442b

4 https://recruitingblogs.com/profiles/blogs/how-to-recruit-and-retain-the-best-talent-retention

5 https://hbr.org/2009/05/why-teams-dont-work

6 https://folk.uio.no/terjegro/materials/Gore_lattice.pdf

A FINAL WORD

Join Us in The Participation Age

The Factory System way of organizing, still in use by most businesses, is out sync with everything we are learning about what makes people free and encourages them to be adults. Statistically, it long ago lost the growth, profitability and retention races to companies that focus first on the human side of enterprise.

The classic top-down hierarchy structure is a tragically broken model, born in slavery, fomented in serfdom, fine-tuned in the factories and modern militaries, and adopted as the most expedient short-term mindset for running an organization. In the emerging work world of the Participation Age, it is time to install a new operating system for how we run organizations.

In the late 1990s, Kodak ignored complexity and change and solved for certainty. They were facing the inevitable demise of 35 mm film, and the response was to focus their best people on how long they could keep selling it. In January 2012, they filed for bankruptcy. It was an example of ignoring complexity and change in a hopeless attempt to cling to the familiar.

For too long our response has been, "I know the Factory System is inadequate, but I don't know what else to do." But now we have many Participation Age companies of all sizes in every industry that have been re-humanized, some that have lived at the top of their industries for nearly seventy years. We can't dismiss them as statistical anomalies or a fad. They have given us a clear vision of where we should go, and the templates and processes to get there.

So we can no longer say we don't know what to do, or how to do it. The only remaining question is, "Will we?" As Kodak reasoned, it might seem easier to hang on to the familiar for now. But thankfully, companies in every industry and profession are racing to embrace the Participation Age. Those that do will thrive. Those that don't will be left behind.

Let's re-humanize the workplace by giving everybody their brain back. Please, come join us in the Participation Age.

APPENDIX

Words That Matter

ALIGNING OUR BUSINESS LANGUAGE IN THE EMERGING WORK WORLD

Words are verbal representations of deeply held beliefs. We represent new beliefs with new words. Otherwise, they are likely not to replace the old beliefs.

As we move from a Factory System model to a Participation Age model of leadership, we need words to express these replacement beliefs. Post these — keep them in front of people. Using these words (or your own replacements) can speed up the process of rehumanizing the workplace by giving everyone their brain back.

Make a game out of this with staff. Search and replace in our heads...

WAS	BECOMES
Manager — only a few	Strategic leader or tactical leader, or combinations (everyone leads)
Department	Function
VP, director, manager, supervisor	Functional title (per my major contribution), or we're all just Stakeholders, staff, etc.
Production people	Tactical leaders
Bosses	Strategic leaders (servants — can be multiple or one team, not always one "team leader")
Lone rangers or production teams	Interdependent DDM workgroups — -Teams make decisions together. The power of many.
Owner (of process, process step, etc.)	Champion/guardian/steward (servant)
Employee	Stakeholder (a self-managed adult decision-maker)

Old Hierarchy Mindset	New Participation Age Mindset
Top-down hierarchy — The Factory System model, developed in slavery, through serfdom, through the military, into the factory	DDM workgroups — A network of Distributed Decision-making teams released to take action. Decisions made locally
Top-down, bottom up	Center out (strategic leaders), edges in (tactical leaders)
Working for (the boss)	Working with (other DDM workgroup leaders)
Imposed hierarchy — Manager choose reports, no one really knows if anyone is following because it's not voluntary	Organic leadership — Followers choose leaders; we voluntarily follow other strategic leaders
Boss-centered — we serve our boss (or "our" dept)	Mission-centered — "I'm not your boss. Who's your boss? (the mission statement). We all just serve the boss, including me."
Decisions by managers (top-down)	Distributed decisions by all, locally — Leader-leader and two-step decision-making
Managers tell.	Leaders ask.
Managers solve, decide, and constantly monitor the process	Leaders train others to solve and decide and then get out of the way (to pilot the results, not the process)
People are managed. False assumption — managers make people more productive.	Only non-human things are managed. Manage stuff. Lead people.
Bonuses (time-based, I sat in the chair another year, I deserve a bonus)	Incentives — Money is only one of seven, and they are all results-based
Top down (hierarchy, boss) — The top makes decisions that govern the bottom	Center out — strategic to the tactical functions
Bottom up — the bottom feeds data to the top for decision-making	Edges to the middle — tactical makes decisions that inform the strategic function
Hourly and salary pay (time-based)	Results-based pay — Incentives
Operations manual/SOP	Offer letters, freedom maps, process descriptions, Commitment Letters
Accountability (chasing/motivating people to make them get things done	Support — helping them get done what they own. Input=Ownership